Free-Choice Learning and the Environment

LEARNING INNOVATIONS SERIES

SERIES EDITORS

John H. Falk
Lynn D. Dierking

BOOKS IN THE SERIES

In Principle, In Practice: Museums as Learning Institutions, edited by John H. Falk, Lynn D. Dierking, and Susan Foutz

Free-Choice Learning and the Environment, edited by John H. Falk, Joe E. Heimlich, and Susan Foutz

ABOUT THE SERIES

Museums, libraries, broadcast and print journalism, the Internet, and community-based organizations all represent distinct and important sources of public education that learners can choose from at will. The Learning Innovations Series publishes books pertaining to this broadly defined area of free-choice learning for use in college and university courses or by scholars and professionals in the social sciences and humanities. Each volume in the series focuses on a different institution or subject area, highlighting the many ways in which the free-choice sector facilitates learning in our society.

ABOUT THE ORGANIZATION

Established in 1986 as a not-for-profit learning research and development organization, the Institute for Learning Innovation is dedicated to changing the world of education and learning by understanding, facilitating, advocating, and communicating about free-choice learning across the life span. The Institute provides leadership in this area by collaborating with a variety of free-choice learning institutions such as museums, other cultural institutions, public television stations, libraries, community-based organizations such as scouts and the YWCA, scientific societies and humanities councils, as well as schools and universities, striving to better understand, facilitate, and improve their learning potential by incorporating free-choice learning principles.

Free-Choice Learning and the Environment

Edited by John H. Falk,
Joe E. Heimlich, and Susan Foutz

ALTAMIRA
PRESS

A Division of
ROWMAN & LITTLEFIELD PUBLISHERS, INC.
Lanham • New York • Toronto • Plymouth, UK

AltaMira Press
A division of Rowman & Littlefield Publishers, Inc.
A wholly owned subsidary of The Rowman & Littlefield Publishing Group, Inc.
4501 Forbes Boulevard, Suite 200
Lanham, MD 20706
www.altamirapress.com

Estover Road
Plymouth PL6 7PY
United Kingdom

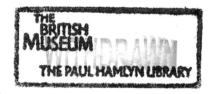

British Library Cataloguing in Publication Information Available

Library of Congress Cataloging-in-Publication Data

Free-choice learning and the environment / edited by John H. Falk, Joe E. Heimlich,
and Susan Foutz.
    p. cm. — (Learning innovations series)
  Includes bibliographical references and index.
  ISBN: 978-0-7591-1122-6 (cloth : alk. paper)
  ISBN: 978-0-7591-1123-3 (pbk. : alk. paper)
  eISBN: 978-0-7591-1333-6
  1. Environmental education. 2. Active learning. I. Falk, John H. (John Howard), 1948–
II. Heimlich, Joe E., 1957– III. Foutz, Susan, 1979–

  GE70.F74 2009
  333.7071—dc22   333.7071 FAL   2008044418

Contents

Acknowledgments   vii

Introduction   1

    John H. Falk, Joe E. Heimlich, and Susan Foutz

I. Background and Theory

1   Free-Choice Learning and the Environment   11

    Joe E. Heimlich and John H. Falk

2   Who is the Free-Choice Environmental Education Learner?   23

    John H. Falk and Joe E. Heimlich

3   Fostering Empathy with Wildlife: Factors Affecting
    Free-Choice Learning for Conservation Concern
    and Behavior   39

    Olin E. Myers Jr., Carol D. Saunders, and Sarah M. Bexell

4   Behavior Change Theories and Free-Choice
    Environmental Learning   57

    Nicole Ardoin

II. Informing Practice

5   From Mission to Practice   77

    Tim Merriman and Lisa Brochu

6 Tools of Engagement: How Education and Other Social
Strategies Can Engage People in Conservation Action   87
Judy Braus

7 How Can Participatory Action Research Inform
Free-Choice Learning Pedagogy and Research
in Environmental Education Contexts?   105
Michael Brody

8 Environmental Literacy through the Lens of Aquarium
Ocean Literacy Efforts   123
*Jerry R. Schubel, Corinne Monroe, Kathryn A. Schubel,
and Kerry Bronnenkant*

III. Envisioning the Future

9 Free-Choice Environmental Learning in Practice:
Research to Inform Environmental Education Practice   141
Elaine Andrews

10 Future Directions for Research in Free-Choice
Environmental Learning   157
Roy Ballantyne and Jan Packer

11 The Federal Government and Free-Choice Learning   171
Janet Ady and Ginger Potter

References   181

Index   207

About the Contributors   211

Acknowledgments

The editors thank all the professionals whose discussions at the 2005 Learning Innovation Initiative Conference on Free-Choice Learning and the Environment inspired this book, the chapter authors for their contributions, and those members of the field who gave feedback on the chapter drafts, including Kerry Carlin-Morgan, Alphonse DeSena, Lynn Dierking, Justin Dillon, Christian Itin, Gus Medina, Jackie Ogden, Tim Sandsmark, William Scott, Beverly Sheppard, Russell Stevens, Tara Teel, Karen Tingley, and Jack Whitehead. We also thank our colleagues at the Institute for Learning Innovation for their support as well as the editors at AltaMira Press.

Introduction

John H. Falk, Joe E. Heimlich, and Susan Foutz

In April 2005, roughly one hundred people gathered at the U.S. Fish & Wildlife Service's National Conservation Training Center in Shepherdstown, West Virginia, for an unusual environmental education meeting. Everyone there was an environmental education professional, but from diverse parts of the community. There were professionals from the United States, Canada, Australia, Greece, and the United Kingdom; from federal agencies, nongovernmental environmental groups, universities, nature centers, botanical gardens, zoos, aquariums, natural history museums, and science museums. They included educators, administrators, as well researchers, evaluators, and funders; professionals from large institutions and ones from smaller institutions. And since this was a diverse cross section of individuals from the environmental education community, most knew only a few colleagues in the group. Within an hour of convening, all of these individuals self-organized into roughly a dozen discussion groups and were deeply engaged in conversation and debate. The topics for discussion had not been predefined, but everyone seemed able to find something of interest among questions that ranged from "What do we want to accomplish with community focused, asset-based environmental education?" to "How does environmental education contribute to conservation actions?" and "What counts as knowledge in environmental education?" There were small groups everywhere, scattered around the grounds of the conference center and in the meeting rooms. Although most of these professionals had not known each other at the beginning of the session, and came from varied backgrounds, they all had something in common. They shared a thirst to know more about how the public's environmental understanding, attitudes, and behaviors could be enhanced through free-choice learning; all possessed a sincere desire to use this information to support and enhance the public's environmental learning. These are the very reasons that motivated us to create this edited volume and we suspect are the same reasons that have motivated you to read this book.

To understand and make best use of this book, however, you should know that there is a story behind the volume. Beginning in 1994, the Institute for Learning Innovation has organized and hosted national conferences and published extensively in the area of free-choice learning. The goal of these Learning Innovation Initiatives, as we refer to them, is to serve as a catalyst for significant improvements in practice and learning research and in evaluation endeavors. In the process, these initiatives have spawned dozens of master's theses and doctoral dissertations and continue to guide practice, research, and theory in the burgeoning field of free-choice learning.

The past decades have been a time of significant research and great advances in our understanding of learning in out-of-school environments. Despite this progress, the environmental education community continues to struggle to meaningfully document the impact of its various programs, exhibitions, websites, and other educational efforts, and to apply those findings to the creation of useful and valid frameworks for exemplary practice. To move this process forward, to consolidate our understandings from existing learning research efforts in this area, and to lay out the issues that need to be addressed in the decade ahead, the Institute, with major support from the U.S. Environmental Protection Agency and other funders including the U.S. Fish & Wildlife Service, the National Oceanic and Atmospheric Administration, Disney's Animal Kingdom Theme Park®, the journal *Environmental Education Research*, the National Park Foundation, the National Environmental Education Training Foundation, the North American Association for Environmental Education, and the Ohio State University Extension, launched a new initiative called *Free-Choice Learning and the Environment*. This initiative had several parts, including a preconference special issue of *Environmental Education Research* (Volume 11(3), July 2005); a national conference of over one hundred environmental education professionals representing a diverse cross section of roles and responsibilities, institutions, geography, and of course perspectives; and now this book.

Our goal throughout this initiative was to gather together in a single place an accessible compendium of what we currently know about free-choice learning and the environment, to inquire where that knowledge leads us in terms of practice and community, and, finally, to ponder what still needs to be learned by the environmental community as we move into the uncertainties and challenges of a new millennium. This book, then, is actually the product of a very long process. These ideas are the distillation of more than three years of effort to bring a useful volume to the environmental education community—useful being defined here as one that provokes thought and discussion within the field. Most important, the ideas presented here are not merely the products of the authors, but actually represent the collected ideas of a diverse and representative cross section of the free-choice environmental learning community. Although this volume has a decidedly U.S. bias, we believe that the vast majority of the ideas included here have relevance to environmental professionals wherever they work.

The past decades have seen not only a growing desire for this information, but a growing sense of urgency and need. Despite the fact that utilization of free-choice environmental education resources through visits to national parks, nature centers, natural history museums, zoos, and aquariums, and similar organizations are at all time highs, few within the environmental community are feeling sanguine. This is because the environmental challenges to the planet, not the least caused by worldwide climate change, seem to grow exponentially, while solutions to these problems lag seriously behind. The urgency to get "good" at what we do has never been greater. We believe that the contents of this book, with its focus on visitor learning and behavior change, will provide environmental professionals of all types with important new tools that will aid them in their efforts to help protect the planet and its precious biological inhabitants.

We have divided the book into three major sections: Background and Theory, Informing Practice, and Envisioning the Future. Although this book was designed to be read cover to cover, like any edited volume, we understand that not all readers will find all chapters equally useful or compelling. Thus, we encourage readers to freely sample, selecting the section, or even the individual chapters that best meet their immediate needs. Please use the book as a reference and, if so inspired, perhaps even as a focus of discussion within your institution or class.

The first major section of the book, Background and Theory, provides the theoretical framework for free-choice learning in environmental education. The section begins with an exploration of the myriad contexts in which free-choice environmental education occurs. Next is a chapter on the free-choice environmental education learner, the audience for free-choice environmental education. Following are two chapters focusing, respectively, on the vitally important but poorly understood issues of the affective and behavioral outcomes of free-choice environmental learning. Although not an exhaustive synthesis of what we currently understand about this extremely challenging subject, the four chapters in Section I provide a fairly comprehensive overview of some of the most important findings from the past decade of research. The first two chapters set the stage by defining the where, when, and who of free-choice environmental learning. The final two chapters in the section provide an impressive summary of our current understandings of key outcomes of free-choice environmental education efforts as well as the gaps in our current understanding. As the four chapters in this section attest, considerable progress has been made over the past several years in our understanding of free-choice environmental learning, and readers will certainly come away with a better sense of what we currently do and do not yet understand about environmental learning outside of the classroom.

Building upon the theoretical foundations of the first section, the second section, Informing Practice, expands on the field's knowledge in order to describe ways to improve practice. The initial chapter explores how clarification of mission can and should lead to better practice by leading to outcome-driven conservation education efforts. The next chapter focuses on understanding how specific conservation actions can be achieved through educational efforts; how current research on conservation education, behavior change theory, and free-choice learning can be and has been applied to practice in programs, exhibitions, films, on the Internet, and through other educational media. This is followed by a chapter on participant action research, the process whereby organizations seek to extend the impact of their free-choice environmental education efforts by directly involving participants in critically evaluating the impact of their own actions on changes on their lives and in their communities. Finally, the last chapter in this section uses the marine environment as a case study to explore how free-choice learning principles can be directly applied to solving specific environmental issues. Ocean literacy is used as an example of how environmental literacy can be "deconstructed" in ways that improve the likelihood of achieving broad-scale success.

Appropriately, the third and final section of the book, Envisioning the Future, frames free-choice environmental learning within the context of the significant changes going on in our twenty-first-century world. The final three chapters of the book attempt to provide a road map to the future of free-choice environmental education; a road map to better educational practice, research, and policy. Each chapter looks to the future and explores the ways that the field might change its current practices in order to maximize the long-term potential and benefits of free-choice environmental learning; each chapter also directly addresses the challenges free-choice learning organizations face as they attempt to significantly improve the impact they have on the public's knowledge, attitudes, and behaviors toward the environment. This last section of the book mirrors the first section, but takes it a step further: Whereas the first section provided an overview of what we have learned about the nature of free-choice environmental learning, the final section provides an agenda for what lies ahead in order to ensure a tomorrow of improved research and practice.

As suggested above, we believe this book is an important marker in the development of the free-choice environmental education field; a time capsule of current best thinking from a representative cross section of some of the best minds in the environmental education community. We certainly do not assume that everyone will agree with all of the ideas postulated here. However, we purposely encouraged authors to be bold, and we believe we have assembled a provocative and thoughtful view of the future of the environmental education field. We will feel successful if the writings assembled here stimulate both reflection and debate and ultimately raise more questions than answers.

DEFINITIONS

The goal of the *Free-Choice Learning and the Environment* Learning Innovation Initiative was to apply new understandings of free-choice learning to the development of visionary frameworks for improving the practice, evaluation, and future research efforts of the environmental education community. A major first step in this process was the bringing together of the varied parts of the community—diverse roles within the community (e.g., researcher, evaluator, practitioner, policy maker); diverse in venue and discipline (e.g., national park and refuges, nature centers, natural history museums, aquariums, zoos, conservation organizations, universities); and diverse in stage of career (e.g., participants included established leaders and emerging ones). In so doing, we hoped to provide a shared platform for understanding and communication while at the same time encouraging divergent thinking. Because of this diversity, it was essential that we shared a common vocabulary and set of definitions. What follows are a few key terms that we identified as important. We stipulated that all authors were to build from and use these definitions.

> informal/nonformal: terms used to describe institutional settings other than schools; for example, museums are typically referred to as informal settings while parks are often talked of as nonformal settings. Although definitions exist that distinguish these two terms, they are frequently used as synonyms; that is how they are treated in this volume.
> free-choice learning: the term we use to describe the learning that occurs in environmental education settings when the learning is largely under the choice and control of the learner—most casual visitors who do not participate in structured programs engage in free-choice learning. When

children in school groups take field trips where there is a predefined and highly structured lesson with limited or no choice or control over goals and activities, this is not free-choice learning.

learning: Although a difficult term to define, for purposes of this book learning will be defined as a personally and socially constructed mechanism for making meaning in the physical world. Our definition is a broad one and includes changes in cognition, affect, attitudes, and behavior.

environment: In environmental education, the term "environment" generally refers to the biophysical, natural, and built physical environments. Environmental education also incorporates the social environment in terms of using the cultures, people, and institutions of people as a filter to better understand human impacts on and ways to address the physical world.

environmental education (International Union for Conservation of Nature, 1971): Environmental education is the process of recognizing values and clarifying concepts in order to develop skills and attitudes necessary to understand and appreciate the interrelatedness among humans, culture, and the biophysical surroundings. Environmental education also entails practice in decision making and self-formulation of a code of behavior about issues concerning environmental quality.

The objectives of environmental education are to

- foster clear awareness of and concern about economic, social, political, and ecological interdependence in urban and rural areas;
- provide every person with opportunities to acquire the knowledge, values, attitudes, commitment, and skills needed to protect and improve the environment; and
- create new patterns of behavior of individuals, groups, and society as a whole toward the environment.

Belgrade Charter (UNESCO-UNEP, 1976): The goal of environmental education is to develop a world population that is aware of and concerned about the environment and its associated problems, and which has the knowledge, skills, attitudes, motivations, and commitment to work individually and collectively toward solutions of current problems and the prevention of new ones.

Tbilisi Declaration (UNESCO-UNEP, 1978): Environmental education is a learning process that increases people's knowledge and awareness about the environment and associated challenges; develops the necessary skills and expertise to address the challenges; and fosters attitudes, motivations, and commitments to make informed decisions and take responsible action.

U.S. Environmental Protection Agency: Environmental education increases public awareness and knowledge of environmental issues and challenges. Through environmental education, people gain an understanding of how their individual actions affect the environment, acquire skills that they can use to weigh various sides of issues, and become better equipped to make informed decisions. Environmental education also gives people a deeper understanding of the environment, inspiring them to take personal responsibility for its preservation and restoration.

I

BACKGROUND AND THEORY

1

Free-Choice Learning and the Environment

Joe E. Heimlich and John H. Falk

Fiol and Lyles (1985) offer a definition of learning as "the development of insights, knowledge, and associations between past actions, the effectiveness of those actions, and future actions" (p. 811). Dewey (2003), Bloom (1976), Carlsen (1988), Bruner (1973), Maslow (1954), and other seminal writers have all suggested that learning—the process of taking in, organizing, and making meaning of the world—is a natural human process and does not necessarily require structured times, settings, curricula, and routines. It might be possible to attend to life without learning to occur; but for even the most stubborn of individuals, learning happens however incidental or ignored. Learning as a lifelong, natural process happens consciously, subconsciously, and often only coincidentally with the intentions of the individual. Over the course of a life-span, people learn most of what they know outside of school and other formal learning arenas. It is unfortunate, then, that most understanding of learning is based on formal education models of the teaching–learning exchange.

Certainly this is true for environmental issues. Most people would acknowledge that learning can occur from a trip to a museum, zoo, or park; attending lectures; reading books that have more than a good plot; and using information obtained from the radio, television, newspaper, Internet, or magazines. Learning attained in this manner, however, is framed in an understanding of literacy by which experience, stories from elders, cultural practice, and models of engagement can have as much impact as the linear, curricular knowledge accumulated through formal courses of study. Unfortunately, most people neither acknowledge nor are even aware of the significant learning that occurs as we talk to people, read, watch how people do things, listen to a lecture or television special, or simply figure things out over the course of a day, week, or year (Darling, 1986 in Cyr, 1999; Falk and Dierking, 2002).

Another way to conceptualize learning beyond schooling is to attribute it to "socialization" within groups. From this perspective, socialization itself contributes to the environment of how one learns, where one learns, and what is learned outside the formal learning environment. A long evolutionary history supports the fact that humans are first and foremost social creatures; virtually all learning is socially mediated (Barkow et al., 1992; Falk and Dierking, 2000). As technology, global issues, and other events continue to reshape the world more rapidly than ever before, it is important to reflect on the diverse ways people learn about the world around them.

The opportunities for environmental organizations and institutions to use their physical settings and facilities to help their visitors and users learn desired outcome messages are tremendous. However, these opportunities demand that institutions understand the relationships among message, context, and social role of the individual. This chapter focuses on the context in which the environmental messages are delivered: the places where free-choice environmental learning is most likely to occur either by design or default. In order to address the issues, we will first explore how learning in environmental free-choice settings is situated and contextualized and then focus on the range of environmental learning settings, thus providing a framework for the chapters that follow. In addition, the chapter explores the limits put on learning by the nature of the settings and experiences.

LEARNING AND ENVIRONMENTAL SETTINGS

In learning-exchange theory, both the physical and the psychological environments are important constructs (Heimlich and Norland, 1994). In the field of environmental education, a longstanding approach to understanding educational differences is in the contrasts among learning *in* the environment, learning *about* the environment, and learning *for* the environment, as first framed by Lucas (1972). For environmental learning *in the environment,* the setting and the message are necessarily intertwined, and—certainly for the learner—are inseparable. The visit itself and the outcomes from the visit are often seen as the same by the visitor, even if the site has its own defined outcomes.

One of the oft-cited values of education in environmental settings is the inherent "hook" of nature—animals, plants, vistas, smells, textures. Nature provides both a tremendous boost for engaging people and an equally large barrier for being able to focus on the message of the institution, agency, or organization. The context for learning about the environment in a natural, naturalized, or nature setting has been acknowledged since John Dewey wrote about *learning nature in nature* (see, for example, Dewey 1970, 1997). The same lessons about *learning in nature* can be applied to learning about and for the environment. To understand the context, it is important to have a shared understanding about situated learning, free-choice learning, and the messages conveyed.

Situated Learning

Lave and Wenger (1991) posit that what people know in a particular situation is intimately entwined with the tool, community, and activity in which the situation occurs. Situated learning is interacting with others, the tools at hand, and the activity of the present (Hansman, 2001). Ideally, situated learning contextualizes what is to be learned cognitively, affectively, and behaviorally in the physical and social situations in which the learning occurs. The act of situating learning allows meaning for the learner to emerge, in turn making the learning process context dependent. In situated learning, the social dimension of learning is important; knowledge is situated within a context and negotiated or given meaning. Every experience a person has is full of potential meaning because the context in which the experience occurs has a meaning system for the individual (Wolcott, 1991)—experience is interpreted from a particular stand or viewpoint and the meaning is contextualized. Knowledge is located within the framework of the situated community rather than in the mind of the individual. The process of learning, cognition, and knowledge are all context dependent (Lave, 1988). An outcome of viewing learning through a situated lens is an appreciation that the meaning an individual makes from any learning experience derives from the interplay among setting, the means, and the context of the learning event.

It is becoming increasingly appreciated that learning occurs through a process of assimilating experiences and the building of new knowledge structures; learning is a continuous process of constructing meaning out of prior and new knowledge. Marsick and Neaman (1996) describe learning through constructed meaning as beginning with internal or external triggers, reviewing alternative responses, selecting a strategy and action. Throughout the learning process there is implicit filtering of information through selective perception, values, beliefs, and framing. "Learners selectively make meaning of the experience and retain these cognitive constructs as what is learned from the experience" (Marsick and Neaman, 1996, p. 100). In other words, learners do not just passively absorb information but rather actively construct meaning; the result is that each learner's understanding of the world is unique.

Building off of these ideas is a growing body of evidence that learners' epistemological beliefs, not just the information presented, impact both how an individual learns as well as what they learn. Epistemological beliefs have been shown to influence students' approaches to study and problem solving, and motivation and persistence in information seeking. There are also some preliminary research findings that suggest that the structure of learning environments can influence learners' epistemological beliefs (Tolhurst, 2007).

A number of studies have shown that people learn about the environment from a range of different resources. For most people, the primary source of information for environmental issues is from family and friends (Fortner, 1988). Other studies suggest that some issues such as weather, natural phenomenon, and distant issues like rainforests, and in some contexts including immediacy or awareness over time, the dominant source of information on environmental topics is the media including television and movies (Gaziano and Gaziano, 1999; Pierce et al., 1992; Steel, 1997; Steel et al., 1992). However, a recent Pew study (Horrigan, 2006) found that the Internet had now replaced television as the primary source of the public's science information; by inference, the Internet could also now be the primary source of the public's environmental knowledge as well. From leisure studies and recreation, there is evidence that travel provides a source for environmental information (Bodger, 1998; Long and Zoller-Hodges, 1995; Kimmel, 1999). Museums, zoos, nature centers, parks, botanical gardens, science museums, and similar attractions also provide their visitors with opportunities for learning about nature and the environment (Adelman et al., 2000; Packer and Ballantyne, 2002; Falk et al., 2008). Simply stated, people get their information on the environment in many different places and many different ways.

Free-Choice Learning

Many theorists have offered important distinctions among educational experiences typically offered in school and in nonschool settings (Knowles, 1950; Crane et al., 1994; Ramey-Gassert et al., 1994). However, the frameworks introduced by these theorists have come under increasing scrutiny as researchers have begun to focus less on settings and more on the nature of the learning experiences. For similar reasons, also called into question are the various definitions of these terms that include informal, nonformal, incidental, and unintentional education (e.g., Coombs, 1989; Vidart, 1978; Mocker and Spear, 1982; Heimlich, 1993; Bjornavold, 2000). Falk and Dierking have long argued that terms such as informal, nonformal, and formal learning are problematic because they assume that the critical variable in learning is the educational setting or instructional approach rather than attributes of the learner; in particular these categorizations leave out the key variable of learner motivation and agency (cf., Dierking, 1987; Falk and Dierking, 1992, 1998, 2000, 2002).

Free-choice learning provides a means by which "learning"—the role of the learner—can be separated from the approach to teaching for learning. Such a separation allows the educational opportunities to be considered from the perspective of the learner, participant, attendee, subscriber, patron, donor, visitor, member, or guest—the recipient of the messages from the educational organization, agency, institution, or site. The visitor to a state park rarely makes a distinction between learning from a guided hike or from an interpretive sign. Likewise, a nature center program attendee may not classify learning differences between the public forum and the craft-based program. Indeed, one of the ongoing challenges (and benefits) to education in environmental settings is that the many institutional approaches to messaging are compressed within a single visit by the learner (Mony, 2007), which reinforces the fluidity of the constructs of free-choice learning as well as learning in life.

What then makes learning free choice? One recent synthesis offered the following constructs as elements in free-choice learning theory (Heimlich and Storksdieck, 2007):

- Learners' agendas drive their outcomes.
- Outcome goals are often not shared between the learner and the institution.
- Learners have their own motivations.
- Learning is constructed meaning applied by the learner.
- Learning is continual.
- Learning is cumulative.
- Learning is horizontal (synthesized across a variety of learning experiences).

Learning throughout life is about a person going about the business of living. Learning occurs as a seamless blend of events, activities, structures, occurrences, and practices within the individual's life. It is less important that an individual views any particular event as "learning" or "not learning" than it is that the settings and messages for externally derived learning outcomes be shaped to honor how learning really does occur in a person's life.

The Message

The context and the learning structures, however, are not complete without the message being communicated. In many environmental settings, intended messages are related to conservation actions. In others, messages may relate to components of environmental or nature literacy. Although many of the chapters that follow provide insights into the messages themselves, it is important at this point to note that the message is a vital component of situated cognition. Otherwise, as in experience versus experiential education, we would have a situation versus situated learning.

WHERE IS ENVIRONMENTAL FREE-CHOICE LEARNING?

An exhibit is created by someone who has a desired message; an interpreter generates a wayside display after determining what the visitor might learn at that location; teaching–learning exchange theory suggests that good pedagogical, andragogical, and socially mediated instruction all include an educator whether this person is present at the moment of the exchange with the learner or prior to the moment (Heimlich and Norland, 1994; Seevers, 1999). The educators for environmental free-choice learning and often the institutions themselves are determinants in and the sources of information being shared in the learning events.

The number of sources for environmental free-choice learning, and the locations where it happens, are vast: television, magazines, newspapers, newsletters, and the web along with natural settings and parks, nature centers, zoos, aquariums, natural history museums, planetariums, botanical gardens, conservatories, and other environmental museums; and outdoor recreation and ecotourism. Sometimes learning is simply by being at a place; other times it is in the message of the medium.

Sites

People visit places where they feel comfortable, that are nonintimidating, user friendly, and speak in the language of the uninitiated public (Resnicow, 1994). Individuals visit environmental sites with the intent of consciously or subconsciously learning about themselves and their cultural heritage (Kramer, 1994; see also Chapter 2; Falk et al., 2008). If a visitor does not feel grounded in the topic underlying the attraction to the site, the likelihood of that location being viewed as educational is reduced (Falk and Dierking, 2002) and indeed, the likelihood of visiting is minimal.

Do visitors see the purpose of these places as education? For many visitors to environmental sites, the purpose of the visit is far removed from the educational message of the organization, and the value of the visit is to be in the place: this national park, the zoo, the aquarium, the view. Anecdotally, park rangers, zoo educators, and museum docents all have stories about individuals who come routinely to sit under one tree or watch a particular animal, or reflect on a particular sculpture. The value in the site is, for these visitors, the site itself. What they learn may not be the conservation message, but personal insight that can be meaningful.

Jarvis (1987) suggests that any one experience may be meaningful to one learner and meaningless for another. An experience can be either attended to and reflected on, or not attended to (nonlearning); if the experience is attended to, the learning can be nonsignificant or not subjectively valued and hence be short term at best, or the experience can be significant, one in which personal value is highly supported by the experience and thus increases the cognitive impact of the information (Hilton, 1999). One of the benefits of the land-management agencies and site-based nongovernmental organizations is that visitors to these environmental sites come with a predisposition toward an inherent valuing of the site they choose to visit (Hilton, 2002). Visitors choose to visit because they want to be there.

Attractions

Destination sites are frequently viewed as having the potential to introduce people to art, ideas, history, nature, science, and knowledge. These places, however, can do more than create interest or inspire curiosity (Watkins, 1994). They can allow the visitor to become engaged with ideas, even when the visit is for social purposes (Lucas, 1991). In the early 1960s, Houle (1961) constructed three categories of learners based on the relationship of how and why the learner participates: (1) goal-oriented learner; (2) activity-oriented learner; and (3) learning-oriented learner. For many visitors, the "goal" in the learning opportunity is the social exchange, the entertainment opportunity, or the proximity to the information. When a visitor has the opportunity to learn as a part of a destination excursion, the individual's goal may not be the learning as defined by the educator, but instead be the social interaction and the activity itself.

For example, Beer (1987) found that slightly over half the visitors to a museum attended with learning as a purpose; other researchers, however (e.g., Hood, 1983; Miles, 1986; Hood and Roberts, 1994), found much lower numbers. The dominant reason for visits found by these researchers was social; and in one study (Hood and Roberts, 1994), less than a third of these social events were family based. This suggests that institutions' opportunities are based on the social interactions of visitors with family or of visitors with other visitors and that the learning is, at best, a secondary factor in the initial attraction for the visitor. However, as pointed out by Falk (1998, in press), for settings like museums, zoos, and aquariums and likely even parks and many other free-choice educational settings, learning is virtually always an assumed rather than an explicit reason for visiting. In other words, visitors are there to learn even if they don't say that's what they are there for.

How important are these attractions for environmental learning? The Association of Zoos and Aquariums reports that, annually, more than a hundred million people visit their member institutions (Association of Zoos and Aquariums, 2004). The National Park Service reports 272,623,980 recreational visitors in 2006 (National Park Service, 2007). The median visitation to a botanical garden in the United States is over 100,000 while the median annual visit to a nature center is nearly 53,000 (American Association of Museums, 2007). In other words, there are hundreds of millions of visits to these attractions each year, perhaps as many as a billion worldwide, making the potential reach across the full range of environmental free-choice settings tremendous.

The Media

One of the dominant sources for environmental information, whether intentionally for learning or not, is the mass media. Television, radio, newspapers, magazines, and even the Internet are major providers of information for adults (e.g., Fortner and Mayer, 1983; Fortner and Teates, 1980; Ostman and Parker, 1987). The media, then, define for many people what it is important to know and when it is of importance—the agenda-setting model of mass communications (Kline and Tichenor, 1972). How and what is reported by the media can shape specific groups' opinions of issues (Badri, 1991).

Fortner (1988) noted that the media have a "limited news hole" and that only a certain number of stories can be printed or reported as determined by the gatekeeper—the person or group of organizations that determines which stories are considered "newsworthy." Further confounding the agenda-setting theory of media is Fishman's (1982) discovery that reporters "see events by using the same phrase structures that beat [specific reporter assignment] agency officials use" (p. 244). The frames of reference of the institutions or experts being reported are used without further investigation of the information or without providing a basic foundation for the reader/viewer to make sense of the information (Chien, 1996). Borman (1978) suggested that due to a lack of time, space, and other resources, news reporters tend to oversimplify, or ignore some important information. Friedman and colleagues (1999) found that, due to the limited time or space the media have for communicating new, controversial, and uncertain science, much information is lost, in particular the uncertainty of many scientific concepts.

Increasingly, individuals are using the Internet to find answers to questions of immediacy. Some of the most attractive features of the Internet such as speed, lack of restriction, and ease of data retrieval are also the same features that can lead to issues of privacy, fraud, and the proliferation of misinformation (Kerka, 1999). Morrison et al. (1998) found that users of the web generally assumed that whatever was found on-line was indeed fact; Kirk (1999) notes that on the web, excellent resources reside alongside those that are dubious. Heimlich et al. (2004) learned that among environmental educators, more frequent users of the web found the amount and the trustworthiness of the information to be their greatest barriers while those who use the technology less for professional information see trustworthiness and information overload as far less important and thus are far less critical consumers of the science they view on-line.

CONSTRAINTS ON LEARNING

An interesting paradox facing educators in free-choice environmental settings is that the settings for environmental learning often constrain the learning that environmental educators hope to facilitate in these settings. First, the nature of the learner creates many challenges. Most learners come, as is discussed briefly above and in greater depth in the following chapter, for reasons that may or may not be conducive to receiving the messages the educator wants them to get. Even so, there is good evidence that most people who visit environmental sites come with a bias in support of the mission of the organization (e.g., Heimlich et al., 2005). There are constraints imposed by myriad factors of the person: where they are in the lifespan; the social role being played in the present group; the identity-related needs of the individual; and events that support or hinder learning at the moment of instruction (e.g., crowding, distractions, hunger, etc.). The individual's history with the topic, with the educator/institution, and with similar messages makes a difference in how open an individual is to messaging or programming, and supports the need in the larger field of providing supportive, repeated, and consistent messages within and across institutions. All the elements of a person's background and predispositions affect the potential for learning.

Timing can also create challenges to environmental free-choice education as the learners' time frames and references are often not consistent with those of the institution or the educator. One element of time refers to time budgets. Most professionals who have museum, park, center, or attraction experience are able to share numerous explicit stories of people who attend and have only an hour or two hours budgeted to a site that takes many more hours to walk, let alone spend time reflecting, reading, engaging, and interpreting (Falk and Dierking, 2000). The other element of time relates to appropriateness of message and phenomena; a good message at the wrong time—often when something outside of control such as a crying child or a spectacular sighting—is no different than no message at all.

The factors surrounding the nature of the individual within the group can be additional constraints or facilitators to learning. The nature of the group in terms of cohesion and history alters the learning orientation of the individuals within the group. Prior experiences as a group in similar settings (beyond the history of the group in general) can create support for or against "getting" the message or spending the time to hear the message.

A second realm of factors of constraints is in the nature of the setting itself. Educators and others working in these settings can become immunized to the glamour and novelty of the locations. It is easy to become complacent and forget the power the settings or collections may have on visitors. Nature and the environment are amazing and every now and then it is good to be reminded of how powerful they are in directly influencing learning (Falk and Dierking, 2000). A corollary to the power of the settings is the unpredictability of nature. Weather is often a factor in learning settings—too hot, too cold, too windy, too wet, or too dry—all these elements create different learning experiences. Consistency in sightings or in animals being present when needed is not guaranteed. Educational props are commonly used to provide alternatives in the event that nature does not cooperate, but there will always be constraints to consistent educational messages when nature is involved.

The third realm relates to factors of the individual in the group in the natural setting. The intersection between the learner and the group with the setting provides an interesting array of benefits and challenges. Preexisting groups within larger groups have unique histories, relationships, and ways of expressing themselves that may not be positively viewed by others in the larger group. Dynamics of interactions of the group can dramatically have impact on the learning experience and influence what content can be or is covered. The nature of the group interacting with nature also adds a dimension of complexity and influences the cohesiveness of the messages conveyed.

With all these challenges, one could ask if this work is worth doing? The remainder of this book suggests that the answer to this question is yes, while also reinforcing the inherent challenges raised. We'd like to close this chapter with just a couple of observations.

Those who engage in free-choice environmental learning are often prejudiced toward the message being offered. There is no problem in preaching to the converted as even the converted need to hear the message over and over again; but don't forget that the unconverted and converted need to hear different messages. Furthermore, the sheer numbers of those who engage in free-choice learning in environmental settings suggest that if we continually deepen and enrich the learning experiences, we will be reaching a vast number of people.

Teaching in free-choice learning settings is about conveying messages across individuals and the variety of groups in which people participate in the learning events. Even though learning is measured at the individual level, the goal in most free-choice programs is generalized cognitive, affective, and psychomotor learning. This is accomplished through teaching groups at museums, nature centers, parks, conservatories, botanical gardens, zoos, aquariums, natural history museums, and all the other places where free-choice environmental learning occurs, including at home. The greatest challenges are about constructing consistent, strong, cumulative, and expanding messages that provide cohesive learning opportunities for the many different people reached through these settings and programs. Learning in general, and about the environment in particular, is not something that happens just once or in just one place, but something that does and arguably needs to happen continuously across many settings, situations, and circumstances.

Where does free-choice learning about the environment occur? The answer: in virtually every and any environment in which people learn. The more difficult question remains: When does it occur and how can we ensure that the learning that does occur is as effective as possible?

2

Who is the Free-Choice Environmental Education Learner?

John H. Falk and Joe E. Heimlich

The previous chapter talked about where and when free-choice learning about the environment occurs; the focus of this chapter is on the why and whom: specifically, the free-choice environmental learner. We have divided our discussion into two sections. The first section provides an overview of traditional ways of understanding learner characteristics, in particular demographic characteristics; this is the lens of the marketer. Considerable effort has been invested in thinking about the visiting populations through this lens and, consequently, a lot is known about the age, education, social arrangement, residence, and superficial motivations of individuals who visit sites like national and regional parks, zoos and aquariums, natural history museums, and other similar venues and programs. Although users of free-choice environmental settings have been sliced and diced in numerous ways, until recently these methods have yielded relatively little actual insight into free-choice environmental learners. In order to really understand free-choice environmental learning, it is necessary to go beyond *who* visits and actually try to understand *why* people visit environmental education sites.

The second section of the chapter focuses on alternative approaches to understanding free-choice environmental education learners, specifically approaches that emphasize an individual's social roles and personal identities. Research on the social roles, identities, and visit motivations of individuals has yielded considerable insights into environmental learners; not only how these pre-visit characteristics influence the ways individuals utilize a place but also what information they pay attention to and how they connect various pieces of information into long-term meaning. These understandings are critically reviewed in terms of environmental education and the contexts in which free-choice learning about the environment occurs as explored in Chapter 1.

THE FREE-CHOICE ENVIRONMENTAL LEARNER:
A DEMOGRAPHIC PERSPECTIVE

As outlined in the previous chapter, environmentally oriented leisure venues—national, state, and regional parks; zoos, aquariums, arboreta, and botanical gardens; natural history museums; and nature centers—are one of the top out-of-home leisure venues in the United States and the world. While the numbers of visits per annum reported by these sites is impressive, these statistics can be misleading. Despite their popularity, research shows that the use of environmental learning settings, broadly defined, is far from evenly distributed throughout the population. For example, slightly more than half of all Americans visit some kind of environmental setting once per year but fewer than one in five visit with any regularity (Research Resolutions & Consulting, 2007). This raises the question: Who does and who does not go to environmental settings?

Considerable research has been conducted in the United States and elsewhere in recent years in an effort to address the question of who comes to environmental settings. Using the United States as a case study, the preponderance of the data collected from these studies has been based upon demographics. One fairly consistent historical finding was that users of environmental settings are typically better educated and more affluent than the average American. Although this remains true of U.S. heritage and environmental tourists (Research Resolutions & Consulting, 2007), national, state, and regional park users (Mainella, 2001) and visitors to zoos, aquariums, arboreta, botanical gardens, natural history museums, and nature centers (Falk, 1998; Falk and Sheppard, 2006; Smithsonian Institution, 2004), it is also true that as these sites have become increasingly popular, this socioeconomic divide has significantly diminished. Despite increasing popularity among a wider segment of the American public, it is fair to say that, in general, disposable income remains an important factor determining use.

In addition to socioeconomic status, there are two other demographic variables that appear to also strongly correlate with use of free-choice environmental learning experiences. The first is age and the other is race and ethnicity. Use of environmental settings is not evenly distributed by age. Even when the discussion is limited to free-choice visitors, in other words excluding school field trips, a significant percentage of all users in the United States are elementary school-aged children accompanied by parents. For many sites, family groups are the largest single category of visitor. Accordingly, adults between the ages of 25 and 44 and children between the ages of 5 and 12 are disproportionately represented among the visitors to many venues. One of the best-documented settings is the Smithsonian Institution's various museums, including the National Museum of Natural History (NMNH). Nearly two decades of demographic studies at the NMNH indicated that (excluding school groups) about two-thirds of all visitors came as family groups; one in six (16 percent) were adults without children between the ages of 45 and 64 years and less than 4 percent were 65 years or older (Smithsonian Institution, 2004). The visitor demographics at zoos, aquariums, natural history museums, and nature centers are quite similar to the NMNH study; demographics at botanical gardens and arboretums tend to be more skewed toward adults.

Good data also exist for U.S. national parks. A recent summary of several years data from across a variety of national parks reveals that the largest single population were family groups (with children) (52 percent); slightly less than half were visiting as part of all-adult groups. In the latter group, roughly a third were over the age of 50 years (35 percent); 16 percent were over the age of 61 years (Forist, 2003). However, more than half of U.S. tourists who were traveling some distance (at least one night's overnight stay) are over the age of 50 years and were not accompanied by children (Research Resolutions & Consulting, 2007).

Age aside, most visitors to environmental settings come as part of a social group. For example, roughly 90 percent of all U.S. national park visitors arrived as part of a social group (Forist, 2003). Comparable numbers were true for visitors to the Smithsonian's NMNH and the zoo (Smithsonian Institution, 2004), as well as a wide range of other comparable institutions (Falk and Dierking, 2000). Utilization of free-choice environmental settings is overwhelmingly a social experience.

Utilization of free-choice environmental settings is also a relatively novel experience. Despite the high number of visitors year after year, settings such as the Smithsonian and national parks typically are visited by people only once in their life. More than half of all national park visitors (55 percent) state that this is their first visit to these sites (Forist, 2003). This is also true of visitors to the Smithsonian museums (Smithsonian Institution, 2004) and nationally for visitors to all museums (Falk and Sheppard, 2006). Millions of people utilize environmental learning settings, but on average, they only utilize any given setting once or at most twice in their lives.

Considerable attention has been focused in recent years upon the issue of whether environmental settings are underutilized by nonmajority populations, particularly in the United States (African Americans, Asian Americans, and Latinos). Over the past two decades a large number of studies have documented that minority groups underutilize environmental settings, and when they do utilize such settings they tend to use them for "recreational" rather than "educational" purposes (see review by Rodriguez and Roberts, 2002). These findings are reinforced by recent U.S. tourism data indicating that minorities are underrepresented users of heritage and environmental sites (Research Resolutions & Consulting, 2007). Eighty-six percent of tourists to such sites were white. African Americans made up only 5 percent of such tourists, Asian Americans 3 percent, and all other minorities, including Hispanics, only 6 percent. In a study conducted by Falk more than a decade ago on African Americans' leisure habits, African Americans utilized museum-like settings at a rate of 20–30 percent lower than national norms (1993). However, extreme caution needs to be used when interpreting these findings. Although it appears to be true that as a group minorities are less likely than the Americans of European descent to utilize environmental education settings, this simple reality is not as simple as it initially appears. We would assert that it cannot be assumed, as it usually is, that this fact is somehow related to race or ethnicity.

It is essential to realize that the minority populations of the United States are not monolithic. In fact, of the three major minority communities, African Americans, Latinos, and Asian Americans, African Americans are probably the most homogeneous despite being anything but homogeneous. For example, a recent epidemiological study in New York City followed up the finding that African Americans had significantly higher incidences of high blood pressure and heart disease than did European Americans (Hechinger, 1992). When the situation was studied in detail though, it was found that the variations in blood pressure and heart disease were greater *within* the New York City African American population than *between* blacks and whites living in New York City. In other words, a wide range of variables entered into such a finding, including family history, social and economic environment, and individual lifestyle—even in this seemingly very biological measure, biology did not explain most of the variance. Falk's research into the museum-going behavior of African Americans also strongly reinforced this reality. The overwhelming conclusion of the research was that, overall, African American leisure behavior was very similar to European American leisure behavior, while tremendous differences in leisure behaviors existed within the African American community. Where clear differences existed, and there were some differences, race did not emerge as the best variable to explain the differences. Emerging research findings continue to support and deepen our understanding that often those demographics of a visitor we think are meaningful, when explored more deeply, are issues of culture, personal history, and prior experiences (Meyer et al., 2008).

Utilization of environmental free-choice learning settings, like many if not most human behaviors, is far too complex to be understood merely on the basis of demographics. Demographic descriptions of environmental free-choice learners do reveal some interesting patterns, but demographic categories alone cannot tell the whole story. It is true, for example, that European American individuals with higher income and education levels are more likely than are minority individuals with low incomes and education levels to utilize environmental education settings during their leisure time. But it is not true that being white and having a higher income and education level means you *will* utilize an environmental education setting. To understand and be able to predict free-choice environmental site use requires more information than demographics provide.

THE FREE-CHOICE ENVIRONMENTAL LEARNER:
BEYOND DEMOGRAPHICS

What beyond demographics, then, is known about those who participate in environmental free-choice learning? Transcending variables like age, income, and education is the idea that much of any individual's free-choice behavior is influenced by early childhood experiences and parental modeling. From a variety of studies, we now know that a range of adult leisure behaviors in the United States seems to be strongly correlated with early childhood leisure behaviors (Falk, 1993; Kelly, 1977, 1983; Scott and Willits, 1989). These behaviors include reading, taking family trips, and participating in clubs, associations, or scouts and museum-going. One of the best predictors of whether an adult will participate in environmental free-choice learning is whether they were encouraged to participate in these or similar activities *by their parents* when they were a child. Unfortunately, this is an area where not all individuals have had equal opportunity. Staying with the U.S. context, many minorities, recent immigrants, and the economically disadvantaged have historically had less opportunities to visit and participate in environmental free-choice learning as children than have the more affluent majority population. A range of factors conspired to prevent earlier generations of whole groups of Americans from visiting museums, zoos, aquariums, nature centers, national parks, and other similar venues. These factors included racism, growing up in rural areas or foreign countries where few institutions like these existed, and, of course, the ultimate reducer of opportunity, poverty. Overall, it is fair to surmise that proportionately fewer minority, immigrant, and poor children participated in environmental free-choice learning with their parents a generation ago than did affluent majority children. This history directly influences current leisure and learning behaviors.

Of course early childhood experiences, or lack of experiences, are not totally determinant. Individuals do develop new preferences and interests as they mature, and individuals growing up in underenriched environments do rise above their circumstances. However, it is fair to say that embracing leisure or free-choice learning behaviors that are outside one's childhood experience requires additional inputs from one's environment. What might these additional inputs be?

There are a variety of factors, cues, and experiences within an individual's environment that also influence participation in environmental free-choice learning. These "cues" can take on a range of forms. They include the tourist who is visiting a new city while on vacation and asks the concierge, "What are good things to see and do here?" They include the circumstances surrounding a friend or relative coming to visit and a desire to do something special for the occasion. Also in this category would be advertising and promotions from the institution and word-of-mouth recommendations from friends and family.

Most Americans attribute word-of-mouth from friends and family as being the single most important factor in affecting their leisure decision making (Research Resolutions & Consulting, 2007). The more friends and family one has who are free-choice environmental learners, the more likely one is to also be a free-choice environmental learner. For example, Research Resolutions & Consulting (2007) report that more than 80 percent of American tourists used word-of-mouth from friends or family as the primary or secondary reason for selecting a leisure destination. Not only did people hear about destinations through word-of-mouth, it also was the single most important factor in influencing them to actually visit. Similar findings were discovered at such diverse institutions as the California Science Center, Colonial Williamsburg, Henry Ford Museum and Greenfield Village, Anniston Museum of Natural History, Biltmore Estate, and the Virginia Museum of Fine Arts (Falk, 1993). For these same institutions, advertising and publicity programs directly accounted for less than 20 percent of visits.

Brochures, advertisements, and promotions initiated by museums, parks, nature centers, zoos, aquariums, and other similar institutions do make a difference, but rarely, in and of themselves, will they make a nonvisitor into a visitor. Messages aimed at changing behaviors generally work only when someone is ready to be influenced (Prochaska and DiClemente, 1986). On any given occasion, it is often the added incentive provided by a successful promotion that tips the scales and moves an individual toward participating in an activity. Within the population of individuals inclined toward free-choice environmental learning, announcement of a special program, opportunity, or exhibition, particularly if that event relates to a topic of personal interest to the individual, can be sufficient to catalyze the decision to engage in that experience.

As with any leisure experience, time and money, more appropriately thought of as relative "value," enter into the equation. We live within a world of unprecedented leisure opportunity; in fact, there is a glut of things any individual can do in his or her free time. Historically, money was the limiting variable in leisure decision making (which it still is for a proportion of the population). However, for most individuals living in the West, time is now the greater limitation. A recent study in the United Kingdom found that money or "price" was rarely, if ever, a major deciding factor in how most people made their leisure decisions. On the other hand, as people juggled their various leisure options, *time* was nearly always an issue (Curry and Stanier, 2002). Time saving thus becomes a component of all behavioral decisions, particularly for the individuals who feel most rushed. A pervasive example is found in modern child rearing, where a familiar term has crept into our vocabulary—"quality time." Quality time with a child, first and foremost, takes for granted that less time will be spent. In effect, being with the child, which is viewed as a means to an end, can be made more efficient so that more positive things can be accomplished (Godbey, 2005). Going to zoos or aquariums, for example, is frequently considered a "quality-time" activity, particularly for weekend dads. Anecdotal evidence suggests that the number of single dads taking children to free-choice settings on weekends is at an all time high.

Traditionally, leisure has been associated with voluntary activity, something which implies a choice between alternatives. Today, through "time deepening," many people seek to "multitask" so they can avoid the sacrifice of one activity for another, seeking instead to do it all and see it all, and do it and see it now (Falk and Dierking, 2000). We visit national parks to see animals as well as have an opportunity to get some exercise and enhance our fitness. We go on cruises that include lectures and cultural onshore tours so we can improve our minds while on vacation. Passing time in activities that are pleasurable in and of themselves is almost a foreign notion to most Westerners these days. Efficiency rules our work and our leisure. Speed and brevity are ever more widely admired, whether in serving food, the length of magazine articles, conversations, or educational labels at free-choice learning sites. The emphasis is on cramming more (information, quality, enjoyment, etc.) into less time. The public is seeking multiple experiences—quality time with children and education, an environmental experience and a good opportunity to shop and eat, new and fun experiences and convenience. Hence, an increasing number of decisions about whether to participate in free-choice environmental learning come down to how those experiences are packaged.

Money has not disappeared as a decision variable; it has just diminished in relative importance. Relative to most other leisure and entertainment opportunities, free-choice environmental learning is comparatively inexpensive. Even relatively poor individuals are often able to find the resources necessary to engage in leisure activities they deem deeply satisfying. Hence, the real issue, certainly among more affluent consumers (be they Western or Eastern) is *perceived value*. For those individuals who find the experience satisfying, the cost (in dollars and time) will be judged inconsequential; those finding the personal value lacking will find the cost too dear.

All of these things conspire to influence who engages in free-choice environmental learning and who does not. Still, the list so far—demographics and extrinsic factors such as word-of-mouth, advertising, cost and time—only scratches the surface. We would argue that the key to understanding who engages in free-choice environmental learning ultimately comes down to the question of *why* people engage in free-choice environmental learning. This is particularly true for free-choice learning as a whole, since, by definition, this is learning primarily driven by the needs and interests of the learner. Free-choice environmental learning not only begins but often ends with motivation, as suggested by our recent research (Falk et al., 2008; Falk and Storksdieck, in press).

THE FREE-CHOICE ENVIRONMENTAL LEARNER: AN IDENTITY-RELATED MOTIVATIONS PERSPECTIVE

It has long been appreciated that learning and motivation are tightly intertwined, but unfortunately the behaviorist paradigms of the twentieth century, as well as many cognitive paradigms more recently, largely ignored this relationship (Schiefele, 1991; Schoenfeld, 1999). Fortunately, the role of motivation in learning has begun to be rediscovered and reappreciated as more investigators are studying learning outside of the artificial confines of laboratories and schools (Csikszentmihalyi and Hermanson, 1995; Deci and Ryan, 1985; Dweck, 1986; Falk and Dierking, 2000; Leinhardt and Knutson, 2004; McCombs, 1991, 1996; Paris, 1997). Most human learning is self-motivated, emotionally satisfying, and personally rewarding. A number of investigators have found that humans are highly motivated to learn when they are in supporting environments (Deci, 1992; Deci et al., 1981; McCombs, 1991); when engaged in meaningful activities (Dewey, 1913; Maehr, 1984; McCombs, 1991; Salami, 1998); when they are freed from anxiety, fear, and other negative mental states (Deiner and Dweck, 1980; McCombs, 1991); when individuals have choices and control over their learning (Covington, 1992; Griffin, 2004; Paris, 1997; Paris and Cross, 1983; Pintrich and De-Groot, 1990); and when the challenges of the task meet the person's skills (Csikszentmihalyi, 1990a, 1990b). Since most, if not all, of these conditions typically apply in the environmental education contexts we are considering, it follows that these should be highly motivating settings in which to learn about the environment.

Hidi and Renninger (2006) distinguished between the motivations that are intrinsic to the individual and those that are characteristic of the setting; their research suggests that the former are stronger than the latter. However, the vast majority of research on the role of motivation in formal and informal learning has been focused on the short-lived motivations engendered by the learning environment. Recent investigations by Falk and Storksdieck (in press) showed that situational motivations, for example a compelling exhibition or program, did account for some learning. However, the vast majority of what people learned was determined primarily by intrinsic motivations—motivations learners brought with them to the setting (Falk and Storksdieck, in press).

A handful of investigations have explored the motivations educational users possess prior to encountering a learning situation. For example, Leinhardt and Knutson (2004) explored the role of identity (defined as prior knowledge and motivation) in museum learning, and Ellenbogen (2003) investigated the long-term interactions of families across multiple learning environments. Ellenbogen's study revealed that families used their free-choice learning experiences primarily to satisfy their own family agendas—as opposed to fulfilling an informal education institution's learning agenda; the locus of control was with the family rather than the setting (2003). Similar conclusions were reached by Falk and Storksdieck (in press) and more than two decades earlier by Falk and Balling (1982). In other words, motivation was primarily situated in the *learner* rather than in the educational *experience*.

From this perspective, if we are to really understand the nature of the free-choice environmental learner it is essential to understand why the learner is involved in such learning experiences in the first place. This is not a new idea. Falk and Dierking (1992, 2000) as well as Doering and Pekarik (1996; Pekarik et al., 1999) have written that museum visitors do not arrive as *blank slates*, but rather bring with them well-formed interests, knowledge, opinions, and museum-going experiences. Falk and Dierking referred to these entry conditions generically as the visitor's *personal context*, while Doering and Pekarik talked about these more specifically as representing the visitor's *entry narratives*. According to Doering and Pekarik (1996), if we start with the idea that learning, broadly defined, is a major outcome of museum experiences, then it follows that differing learning outcomes are likely to be directly attributable to differing entry narratives; visitor's entering narratives will be self-reinforcing. Entry narratives will direct learning and behavior because visitors' perceptions of satisfaction will be directly related to experiences that resonate with their entering narrative.

An alternative theoretical framework for describing both entry narratives and personal contexts is identity. At the core of any individual's motivations lies their identity. A wide range of investigators from the fields of sociology, cognitive psychology, neural biology, leisure studies, and, most recently, informal education have all converged on the central role and importance of identity as a framework for investigating human behavior and learning. In fact, Lave and Wenger (1991, p. 115) state that "learning and sense of identity are inseparable: They are aspects of the same phenomenon." This relationship is particularly strong when one learns during leisure time, since, like other activities that have a large measure of choice and control, individuals purposefully select actions that allow them to actively affirm the nature of their identities. "Through leisure activities we are able to construct situations that provide us with the information that we are who we believe ourselves to be, and provide others with information that will allow them to understand us more accurately" (Haggard and Williams, 1992, p. 1). The perception of choice and control appears to be fundamental to a heightened sense of self-actualization (Bem, 1972; Csikszentmihalyi, 1990a; Samdahl and Kleiber, 1989; Steele, 1988; Williams, 2002), which in turn sustains the integrity of personal identity.

For over one hundred years, the constructs of "self" and "identity" have been used by a wide range of social science investigators from a variety of disciplines. Perhaps not surprisingly, there is no single agreed-upon definition of either word, though there are a number of useful reviews of these various perspectives (e.g., Baumeister, 1999; Bruner and Kalmar, 1998; McAdams, 1990; Rounds, 2006; Simon, 2004; Woodward, 2002). Highlighting the complexities of the topic, Bruner and Kalmar (1998, p. 326) write: "Self is both outer and inner, public and private, innate and acquired, the product of evolution and the offspring of culturally shaped narrative." Perhaps more pointedly, Simon (2004, p. 3) states that:

> even if identity turns out to be an "analytical fiction," it will prove to be a highly useful analytical fiction in the search for a better understanding of human experiences and behaviors. If used as a shorthand expression or placeholder for social and psychological processes revolving around self-definition or self-interpretation, including the variable but systematic instantiations thereof, the notion of identity will serve the function of a powerful conceptual tool.

It is just such a conceptual tool that we are seeking as we try to better understand why an individual would engage in free-choice environmental learning.

The model of identity utilized here has antecedents in the work of a number of other investigators. Like Bronfenbrenner (1979), Holland et al. (1998), and Simon (2004), we subscribe to the view that identity is the confluence of internal and external social forces—in other words, cultural and individual agencies. Like Bruner and Kalmar (1998) and Neisser (1988), we acknowledge the important evolutionary influence on identity of innate and learned perceptions about the physical environment. From this perspective, identity emerges as malleable, continually constructed, and always situated in the realities of the physical and sociocultural world—both the immediate social and physical world of an individual, and the broader social and physical world of an individual's family, culture, and personal history. Each of us maintains numerous identities, which are expressed collectively or individually at different times, depending upon need and circumstance (cf., Cooper, 1999; McAdams, 1990). Although each of us possesses and acts upon a set of enduring and deep identities—"big 'I' identities"—we also enact a series of what Falk has termed "little 'i' identities" that respond to the needs and realities of the specific moment and situation. This latter kind can be thought of as "situated" identities.

Following on the work of Linville (1985) and Simon (1997, 1998, 1999, 2004), our premise is that most free-choice environmental visitors, as active meaning seekers, engage in a degree of self-reflection and self-interpretation about their visit experience. Most of this self-interpretation revolves around an effort to give coherence and meaning to the experience, including their relationship to the "what" and "how" of the physical environment and the "who" and "why" of the social environment. According to Simon (2004, p. 45), "through self-interpretation, people achieve an understanding of themselves or, in other words, an identity, which in turn influences their subsequent perception and behavior." In Simon's model, self-interpretation involves a varying number of "self-aspects"—a cognitive category or concept that serves to process and organize information and knowledge about oneself. Self-aspects can refer to "generalized psychological characteristics or traits (e.g., introverted), physical features (e.g., red hair), roles (e.g., father), abilities (e.g., bilingual), tastes (e.g., preference for French red wines), attitudes (e.g., against the death penalty), behaviors (e.g., I work a lot), and explicit group or category membership (e.g., member of the Communist party)" (Simon, 2004, p. 46). In other words, individuals make sense of their actions and roles by ascribing identity-related qualities or descriptions to themselves within a specific situation. The researches of Cantor et al. (1982) and Schutte et al. (1985) reinforce this model. They found that individuals do indeed construct identity-relevant situational prototypes that serve as a working model for the person, telling him or her what to expect and how to behave in particular types of situations. We believe that this is quite likely what visitors to natural areas, zoos and aquariums, natural history museums, and other free-choice environmental learning settings also do. Visitors have a working model of what the setting affords and then ascribe a series of self-aspects to their visit experiences. Visitors' self-aspects are congruent with both the situational prototypes of the context and their own perceived identity-related roles and needs. We hypothesize that visitors use self-aspects to justify their visit in advance and to make sense of their visit retrospectively.

While there are a multitude of ways to possibly operationalize identity within the context of free-choice learning (e.g., Leinhardt and Knutson, 2004; Sfard and Prusak, 2005), empirical research by us and our colleagues provides a glimpse into the powerful nature of this lens relative to the free-choice environmental learner. Falk (in press) appreciated that across a wide range of leisure-related free-choice environmental learning situations—use of national and regional parks (Haggard and Williams, 1992; Kelly, 1983; Samdahl and Kleiber, 1989); engagement in hobbies (Azevedo, 2004; Havitz and Mannell, 2005; Kelly, 1983); use of the public library (Falk et al., 2007); and visits to science centers, zoos, aquariums, and botanical gardens (Falk, 2006; Falk et al., 2008; Falk and Storksdieck, 2004; Stein and Storksdieck, 2007; Stein, 2007)—most people's stated motivations for using these settings tended to cluster around a relatively small number of closely related reasons—reasons that were strongly related to their identity-related self-aspects. Although (in theory) users of environmental education settings could possess an infinite number of identity-related "self-aspects," this does not appear to be the case. The reasons people give for visiting a museum setting, for example, tend to cluster around just a few basic categories of reasons and descriptions, which in turn appeared to reflect how the public perceives what a museum visit affords. Based upon these findings, Falk (2006) theorized that it should be possible to cluster museum visitors into just five distinct identity-related categories reflective of suites of self-aspects; he named these five types *explorers, facilitators, professional-hobbyists, experience seekers,* and *rechargers.*

Arguably, these five categories of visitor motivations represent the leisure attributes most people currently ascribe to museumlike contexts. In other words, people who visit museums put themselves in a situation expressive of one or more of these behavior categories. A successful museum visit is one that allows an individual to enact the traits, roles, attitudes, and group memberships associated with one or more of these categories.

In a recent national study of zoos and aquariums we discovered that these large motivational categories successfully captured a range of "i" through "I" visitor identities, as well as a variety of other variables, including important aspects of prior knowledge, interest, beliefs, and attitudes (Falk et al., 2008). Slightly more than half (55 percent) of all summer zoo and aquarium visitors possessed a single one of these five identity-related motivations upon entering the institution. Evidence from research at a botanical garden (Stein and Storksdieck, 2007) and aquarium (Nickels 2008) suggests that off-season percentages might be considerably higher. Grouping individuals by these five basic identity-related motivational categories provided significant insight into visitors' in-institution behaviors as well as short- and long-term post-visit learning outcomes.

For example, as an initial way to determine if zoo or aquarium visitors' entering identity-related motivations influenced learning outcomes, we conducted a two-step cluster analysis using data from the matched pre–post population ($n = 1,855$). First, a cluster analysis was performed on visitors' (post-only) cognitive and affective responses; learning outcomes fell into six unique clusters. Next, a second cluster analysis was conducted to determine what, if any, relationship the five identity-related motivations had with these six naturally forming clusters. The results revealed a strong correlation between visitors' understanding of conservation, their attitudes toward conservation and zoos/aquariums, and their entering motivations. Individuals who expressed a single dominant identity-related motivation ended up clustering with others with similar motivations; this was true for each of the five motivational groups. Five of the six distinct knowledge/attitude clusters were made up almost exclusively (81–100 percent) of individuals with the same entering identity-related motivation. The remaining cluster was a blend of individuals with dual and mixed identity-related motivations. The clustering of these factors provided strong evidence that the nature of a zoo or aquarium visitor's experience, in this case cognitive and affective outcomes, was related to the visitor's entering identity-related motivations (Falk et al., 2008).

Additional evidence of the benefits of segmenting visitors as a function of their entering identity-related motivational categories emerged during the analysis of pre- to post-changes in cognition and affect. The basic analyses of cognition and affect revealed that zoo and aquarium visitors in this study did not show significant change in their conservation-related knowledge but did show significant overall change in their conservation-related affect. However, this "one-size-fits-all" analysis provided an incomplete picture of what actually happened. Some visitors did show significant gains in their cognition; in particular, individuals enacting an *experience seeker* of entering motivation showed statistically significant changes in their understanding of conservation over the course of their visit. The data suggested that so too did most visitors acting as *facilitators*, but there was little evidence that individuals who entered as a dominant *explorer*, *professional/hobbyist*, or *spiritual pilgrim* gained in their knowledge of conservation-related topics during their visit. Similarly, the affective results suggested that visits to zoos/aquariums positively changed visitors' attitudes toward conservation and the role of zoos/aquariums related to conservation. But once again, these results did not tell the complete story. Some visitors, specifically those with motivations *facilitators*, *professional-hobbyists*, and *experience seeker* changed their affect as function of their zoo/aquarium visit; visitors with *explorer* and *recharging motivations* did not (Falk et al., 2008).

CONCLUSIONS

Building on this theoretical and empirical base, we can arrive at what we believe is a fairly rich, though still developing, understanding of who the free-choice environmental learner is. We understand that such learners are demographically diverse—in age, income, race or ethnicity, gender—and access free-choice environmental learning experiences across a wide range of sites and resources. We also understand that the decision to participate in free-choice environmental learning experiences is strongly influenced by leisure variables including word-of-mouth, advertising, and perceived leisure value. We also appreciate that whether or not an individual is inclined to pay attention to these environmental factors is strongly influenced by childhood leisure practices. However, more than anything we have come to appreciate that free-choice environmental learners visit educational venues in order to satisfy specific, usually predefined, identity-related motivations.

We are now discovering that what and how individuals learn in free-choice settings are strongly shaped by a range of very important factors, particularly identity-related motivational factors. Understanding this should allow researchers and practitioners to better understand and serve these learners. Research on free-choice environmental learning, despite an awareness of the diversity of users, has long been handicapped by efforts to treat learners as if all learners could be dumped into a single analytical group. Although some efforts have been made in the past to segment learner groups, many of these efforts have been based upon demographic categories—categories notoriously ineffective at meaningfully separating free-choice learners (e.g., Falk and Adelman, 2003; Falk and Storksdieck, 2005). As our current research shows, segmenting users based on the identity-related motivations they enact yields quite robust results. Moving forward, investigators will need to help refine these categories, appreciating that the current categories are quite course grained and potentially setting specific, or find alternative ways to capture users' identity-related motivations for engaging in free-choice environmental learning. Either way, there should be no going back to the old approaches since we now know they poorly explain why, how, and to what end individuals engage in free-choice environmental learning.

Similarly, free-choice environmental education practice has been diminished by a one-size-fits-all approach. From the perspective of practice, if free-choice environmental learning is primarily shaped by user's identity-related motivations, and only secondarily influenced by situational motivations such as a compelling exhibition or program, then what and how we offer educational programming in free-choice environmental settings needs to reflect this reality. Historically, free-choice environmental educational efforts have been predicated on the assumption that what a user sees and does primarily determines learning outcomes. These experiences have been disproportionately designed using behaviorist learning models, i.e., "if we can get the stimulus right, then everyone will have the same response." Now we appreciate that this is not the case. As described in the previous chapter, all free-choice learners enter an environmental educational setting with their own unique prior experiences, knowledge, needs, interests, social realities, and, as we now are better appreciating, identity-related motivations. These "entering conditions" have a disproportionately large influence on learning outcomes. Thus, understanding and accommodating users' entering conditions becomes of paramount importance because these drive how learners learn in free-choice environmental education settings. We can make sense of learning outcomes and we can get better at customizing user experiences for free-choice environmental learners, but only if we attend to the real motivations, interests, knowledge, and prior experiences of learners. That's the ultimate take-away message.

Fostering Empathy with Wildlife:
Factors Affecting Free-Choice Learning
for Conservation Concern and Behavior

Olin E. Myers Jr., Carol D. Saunders, and Sarah M. Bexell

EMOTION AND FREE-CHOICE LEARNING

Free-choice learning environments prompt us to reevaluate the roles of emotion in learning. A key aim of environmental education is to produce scientifically informed citizens: Without an understanding of ecology, we will not possibly make the best decisions. But any educational approach must also address motivation to act, which is closely related to feeling and emotion, and this is perhaps all the more true in free-choice learning settings where learners often have novel and stimulating multisensory experiences; sometimes positive mediation by experienced facilitators is lacking.

In this chapter we begin with some principles and findings about emotion. Initially we will look at emotion toward nature, including the concept of biophilia. Then we will focus on empathy as a key emotional process for free-choice learning and, in particular, explore how empathy is extended to its most likely targets in nature—wild animals. Finally we will seek to explain basic concepts and processes, describe what is known and what is not, and suggest important ideas for application.

THE NATURE OF EMOTION

Emotion has the reputation for giving life flavor, but also being sometimes a bit too hot, sour, or superficial; emotion has also been viewed as being irrational, unpredictable, and an inappropriate basis for decisions. Emotion employs parts of our brain that are relatively old and shared across mammals. This fact should give us pause in our denigration of emotions, for it suggests how adaptive they may be. The past three decades of research on emotion have changed the way psychologists look at it, from a set of stereotyped and automatic expressive behaviors, to a nuanced, variable, and functional process that integrates many brain areas. Recent research suggests that we humans are very much emotional animals (LaDoux, 1996).

Emotions represent a subset of the broader category of subjective feeling concepts termed "affect." Affect concerns feelings and traits related to them. Emotions are distinguished by being felt in the present (as opposed to being dispositions) and by having definite targets (as opposed to moods). They vary in feeling quality (sorrow versus remorse, etc.), and degree of physiological arousal (Ben-Ze'ev, 2000).

In one of the most widely accepted theories of emotion, Lazarus (1991) explained that emotion recruits cognitive and affective components in order to assess the import of events in the environment for a person's key goals, such as a key relationship, survival, identity, or avoiding moral offense. The brain makes an initial judgment of whether the information it has received bodes "good" or "bad" for such goals. The characteristic feeling of the particular emotion (fear, love, anger, etc.) is then felt at some level of intensity. This is the "primary appraisal" process. It shows that emotion is intrinsically cognitive, although the thinking may be more or less rapid and unconscious. Beyond the evaluation of the event as good or bad, the person may also cognitively generate a plan (the "secondary appraisal"), giving emotion a directive quality; we usually are inclined to act in some way when we have a strong feeling about one of our key goals.

Emotion also mobilizes the person for a response. The quality and degree of this arousal varies with different emotions, and although aroused, a person may or may not act. Action is affected by self-efficacy as well as emotional self-regulation. One type of action is expressive action, showing how emotion is social and serves a communicative function. A person experiencing an emotion might act instrumentally (flee, fight, problem solve), or seek to evoke a response from others. Communication of emotion is constrained by personal and cultural display rules about with whom, and when, a certain emotional expression is acceptable. Expression of emotion can be nearly automatic or very deliberate and conscious.

Recent brain research has confirmed and elaborated this picture of emotion. The brain "sorts" incoming information; that which is "labeled" emotional is routed first to the amygdala and second to the neocortex, where associative thinking takes place (LaDoux, 1996). Adolescent and younger children have a greater "knee-jerk" reaction tendency because the nerves between the neocortex and the amygdala are not yet fully coated with myelin as they are in adults, a process that speeds information transfer and moderates the reaction.

Individuals vary in terms of how much or little of a stimulus is required to evoke a response, how intensely a given emotion is felt, and how long it takes to reach a peak of arousal and to recover from it. The brain areas that support higher cognition also play an especially important role in how well a person can deescalate from negative emotions, and thus in his or her emotional regulation and resilience (Davidson, 2005).

For educators, emotion of the learner is central because it may initiate, prolong, disrupt, or terminate learning. Too much or too little emotional arousal interferes with learning, and positive affect is facilitative while negative affect hinders learning. Humans have a strong drive to make meaning out of experience. The brain stores memories and concepts in networks of meaning. Interestingly, emotion plays a big role in whether an event is experienced as meaningful and thus whether and how it is remembered. If an emotion is engaged, the brain marks the experience as meaningful and stores memory of it in the networks activated by the emotion and similar experiences. What a person remembers is thus largely determined by previous emotional arousal, and vice versa. Such experientially based networks produce fairly stable sets of responses, which help account for how people interpret and respond to different kinds of opportunities to learn.

In summary, emotion is adaptive because it helps us identify significant events, often provides the best initial assessment of the proper manner in which to respond, and it generates an influential repertoire of bodily and verbal ways of communicating (Thompson, 1993). We can be sure few people will respond to information unless it also arouses. Arousal, however, depends on a host of person-specific factors including emotional traits, experiences, social context, and meaning networks. If the setting arouses greatly, the emotional brain will dominate. If the person has only their own coping skills and style to depend on at that point, we have little influence over what is learned.

EMOTION AND NATURE

Biologist E. O. Wilson (1984) introduced the idea of "biophilia," which was then elaborated in several ways by authors in a volume edited by Kellert and Wilson (1993). The term was meant by Wilson to suggest that humans have an innate tendency to take an interest in, or to affiliate with, "life or life-like processes." In 1993, he stated that "were there no evidence of biophilia at all, the hypothesis of its existence would still be compelled by pure evolutionary logic. . . . In short, the brain evolved in a biocentric world. . . . It would be therefore quite extraordinary to find that all learning rules related to that world have been erased in a few thousand years" (p. 32). The strongest evidence for such predispositions for learning, however, is about fear responses to spiders and snakes, which, once reinforced, are very resistant to unlearning (Öhman, 1986; Ulrich, 1993). Socialization also plays a role; without role models, preparation, and knowledge some people find some aspects of the outdoors disagreeable (Bixler and Floyd, 1997; Bixler et al., 2002). Cultural beliefs and mass media may reinforce this impression.

But evidence is accumulating that supports positive affect in nature as well. Studies of people's responses to landscape photographs show that water features, views, and refuges are preferred (Kaplan and Kaplan, 1989). Early researchers thought this supported a "savannah hypothesis" about the origins of humans' landscape preferences (e.g., Balling and Falk, 1982), while other studies showed preferences for forests (e.g.,Woodcock, 1982). According to Han (2007), factors of openness, complexity, and water appear to be stronger than biome in influencing preference. Although the debate about which elements are most compelling continues, what is not in dispute is that people find certain environments restorative. Specifically, people's capacity for focused attention can become fatigued in everyday life but can be restored when an environment spontaneously fascinates us. According to Kaplan (1995), restorative environments offer the mind a balance of coherence and complexity, give one the sense of being "away" from usual stressful settings, are fairly spatially extensive, and feel compatible with the person's goals. Evidence is accumulating that exposure to natural environments offers mental and physical health benefits (Frumkin, 2001); people may not always be conscious of these benefits, although they typically report positive mood and emotion in such environments.

One limitation of biophilia, if it is conceptualized as an innate result of natural selection, would be that while it may predict attraction to certain natural features for the benefits they offer the individual, it does not explain how people come to care about nature or develop self-restraint in their actions toward it. Developmental psychology is usefully recruited when such issues of "nature versus nurture" arise. Developmental psychologist Kahn (1999) pointed out that, even if there are biophilic learning rules, they only have their effects through the person's active creation of understandings about their experiences. Kahn discusses how, through development, individuals may integrate biophilic and biophobic tendencies in higher-order meaning networks. Essentially, we can come to understand how we fit into the whole of nature, including the elements that are not immediately pleasing to us. Kahn has found evidence across several cultures that children and adults perceive responsibilities not to abuse natural resources as moral obligations (as opposed to being wrong because of social convention or personal preference). Such obligation is owed not to innate biophilia, but to the dynamics of cognitive-socioemotional-moral development. It is fostered through motivated dialog and reflection about meaningful events and questions.

While our focus in this chapter will shortly turn to empathy toward wild animals as a special case of emotion in free-choice learning environments, it is worth noting that not only can landscapes and animals evoke positive emotions, but so too can individual plants. Gross and Lane (2007) interviewed gardeners and found three emotionally relevant themes in their experiences: (1) *escape,* feeling removed from their usual worries and demands; (2) *identity,* the garden is a public display of one's own effort, skill, and preferences; and (3) *ownership,* meeting the desire to exercise control over a space. Even on the microscale, nature can have an impact on our emotions. The mere presence of an interior plant appears to facilitate cognitive function and positive emotion. Sommer (2003) examined studies on emotions about trees, concluding that "there is something deeper, spiritual, and almost ineffable about people's attachment to trees" (p. 180). Recent research found that people's levels of restorative experience and positive emotions related to place were positively correlated with the objective species richness (biodiversity) of urban parks (Fuller et al., 2007). Even indoor plants suggest biophilia. Shibata and Suzuki (2004) found that undergraduates doing a cognitively demanding task in a room with a plant showed more calmness, less distraction, and more tranquility.

The message here is that while biophilia probably is real, and that our still very embryonic understanding of it will increase, practitioners should not depend on biophilia alone as a strong spontaneous force in connecting people to nature. Rather, its effect comes through person–environment interaction, usually as mediated by other people, information, and institutions. Some guidelines for playing to people's positive emotions toward nature might be

- Facilitate access to natural areas by all demographic groups and provide diverse, rich natural stimuli and settings.
- Realize that comfort in nature (a prerequisite for positive emotions) sometimes requires the aid of an experienced and knowledgeable mentor.
- Highlight the positive feelings and benefits from restorative time in nature.
- Design natural spaces that heighten biophilic potential; balance coherence and complexity and inherently fascinating varied natural stimuli.
- Be aware of where innate learning rules and cultural meaning networks associate aspects of nature with fear. In these areas, create settings where

these aspects are encountered in a setting of low-arousal emotions such as wonder, and tie the natural object with positive mental networks.
- Creating empathy with nature may be a mechanism for creating positive emotional relationships with nature.

EMPATHY AS A KEY AFFECTIVE PROCESS

"Environmental sensitivity," or an empathic orientation toward nature, has been suggested as a key prerequisite for environmental education (Hungerford and Volk, 1990). Unless we care about nature, we will not be motivated to protect it. Certainly there are strong egocentric and human-centered reasons to protect nature, but they may not motivate a sufficiently long-term and thoughtful environmental ethic. As Leopold (1949) said, "It is inconceivable to me that an ethical relation to land can exist without love, respect and admiration for land and a high respect for its value" (p. 223).

Wildlife is a commonly used "other"-focused, emotion-evoking, center point of environmental education programming. Empathy with wild animals, particularly in free-choice learning settings, may provide a starting point for the development of active care for nature more broadly (Myers and Saunders, 2003).

The empathy literature typically describes the person feeling the empathy as the "subject," and the one about whom empathy is felt as the "object." This distinction is reinforced by psychologist Martin Hoffman's (2000) definition of empathy: "an affective response more appropriate to another's situation than one's own" (p. 4). Empathy thus involves "state matching," and if the object is in distress (the most common scenario in which it is discussed), it may result in "empathic distress." In comparison, sympathy or compassion occurs when there is a (nonmatching) feeling of wanting to help the object. If, instead, one becomes empathically overaroused, then "personal distress" may be experienced.

It is helpful to further distinguish between empathy and sympathy. Sympathy is more a "feeling for" an object, such as feelings of sorrow or concern for another's welfare. Empathy is more like a "feeling with," or sharing the perceived emotion of the other. Some people conceptualize empathy as making inferences about others by simply projecting our own feelings. But the self-in-relation perspective holds that the self is constituted through its relations with others. It is not true that we sense others only in terms of our own experience. We can sense that we don't know what others feel. Gilligan and Wiggins (1987) describe this as "co-feeling," or the ability to participate in another's feelings. There is often a bodily-felt sense that a given animal or person might approach us, for example, or is relaxed, or that it moves and behaves with an injured, disorganized quality.

Taking a broad view, empathy can be considered as one of a family of processes having to do with detecting the feelings of others, understanding others, and feeling concern for others. Some of these processes seem quite direct and almost automatic, whereas others depend on cognitively processing information about the other. Recent research allows us to create a differentiated picture of this family of processes that helps explain how the automatic and the more deliberate aspects relate.

Mirror Neurons and Perception-Action Matching Theory

Emerging social and cognitive neuroscience work has allowed researchers to detect which areas of the brain are activated in different empathy-related states and to interpret this information in terms of earlier psychological theory. While this area of research is still young, the findings support a clarified concept of empathy.

A fundamental basis for empathy lies in what has been described physiologically as the "mirror neuron" system. Simply put, perceiving another do an action or have an emotion appears to automatically activate the same parts of the brain that are activated when one does that action or has that emotion oneself, in a sort of "mirroring" (Decety and Chaminade, 2003). The brain processes others' actions by mapping them to the same systems used in generating the self's actions. This general process has been termed the "perception-action model" (PAM) (Preston and de Waal, 2002).

According to PAM, the link between another's action and one's own is immediate and automatic. This capacity is displayed by a wide variety of animals, has a plausible evolutionary basis (see Preston and de Waal, 2002), and is developed to a high degree in humans. While the PAM matching process underlies a wide variety of social phenomena, it is displayed in people in its most automatic form in processes including neonatal imitation, emotion contagion, and vicarious emotion. Very similarly, Hoffman (2000) lists three involuntary modes of empathic arousal in which an action or emotion of another is matched (and may be displayed) preconsciously, without self–other distinction. Examples include babies crying in response to each others' cries and spectators leaning in synchrony with a performer's efforts.

An implication of PAM is that the self is the model for understanding others. Preston and de Waal (2002) argue that "there is no empathy that is not a projection, since you always use your own representations to understand the state of another" (p. 17). But empathy clearly is not only projection, and it is not always automatic. In other words, there is more to empathy than perception action.

The Bases of Perspective Taking

Unlike emotion contagion, empathy requires the ability to distinguish between self and other. Empathic responding increases in early childhood development in synchrony with advances in self–other relatedness, with true empathy emerging in the second year (Hoffman, 2000). When "other" is differentiated from the "self," then we may think about what is happening to the other, and what it is like to be the other. This is called perspective taking, and it requires cognitive processing and flexibility. A person's intuitive "theory of mind" (including understanding beliefs about feelings, attitudes, desires, and intentions) and the ability to draw inferences from social situations are important in social cognition and empathy, as demonstrated by the consequences of their absence in neuropsychiatric disorders and neurological studies.

Emotional self-regulation is also a component of empathy, without which the object's state or situation may overwhelm the subject, who then experiences unpleasant personal distress leading to self-focused emotional coping (Lazarus, 1966; Rippetoe and Rogers, 1987). Fear and personal distress inhibit a person's ability to feel empathy toward and the ability to help another (Eisenberg et al., 1994). In sympathy and compassion, self and other are kept distinct and the subject registers the distress or pain of the object, but self-regulation prevents a debilitating match of the other's state; instead the subject consciously feels sadness or concern for the object. Interestingly, despite the inverse relation of personal distress and sympathy, people—even young children—can experience both at once if they are not too aroused, simultaneously feeling distress over the other's plight but also helping them (Denham, 1998).

Variables Affecting Empathy

Studies examining the effects of different variables on empathy have shown familiarity, similarity, emotionality, past experience, cue salience, learning, motivation, and socialization practices to be important. These factors have implications for programming.

Familiarity refers to the degree to which the subject knows the object well (for example, as a friend or relative), or has well-developed mental representations that include the object's features, behaviors, voice, emotions, reactions to different situations, and so on. High familiarity does not necessarily mean empathy is more likely nor that it will manifest in prosocial behavior, but it can enhance the likelihood and strength of both and may partly explain helping in intimate groups.

Similarity has long been observed as enhancing empathy; the more similar the subject perceives him or herself to be to the object the more likely that empathic identification will occur. Similarity may take second place to familiarity, for example, when there is emotional attachment to a highly familiar other. This is not only the case between humans, as Preston and de Waal (2002) note cases where nonhuman animals comforted humans with whom they were intimate.

Overall *emotionality* affects empathy; in particular "situation-appropriate" emotions. For example, preschoolers who have more positive temperaments and interactions with peers exhibit more compassion, helping, and comforting, and children who are more typically angry or sad respond less to other children's emotions. Experience of emotions, particularly positive ones, appears to be an important early mediator of empathy (Denham, 1998). The emotional tone of the physical environment is important too. Children from homes where hostile negative emotions are frequently expressed show lower empathy (Denham, 1998). The degree of empathy felt is also dependent on emotional relations between subject and object. Fear or dislike of the object is likely to interfere with empathy.

Empathy is more likely a response to *cues that are salient*. This is partly because salience increases attention, and empathy requires that a subject attend to the object's feelings or condition. Salience may be heightened by perceptual vividness or intensity, emotional meaning to the subject, and whether the cue makes the person feel a need to act (Preston and de Waal, 2002). Stimuli that are multisensory and naturalistic are more salient also.

Past experience and learning affect empathy directly or indirectly, on several levels. Hoffman (2000) shows that automatic or involuntary empathy may be stimulated by direct association of cues with the subject's own past experience (e.g., if the subject had previously experienced pain from the same stimulus). The higher-order cognitive modes of empathic arousal do not occur just in response to the spectacle of another's plight—they can occur in response to a description of the object or the object's situation. Learning underlies with whom one will experience empathy, the states with which one can empathize, and whether one will empathize or respond counterempathically (as, for example, in racial hatred) (Bandura, 2002). Finally, the subject's emotional or instrumental responses to empathic feelings are matters that may be affected by learning, cultivation, and adoption of societal ideology (Bandura, 2002).

The personal action model assumes that the stimulus will automatically engage empathy. Further evidence and reasoning, however, suggest that *motivation* is also important. Generally, if the function of empathy is the facilitation of social bonds (by coordinating actions, increasing mutual understanding, and signaling solidarity), then a subject should be more motivated and empathy is more likely to occur among members of a social group (Anderson and Keltner, 2002).

Research on socialization of empathy and moral responding shows that *positive social behavior should be modeled,* and models should express their empathic and sympathetic feelings openly and verbalize their attributions of the cause of the victim's distress (Hoffman, 2000; Eisenberg et al., 2006). Modeling that points out examples of empathic persons, expresses admiration of them, and stresses the good feelings that come from caring about others is likely to increase empathy (Schulman and Mekler, 1985).

Encouraging both self- and other-focused perspective taking fosters cognitive empathy. That is, reminding the subject of his or her own similar experiences or how he or she would feel (self-focused), and alternately directing the subject's attention to the object's condition and circumstances (other-focused) are both effective techniques. Focusing on the person's role in causing the distress is not regarded as necessary or productive, assuming empathy is activated (Hoffman, 2000).

Role-playing and perspective taking are endemically available in children's pretend and dramatic play, and adults can use them to inject scenarios that may be lacking in children's emotional repertoire (Hoffman, 2000). Adults also benefit from experiences that help them assume the other's perspective.

Empathy and Behavior

Our discussion so far has focused on empathy with the object. But empathy is of interest because of its possible role in response to the object. Of particular interest are prosocial behaviors, which are those voluntary behaviors intended to benefit another (Eisenberg et al., 2006). Motivations for such behaviors can be based on the perceived benefits to oneself or perceived benefits to another. Hoffman (2000) has spelled out a developmental sequence based on transgression situations, where empathy may be used by socialization agents (the model referred to above, which is often the parent, a teacher, or an older youth) to produce empathic guilt after a child has committed a misdeed. The parent (or other) should highlight direct, observable consequences of the action, as well as feelings toward the object. This not only communicates disapproval, but also taps the child's empathic capacities, producing empathic distress, and highlighting the child's role, producing empathy-based guilt. Because such "inductions" explain rather than blame, they deemphasize the parent's demandingness, and because they focus not on the person but on the act and its effects, the challenge to self-esteem is more likely to come from within (Hoffman, 2000). Parents then help the child to carry out appropriate reparations. It is notable that this process may not be cross-culturally applicable (Fung, 2006).

EMPATHY FOR ANIMALS AND CONSERVATION BEHAVIOR

Prosocial behaviors of interest to free-choice learning include stewardship and conservation behaviors, and empathy may play a role in promoting such behaviors. The connections of empathy, concern for nature and animals, and conservation behavior are not simple and they change across development and context. It is known that wild animals figured in the ecological identity development of landmark environmentalists including Darwin, Muir, Leopold, Marjory Stoneman Douglas, Hazel Wolf, Rachel Carson, James Lovelock, and E. O. Wilson (Seydel, 2006). How do emotion and empathy connect us to wild animals, especially in free-choice learning environments?

Empathy and protective attitudes toward animals appear to be associated (Taylor and Signal, 2005). Kals et al. (1999) identified three variables that explained much of nature protective behavior. Two of the factors may relate to empathy—emotional affinity with nature and indignation about harm to nature. In an experiment, Schultz (2000) showed that empathy produced by instructing subjects to take the perspective of a distressed animal increased the levels of subjects' biospheric concerns. In evaluating a Chinese conservation education curriculum centered on observing animal behavior, attributing subjective states to animals, and learning about animal care and conservation, Bexell (2006) found that empathy flowered and motivated marked changes in attitudes toward animals.

Myers and Saunders (2003) proposed that caring about individual animals may be the starting point of a development pathway toward caring about habitats, species, and ecology more broadly. One study of 171 children ages 4 to 14 established that children do form conceptual links between a favorite zoo animal and its habitat and other needs; children constructed their ideas around concepts reflecting ecology, conservation, aesthetics, or a psychosocial conception of animal needs (Myers et al., 2003; 2004b). In addition, there is some evidence for a relationship between emotions and behavioral intentions. Myers et al. (2004a) found that adult zoo visitors' emotions of caring, love, sense of connection, special privilege, beauty, wonder, and respect were strongly correlated with a desire to save the observed animal. Except for wonder and respect, visitors did not experience these emotions equally across

all animals, so zoos and aquariums and other similar free-choice learning organizations will need to work harder to encourage most preservation-oriented
emotions and capitalize on the "equal opportunity" ones.

Empathizing with Wild Animals

There has been much written on the sentience of animals, and for this chapter
we are framing our discussion on the assumption growing from ethological
research that animals are thinking, feeling beings. Flowing from this idea,
empathy and other emotional responses to other animals are widely used in
conservation campaigns and education. Much of the human-to-human process of empathy applies to people's relations to animals. Many animals are
objects for empathy because of intelligible behavior, facial features, patterns
of arousal and mood, observable social relationships, and bodily motion.

The general ability for humans to relate to animals as psychological, empathically relevant others is supported by research on humans and domes-
ticated tame and wild animals. Myers (2007) argued that the basis for such
empathy is the developmental plasticity of human modes of social interaction. Early empathy with animals is based on the "translation" of the child's
body to the body plan of the animal object, as well as affective attunement
and inferred intersubjectivity. Cognitive perspective taking carries the process further. No neuropsychological research has yet been conducted on how
the mirror neuron system is used to perceive other species. Preston and de
Waal (2002), however, speculate that the more dissimilar the other animals'
morphology and biomechanics compared to humans, the less mirror representations would be activated. But the vaulted ceiling of imagination should
not be underestimated. Anecdotally, scientists have reported empathizing
with organisms under the microscope (Naess, 1988). Among many other
examples, children pretending, dancers and martial artists performing, and
hunters stalking translate their bodies into the shapes and movements of other
species. According to the anthropologist Guenther (1988), Nharo Bushman
hunters of Botswana tune themselves to their prey species before the hunt,
gathering presentiments of what would happen:

> These presentiments . . . activated the hunter's entire body; they were felt at
> his ribs, his back, his calves, his face and eyes. His body would be astir with
> the "antelope sensation," at places on his body corresponding with those of the
> antelope's. (p. 199)

It is not known whether the necessary translations happen within the mirror
neuron system itself or via cognitive mediation, but all the variables affecting
empathy listed earlier no doubt apply.

EMPATHY FOR WILD ANIMALS IN
FREE-CHOICE LEARNING ENVIRONMENTS

The extent to which empathy with animals is activated in a free-choice learning environment will depend on the species and the context of how wildlife is encountered. According to Kola-Olusanya (2005) this context may range from (1) direct encounters; (2) encounters mediated by institutions such as zoos or media; to (3) vicarious, abstract, or symbolic encounters. In the following, we use this rough typology of contexts to organize evidence for empathy with wild animals.

Direct Wildlife Encounters

Emotion and empathy in direct encounters are mediated by the animal's activities relative to the subject. These activities include psychological features such as knowledge, feelings, beliefs, intentions, and the person's immediate social group (if any). Evidence of empathy for wild animals when both subject and object directly encounter each other in wild settings has been reported by field biologists. In these cases, empathy may be implicitly part of the observational protocols used, or it may be more overt (Moore and Hannon, 1993). Bodily based imitation and cognitive perspective taking were approaches used by men who had intimate knowledge of wild black bears, whether that knowledge came though everyday experience, tracking, bow hunting, or professional biology work (Myers and Russell, 2004).

Fiedeldey (1994) and DeMares (2000) documented positive emotions in response to wild animal sightings by nature tourists, although empathy was not measured. Indeed, a large number of Americans indicate interest in viewing wildlife. In 2006, 31 percent of Americans over 16 years of age reported watching wildlife in some way, an increase of 8 percent since 2001 (U.S. Fish & Wildlife Service, 2007). Such statistics do not tell us about empathy directly, but can indicate the presence of necessary conditions such as prevalence of encounters, attention, and motivation.

Significant threat from or conflict with wildlife may diminish empathy and probably reduce sympathy. A study of sheep farmers in Norway found that farmers with deeper attachment to their sheep had more negative attitudes toward carnivores (bears, wolves, wolverine, and lynx) (Vittersø et al., 1998). In another study, farmers from a region with high losses of sheep showed more negative attitudes toward predators than farmers from a region with lower losses. Interestingly, however, when farmers' anticipated personal losses were controlled for, farmers from the high-loss region expressed more positive attitudes toward the predators (Vittersø et al., 1999). The authors speculated that farmers from high-loss regions had more sophisticated cognitive representations of the predators. This agrees with the role of familiarity and knowledge in boosting perspective taking and cognitive empathy.

Similarly, threats to one's safety can influence attitudes toward animals and support for wildlife management strategies. Kaltenborn et al. (2006) asked residents around Serengeti National Park in Tanzania about their responses to several predators. There were three hypothetical conditions presented in the study: the animal was sighted near the village, it killed domestic livestock, or it threatened humans. The researchers asked whether villagers would do nothing, scare the animal off, report the incident to a game officer, or kill the animal. Across the worsening threats, higher percentages favored the more severe responses. The animal species had some effect; stronger negative responses were reported for lions, cheetahs, leopards, and especially the highly disliked hyenas. If an animal were a liked or preferred species, less stringent measures were favored, but this effect was shown only for the low-threat situations.

Institutional Wildlife Encounters

There are indications of empathy for wild animals in captive and institutional settings from researcher reports and visitor studies. In an example of the former, according to Burghardt (1992, p. 377), captive black bears are capable of "mutually close, trusting, and playful relationship[s] between experimenter and bear." Myers et al. (2004a) conducted an experience sampling study at a zoo utilizing electronic pagers and a response sheet to measure visitors' emotions and personality variables. They found that the type of animal (out of the three utilized: gorilla, okapi, or snake) significantly affected whether subjects felt they could imagine what it would be like to be the animal, and whether they wondered about the animal's feelings. In response to both questions, people rated the gorilla above the okapi and both the gorilla and okapi above the snake. Empathy as a personality variable was measured and found to predict experiencing the emotions of "special privilege," love, and sympathy upon viewing the animals. On average, women were higher on empathy than men (3.65 versus 3.11; $p < 0 .001$, on a scale of 1–5), as has been often found.

Clayton et al. (2006) listened to zoo visitors' conversations, and reported that 25 percent made some inference about the animal's state; 15 percent attempted to interact with the animals; 6 percent made some comparison to humans; 4 percent spoke as if from the animal's perspective, and 2.5 percent expressed sympathy for the animal. They interpreted their results to suggest that visitors experience a sense of connection to the animals, which is suggestive of empathy.

Vicarious Wildlife Encounters

Empathy can also be evoked by vicarious experiences and symbolic represen-tations. The use of still or moving images of animals to motivate or sustain conservation attitudes is widespread in advocacy, fundraising, and journalism. Such images often appear designed to invite empathy, sympathy, empathic anger, or action on behalf of depicted victims. Images often distill the point of the story, present familiar and attractive creatures, and are accompanied by narrative that provides perspective taking. Roberts (2005) looked at how conservation groups use imagery and found some of the motivational goals in their uses of photographs contain empathic components. Examples of such goals are to inspire, fill with emotion, arouse, and elicit action; to explain "why" without words; to evoke a favorable emotion; and to stir excitement. Animals can be construed empathically even more readily in literature and narrative. Close emotional connection with nonliving nature or plants that do not elicit mirroring may begin with such depictions, imaginatively and/or culturally conveyed.

IMPLICATIONS FOR FREE-CHOICE LEARNING SETTINGS WITH CONSERVATION MISSIONS

Empathy is of interest in free-choice learning settings from several angles. It may be both an outcome of learning, as well as an important motivator to both learning and action.

- Empathy with other life forms may be an important component of "envi-ronmental sensitivity," which is considered to be a critical motivational component in environmental learning (Hungerford and Volk, 1990; Chawla, 1998). Thus it is an example of the "broader outcomes" of free-choice learning delineated by Storksdieck et al. (2005).
- Free-choice learning settings may validly aim to "preach to the choir," to help people affirm their identities (Falk, 2005), or to reinforce those in the audience who already "believe" (Storksdieck et al., 2005). The experience of having one's empathy or sympathy with wild animals af-firmed may be an important outcome of free-choice learning, particularly to the extent that such empathy is dissonant with predominant cultural discourses.
- In free-choice learning settings, people have discretion over whether to attend to any aspect of the setting. As we have seen, some forms of empathy may be fairly automatic, but, even for those, the person must minimally attend to the object.

- The chances of attending to an object are increased when the object is highly salient. This is related to the common practice of using empathy-inducing imagery and other strategies to get the person to attend to the situation of a key figure (human or nonhuman).
- Mere empathy is not directive, but if the person also sympathizes or feels compassion, appropriate behavior is more likely. Thus empathy needs to be viewed as a component in a larger approach to behavioral change.
- Directing attention to animals' behaviors, encouraging perspective taking, building connections from behavior to the animals' environmental needs, and demonstrating respect and empathy with wild animals are important in an educational setting. The fact that people's desire for contact with animals is not always consistent with animals' welfare is itself a question that needs to be approached by encouraging cognitive empathy.
- Practitioners need to be mindful of what might be called the psychic economy of empathy; the most intimate human attachments may be costly, and constant empathizing would be emotionally burdensome. Some of the costs of empathizing with a distressed object include matching of negative feelings and anxiety for the object, its situation, or one's ability to respond, leading to personal distress. Overexposure to distressed "others" provokes psychological defenses that may cause even advocates to act counterproductively (Pantesco et al., 2006).

FURTHER RESEARCH NEEDS

We are a long way from having a complete picture of how empathy and other emotions, and the facets of moral or prosocial responding they support, can contribute to appropriate action on behalf of wild nature. Among the most obvious gaps and possible blind spots in our knowledge are

1. How do the basic processes of mirroring work when nonhuman animals are the objects?
2. What frameworks and knowledge are most important in helping people take the perspective of animals (i.e., belief in animal mind), and how can these be conveyed in free-choice learning environments (for an example, see Sickler et al., 2006)?
3. Which socialization and education practices are most helpful in moving from empathy with animals to moral inclusion? In what specific ways can emotion and reason work together most effectively?
4. How can direct, mediated, and vicarious or symbolic encounters with wildlife best be used to encourage and build on empathy?

5. How can the empathy-lessening effects of perceived conflict and competition with wildlife be dealt with?
6. When is empathy *not* an appropriate strategy?
7. What are the possible pitfalls of "using" empathy in free-choice learning settings, and how can they be avoided?
8. Is empathy with wildlife as a motivation for conservation behavior effective across cultures? How does empathy vary in situations where basic human survival needs are not met, but people live closer to wildlife and hold a better understanding of their needs and importance?

CONCLUSION

In this chapter we have summarized the current science of emotion and empathy and have briefly examined ideas and evidence about how these very dominant human ways of relating to the world apply to our relations to nature. Biophilia stands as a vague but promising umbrella term for emotional relationships with nature. Like all emotion, it is evaluative—we may have feelings of liking a part of nature or we may dislike it. Free-choice educators should attend to the directive and communicative effect of the emotions people experience. Evidence that some people (at least modern urban dwellers) obtain health and psychological benefits from time spent in natural settings may explain some positive emotions toward nature, and may suggest which natural settings will facilitate learning through positive affect.

Since much of our emotional life pertains to our social relations, free-choice learning settings need to consider the social group as the unit of emotional exchange and learning. Applying one of the most powerful foundations of our social emotional life, our capacity for empathy, to our relations to nature could help free-choice learning environments centered on wildlife be more effective. Empathy with animals may work in direct, indirect, and vicarious free-choice learning settings, and would be affected by all the main variables known to influence empathy. Empathy is of special interest for environmental education because it may be linked to behavior on behalf of the other, in this case including empathically salient wild animals.

4

Behavior Change Theories and Free-Choice Environmental Learning

Nicole Ardoin

$\mathbf{A}$ great deal of environmentally related free-choice learning takes place at institutions that explicitly have as their mission conserving wild species and habitats, unabashedly committed to the importance of encouraging conservation behavior (Falk et al., 2007; Groff et al., 2005). Many of these organizations rely on the active support of members and visitors to help achieve conservation-related institutional missions; they work to engage individuals in general while also promoting specific pro-environmental behaviors. This position may sometimes be considered contrary to traditional environmental education, where questions arise as to the appropriateness of encouraging environmental action, and critical thinking and environmental literacy may be considered the most appropriate outcomes (Courtenay-Hall and Rogers, 2002). However, many free-choice learning institutions are guided by conservation or action-related missions and do not struggle as fiercely with this perceived contradiction.

Although the undertaking of stewardship behaviors is frequently cited as an important, indeed central, component of environmental education, environmental action traditionally has been narrowly defined and inadequately measured. Consequently, environmental action and behavior have remained elusive concepts. Some researchers emphasize the importance of framing environmental behavior in terms of action competence (Jensen and Schnack, 1997; Stevenson, 2007). Others argue that critical thinking and action competence are not necessarily predictors of or proxies for pro-environmental behavior, which is often suggested to be an important goal of environmental education (Hungerford and Volk, 1990).

Another consideration that arises with regard to environmental action in the context of free-choice learning is the significance of individual efforts versus those pursued more broadly through communities, corporations, or society as a whole. In other words, do individual-level pro-environmental behaviors culminate in a truly beneficial impact on the environment, or are the promises of individual efficacy disingenuous?

This chapter examines how best to address these and related issues with the intention of assisting free-choice learning practitioners and institutions in considering whether and how to address behavior in working toward mission achievement. Situating environmental behavior and action within the context of broader environmental education goals, this chapter explores the relationship of affect, cognition, and skills with environmental behavior and addresses the role of individual actions within the broader context of large-scale conservation benefits.

DEFINING ENVIRONMENTAL ACTION

Free-choice learning settings, such as zoos, aquariums, natural history museums, parks, and others[1] often strive not only to clarify environmental attitudes and enhance knowledge, but also to teach skills and encourage the undertaking of direct conservation action (Groff et al., 2005). Speculating on the future of zoos and aquariums, Rabb and Saunders assert that, "Having a positive effect on the conservation outlook and behavior of visitors and other audiences is a distinct opportunity and obligation for our institutions" (2005, p. 6).

Behaviors emphasized in these types of settings frequently relate to pressing environmental issues highlighted in exhibitions or programming, such as endangered species, climate change, and habitat conservation (Dierking et al., 2002). While the action-related component of programs may sometimes be controversial (Courtenay-Hall and Rogers, 2002), these institutions recognize an essential value of education (as well as other social strategies, such as social marketing and communications) as being the ability to engage the public in undertaking pro-environmental behaviors, which may ultimately support goals such as biodiversity conservation and habitat preservation. Therefore, in free-choice learning settings, conservation behavior is not simply the beneficial by-product of an institution's activities; rather, achieving those behaviors represents a carefully calculated element of the overall design of public engagement efforts, undertaken with the organizational mission in mind (Falk et al., 2007; Groff et al., 2005). Programs structured to address behavior may present information about specific issues, showcase people undertaking the desired behaviors, highlight the value of the actions, and provide an opportunity to commit through signing a pledge or taking action on site.

In the context of free-choice learning settings, defining behaviors and actions can be difficult because the diversity of organizations and institutions, along with their respective missions and objectives, is immense. Generally speaking, an environmental behavior refers to an action, such as recycling, which may require a number of steps to complete. Each of those steps may necessitate individualized information and have different barriers (Monroe, 2003; McKenzie-Mohr and Smith, 1999). In contrast to reflexive or intuitive behaviors,[2] conservation behaviors are usually conscious, meaning they "require explicit thought to complete" (Heimlich and Ardoin, 2008). Moreover, conservation behaviors are not isolated, but instead are embedded in broader patterns, habits, and routines. Therefore, encouraging environmental actions requires consideration and alteration of the broader context in which the behavior occurs.

Conservation behaviors promoted through free-choice learning experiences may be categorized in a variety of ways. According to Monroe (2003), examples of behavioral categorizations can be direct and indirect (e.g., driving a hybrid versus supporting a law to encourage hybrids); individual or societal (e.g., using native plantings in one's yard versus participating in a community habitat restoration effort); and one-time versus habitual (e.g., turning off the water while brushing teeth versus using a brick to displace water in the toilet tank). Monroe also cites a combination of Stern's (2000) and Winther et al.'s (1994) behavior typologies, which include environmental activism, nonactivist political behaviors, consumer behaviors, ecosystem behaviors, and professional or workplace-related behaviors. Storksdieck and colleagues (2005) describe personal actions, or those that individuals take to directly address a specific issue (e.g., recycling or purchasing environmentally friendly products), and global actions, defined as "general and non-personal actions" (e.g., lobbying or providing financial support to organizations).

Persuasive arguments can be made for the range of classification systems. In the end, it may not be the classification system that deserves emphasis, but rather related questions. For example, an organization or institution with a conservation mission may be most interested in how pro-environmental behaviors collectively accumulate to a measurable bottom-line impact. Researchers must then explore mechanisms that compound the behaviors and what affect those sustainable behaviors may have on the overall quality of life and the environment.

MEASURING ENVIRONMENTAL BEHAVIOR AND ACTION

A challenge when examining behavior is that it is difficult to know which, if any, future actions may be attributable to, or influenced by, participation in a free-choice learning experience (Dierking et al., 2004; Groff et al., 2005). Free-choice learning events are not isolated but instead occur within the rich tapestry of a visitor's life. This complicates the assessment of impacts as vastly different backgrounds and expectations can lead to a variety of learning and behavioral outcomes (Falk et al., 2007; Falk and Storksdieck, 2005). Free-choice learning often takes place in informal settings and for a limited amount of time; the experience, as well as subsequent behaviors, are always strongly influenced by participants' prior motivations, interests, and personal contexts (Falk and Dierking, 2000). Related reinforcing experiences are also important elements in enhancing the prospective impact of free-choice learning (Adelman et al., 2000).

Nevertheless, because institutions where free-choice environmental learning occurs are frequently driven by conservation missions, it is critical to consider the impact of these educational experiences on the bottom line: whether participants and visitors take action and whether those actions have true conservation benefits. Theoretical models can be useful in predicting what short-term shifts in visitors' attitudes, values, knowledge, and intentions may mean for long-term behavior change. Those models also help predict what is likely to occur with a particular learner based on the personal context and using current intentions to project future action. Research assists in documenting shifts that occur related to free-choice learning experiences and explores how those either exemplify or challenge behavior change models (e.g., Adelman et al., 2000; Dierking et al., 2004; Quadra Planning Consultants, Ltd. and Galiano Institute, 2004).

Questions also remain with regard to the benefit of individual actions versus larger-scale or societal shifts. While some actions are personally meaningful (such as purchasing organic produce, which may have direct health benefits as well as broader benefits to the environment and farm workers), other token behaviors may lay the groundwork for people undertaking more difficult and consequential behaviors, while still others may require industrial-scale action. Leon and Brower (1999), for example, suggest that some actions are important at an individual scale, versus others that are more appropriate for organizations or corporations. They emphasize that certain consumer behaviors (such as home efficiency, heating, and cooling; personal transportation choices; and meat consumption) carry substantially greater weight than others (such as the paper-versus-plastic-bag and cloth-versus-disposable-diaper debates). Similarly, Stern (2000) suggests that, at times, the most meaningful individual actions may be to exert pressure on companies, organizations, and governments to make large-scale changes rather than focusing on consumer decisions.

In light of this triage strategy (individual consumer actions, individuals putting pressure on larger entities, larger entities making changes), it is important to consider to what extent actions promoted through free-choice learning settings are meaningful with concrete environmental benefits or to what extent they prepare visitors to commit to undertaking bigger actions (referred to as the "foot-in-the-door strategy").[3] By extension, free-choice learning institutions must consider whether individual actions are the appropriate leverage point or whether influencing organizations and governments that operate on a collective scale is more meaningful for the issue of interest. When individual action is the most suitable, the importance of priming people for future action should not be underestimated: Laying the groundwork for conservation behaviors, particularly through focusing on the affective realm may assist in preparing visitors to commit to continued and evolving engagement in conservation issues (Ballantyne and Packer, 2005).

WHY BEHAVIOR MATTERS

As discussed, questions may arise as to the utility of individual actions in the larger scheme of environmental change. Conservation organizations may wonder whether scarce funds are better spent on lobbying or marketing efforts, and zoos may consider whether direct investment in habitat restoration would be more productive for on-the-ground conservation. While the ideal is to employ a range of strategies simultaneously, finite resources always demand difficult choices. Managers inevitably must look to questions of efficiency and effectiveness in deciding which strategies to pursue.

For these and other reasons, mission-driven institutions and organizations, such as parks, zoos, and environmental groups, must consider the varying leverage points for action. Initially, it is essential to assess the impacts of educational initiatives and consider their benefit in conjunction with direct conservation measures, such as protecting species or restoring degraded habitats. Moreover, the impact of individual actions must be considered in the short and long terms, which is where substantial differences occur between direct conservation activities, such as habitat restoration, and social strategies, such as education, communications, and social marketing.

To best allocate scarce resources, the more immediate benefits of direct action or focusing on policy must be balanced with the future benefits of education—which develops citizens poised to make responsible environmental decisions in light of changing circumstances. Education can also help attract and retain members, serve the community, and build audience, among other tangible and intangible benefits.[4]

Several persuasive arguments exist for encouraging individuals to undertake pro-environmental behaviors that help achieve conservation outcomes. One is that encouraging easily implemented behaviors may develop self-efficacy and enhance a sense of personal control, shown to be important predictors of whether an individual undertakes pro-environmental behavior (Cleveland et al., 2005). Pursuing achievable actions may empower individuals by demonstrating that their actions can indeed make a difference, enhancing internal locus of control while also inspiring larger-scale lifestyle changes (Cleveland et al., 2005).

A second reason is that, for some issues and in certain circumstances, smaller actions can accumulate to create greater benefits. Stern (2000, 407) asserts that "private-sphere behaviors . . . have direct environmental consequences. The environmental impact of any individual's personal behavior, however, is small. Such individual behaviors have environmentally significant impact only in the aggregate, when many people independently do the same things."

Clearly, a balance exists between encouraging smaller actions that cumulatively have a consequential impact versus feel-good actions with uncertain outcomes. As Leon and Brower (1999) note, it is difficult to find actions that do not require tremendous sacrifice on the part of individuals but still produce substantial outcomes. Several efforts have attempted to assess the impact and contribution of individual action to large-scale issues, such as climate change and habitat loss (Monroe, 2003),[5] while others have addressed the psychological benefits that may accrue from asking people to take smaller behaviors, with the assumption that larger, more meaningful behaviors will follow (Burger, 1999).

Finally, as has been repeatedly demonstrated, the support, engagement, and active involvement of local populations are necessary for conservation efforts to succeed in the long term (Byers, 1996; Rabb and Saunders, 2005). Involving people in decisions about their environment and natural resource use is central to developing long-term conservation initiatives that are sustainable and sensitive to on-the-ground realities (Wagenet and Pfeffer, 2007; Western and Wright, 1994). Free-choice learning experiences that nurture involvement in local decision-making processes may affect the bottom line of environmental conservation by engaging local actors and honoring the delicate but dynamic relationship among economics, environment, and social equity. In turn, this may lead to better solutions, longer-term buy-in, more persuasive advocacy efforts, and a competent and empowered citizenry.

THEORIES OF BEHAVIOR CHANGE

The question of how to encourage pro-environmental behavior is informed by theories arising from diverse fields including psychology, education, and social marketing, among others. Monroe (2003) notes that "the abundance of competing [behavior change] theories and models can be daunting to the practitioner attempting to understand and explore human behavior" (pp. 114–15). Thus this chapter highlights only a few, emphasizing those that are appropriate to or frequently cited in either free-choice learning or environmental education research.[6] The theories presented herein explore what makes people voluntarily choose to become involved and undertake pro-environmental behaviors.

In the context of this book, consideration must be given to the unique qualities of free-choice learning experiences, including how those qualities affect environmental behaviors. First, by definition, free-choice settings encourage self-directed learning, which is rarely linear. Second, free-choice learning is predicated on a range of motivations (Falk and Dierking, 2000; Falk and Storksdieck, 2005). Whether the learner's primary motivation is to socialize with family or capitalize on a passion for birdwatching can impact what is gained from the experience. Subsequently, what the learner takes away influences whether she or he undertakes behaviors motivated by the experience. Third, a free-choice learning event may represent one in a series of experiences loosely focused on a similar topic, or by contrast, it may be unique and unlikely to be immediately reinforced. For these and other reasons, behavior models applicable to free-choice learning may differ from those appropriate in formal education settings, where learning and teaching are sequential and sustained, or in marketing campaigns, which may target a well-defined audience with a specific desired behavior (Grimm, 2006a; McKenzie-Mohr and Smith, 1999).

Many behavior models include similar components, but the interactions vary among those and the final determination of whether action is likely. Most behavioral researchers agree that action is spurred by the interaction of emotions, cognition, and values, coupled with the possession of the appropriate skills and opportunities for taking action (Heimlich and Ardoin, 2008). Many also agree that the sociocultural context is important in predicting whether and how people become involved in addressing environmental issues (Cleveland et al., 2005; Kaplan, 2000). These characteristics are of particular interest in free-choice learning as the flexible setting may provide enhanced opportunities for taking action, and the self-directed learning may vastly differ from that of formal education.

THE RELATIONSHIP OF AFFECT, SKILLS, AND COGNITION WITH BEHAVIOR

A complex relationship exists among the affective, cognitive, evaluative, and skills-based realms when considering environmental behavior. A number of theoretical models attempt to clarify this web of interrelated factors. Stern (2000) describes four variables that influence environmental behaviors: attitudinal, personal capabilities (skills), contextual factors, and habit and routine. Environmental learning is a "meaning-making process" incorporating elements of knowledge, awareness, and behavioral intentions, culminating in action based on cognitive and affective precursors (Ballantyne and Packer, 2005; this book chapter 1).

Knowledge about environmental issues is believed by many to be an essential basis for undertaking pro-environmental behaviors, particularly those related to altering currently comfortable and seemingly rational behaviors. The long-standing privileging of the cognitive realm often leads to a focus on environmental information as an avenue to environmental behavior (Schultz, 2002). Although this direct knowledge–behavior link has long been questioned, it continues to permeate many environmental education experiences. Kollmuss and Agyeman (2002) note that "most environmental non-governmental organizations (NGOs) still base their communication campaigns and strategies on the simplistic assumption that more knowledge will lead to more enlightened behavior . . . [and] even governments use this assumption . . . [which] is surprising because common sense tells us that changing behavior is very difficult" (p. 241).

Causal mechanisms governing the knowledge-and-behavior relationship are unclear. Schultz (2002) asserts that, while knowledge may assist in predicting behavior, it does not necessarily cause action. He illuminates three potential causal relationships, any of which could be true: First, knowledge may cause behavior; second, behavior may cause knowledge; or third, an outside factor may influence the two. Shultz provides examples related to recycling: Knowledge of recycling may lead to the recycling behavior, or undertaking recycling may spur interest in learning about it. Alternatively, an outside influence, such as a city regulation that requires recycling, may cause the behavior without requiring any knowledge.

Schultz and others recognize additional elements that work in consort with knowledge. Affect or emotions help lay the groundwork and provide an emotional context for behavior. Ballantyne and Packer (2005) postulate that "rational decision making processes are not sufficient to explain engagement in such behaviours without taking into account the power of emotions such as feelings of guilt, fear, or emotional affinity toward nature" (p. 288).

However, extensive research has demonstrated that general pro-environmental attitudes do not predict behavior (Cleveland et al., 2005; Lee and Holden, 1999) and that knowledge alone does not lead to pro-environmental behavior (Kollmuss and Agyeman, 2002). Essentially, affect, like cognition, does not operate independently. While attitudes are important to forming perceptions and understandings of environmental issues, the move from attitude to action involves a number of steps linked with motivations and contextual factors, as well as skills and competence. Cleveland et al. (2005) suggest the importance of a strong internal locus of control, noting that "personal control has been shown to be the only predictor of [pro-environmental behaviors]" (p. 199). To capitalize on the sense of empowerment, individuals must also be equipped with the appropriate skills to take action. DeYoung (2000) warns: "We make the error of assuming that once people know what they should do and why they should do it, they will automatically know how to proceed" (p. 521). Rather than relying on empowerment alone to motivate and create a path toward action, specific skills must be taught to build on self-efficacy.

Selected Behavior Change Models

Behavior change theories address the relational interactions among the affective, cognitive, and skills-based realms, exploring cause-and-effect as well as feedback mechanisms. However, because predicting human behavior is complex and dependent on myriad factors, models that coherently and correctly predict at least some portion of behavior are varied and may be contradictory.[7] Lindsay and Strathman (1997) attribute this to the fact that, when examining a range of environmental behaviors, research has "indicated that these various behaviors probably do not result from the same antecedent variables, [thus suggesting] that ecologically responsible behavior is not a cohesive construct in itself, but actually consists of multiple subdomains" (p. 1799). Indeed, environmental behaviors can be as small as buying a compact fluorescent light bulb or as all encompassing as pursing an environmental career. Clearly the motivations for these behaviors may vary tremendously and, therefore, models for predicting behavior necessarily reflect this diversity.

Nevertheless, some convergence can be found among a number of models, particularly when considering those most frequently employed in environmental education, health education, and social marketing. One commonly cited model is the theory of reasoned action and its derivative, the theory of planned behavior (Ajzen and Fishbein, 1980). These theories assume that people are rational actors and, while attitudes play an important role in determining behavior, they do not operate independently; rather attitudes help form intentions, which impact actions. Attitudes are a product of precursors situated within a social context; therefore, "the ultimate determinants of any behavior are the behavioral beliefs concerning its consequences and normative beliefs concerning the prescriptions of others" (p. 239). Behaviors and normative beliefs then influence attitudes and subjective beliefs, which affect intentions to perform a behavior (Denison, 1996).

Kollmuss and Agyeman (2002) suggest that the theory of reasoned action has "been the most influential attitude-behavior model in social psychology" and that while "the model certainly has its limitations—for example, the underlying assumption that people act rationally—it is useful because of its clarity and simplicity" (p. 243).

The social cognitive theory (Bandura, 1977) agrees that attitudes are insufficient predictors of behavior. This theory postulates that behavior derives from complex interactions among personal, environmental, and behavioral factors, with personal factors arising from psychological as well as biological characteristics; environmental referring to the physical and social context; and behavioral describing the physical and psychological processes manifested in visible actions.

Initially grounded in the behaviorist belief that actions are motivated by expected and received responses (Bandura, 1986), the social cognitive theory has evolved to more strongly emphasize elements of human agency, including the importance of self-reflexivity, belief in self-efficacy and locus of control, and emphasis on life purpose, among other individual factors (Bandura, 2001). Another central element is that individuals must perceive that the benefits of taking a particular action or regularizing a behavior outweigh the costs and drawbacks (Bandura, 1986). The social cognitive theory also recognizes that personal agency does not occur in a vacuum, but is influenced by social structure (Bandura, 2001). Through all this, Bandura (1986) stresses the significance of learning from others, including models whose behavior can be observed and mimicked, making this theory particularly relevant to group learning settings and when considering collective agency (M. Monroe, personal communication, September 20, 2007).

The health belief model (Rosenstock et al., 1988), also predicated on weighing benefits and drawbacks, explores mechanisms that prompt individuals to maintain good health behaviors. Health behaviors are considered to be similar to pro-environmental behaviors as both are voluntary, require consideration of positive versus negative consequences, and may necessitate sacrifices in the sense of inconveniences or financial investment (Lindsay and Strathman, 1997). The health belief model's central elements include perceived threat (perceived susceptibility to a threat and the perceived severity of that threat); perceived benefits (belief in the efficacy of proposed strategies); perceived barriers (concern about potential negative consequences); cues to action (physical or environmental manifestation of the issue); and self-efficacy (locus of control, or the belief that one's actions can make a difference) (Rosenstock et al., 1988).

In addition to predicting behavior, the health belief model also illuminates some of the most serious deterrents, even when individuals believe that a certain behavior is valuable (Lindsay and Strathman, 1997). Common deterrents, such as the action being too difficult, too inconvenient, or too expensive, may mean that the behavior will not be performed, particularly when it is related to the environment rather than health. Health-related actions generally have more immediate personal outcomes, while environmental actions may have longer-term, more diffuse, and less individualistic benefits and outcomes. These differences can change the strength of motivation required for compliance (M. Monroe, personal communication, September 20, 2007). In addition, critics have suggested that the health belief model does not appropriately consider environmental or economic factors, nor does it give adequate weight to social norms (Denison, 1996).

Another prevalent theory relates to the transtheoretical model of behavior change, based on five behavior change stages (hence the common name, the stages of change model). The stages are *precontemplation*, during which individuals are not interested in changing behavior or may not be aware of the need to change; *contemplation*, where individuals consider changing their behavior sometime in the unspecified future; *preparation*, during which individuals have a timeline and distinct plan for changing behavior; *action*, where the new behavior is actively practiced; and *maintenance*, referring to sustained commitment to the new behavior (Prochaska and DiClemente, 1986). While this model is frequently applied in health settings, its efficacy in environmental settings is uncertain. Individuals may be more motivated to take health-related self-preserving behaviors, whereas environmental behaviors may seem less immediately necessary and, hence, this motivation may be less powerful (M. Monroe, personal communication, September 20, 2007). Moreover, the model may insufficiently weight structural and contextual issues that affect whether individuals undertake and sustain behaviors (Denison, 1996). An additional concern is that it is descriptive, rather than causative, lacking adequate detail and grain size to identify movement within a stage that then might influence movement between stages (Dierking et al., 2004).

In an attempt to streamline theories, the model of responsible environmental behavior (Hines et al., 1987) is built on a meta-analysis of environmental behavior research (Sia et al., 1985). The associated psychosocial variables considered in this model include (from strongest to weakest level of influence) intention, locus of control, attitudes, personal responsibility, and knowledge (Hines et al., 1987).

After initial development of this model, Hungerford and Volk (1990) applied these determinants to formal education settings, finding that skills-building opportunities were also essential to impacting individuals' perceived sense of personal responsibility and intention to act (M. Monroe, personal communication, September 20, 2007). They then consolidated all of the elements into three categories: (1) entry-level variables, such as sensitivity to the environment as well as general attitudes and knowledge; (2) ownership variables, including in-depth knowledge, personal commitment, and resolve; and (3) empowerment variables, including action skills, locus of control, and intention to act. While based on the theory of planned behavior and taking the three categories of variables into account, some contend that this model lacks sufficient attention to what Hines et al. (1987) call situational factors: "economic constraints, social pressures, and opportunities to choose different actions" (Kollmuss and Agyeman, 2002, p. 244).

The Social Marketing Perspective

The models presented thus far represent psychosocial theories common in psychology, environmental education, health education, and others. Monroe (2003) presents a slightly different framework for considering how to target conservation behaviors. Monroe's "two avenues" include environmental education, with the goal of environmental literacy (and linked with the aforementioned models), and social marketing with the goal of influencing specific behaviors.

Social marketing capitalizes on the contextual and barrier-related limitations of the behavior theories presented earlier. As recognized in many of those models, various hindrances to pro-environmental behavior may prevent individuals from taking initial steps toward action. McKenzie-Mohr and Smith (1999) observe that many individuals with environmentally sensitive attitudes, knowledge of an issue, and the desire to do the right thing still do not engage in pro-environmental behaviors. In recognition of that disconnect, the social marketing approach focuses on identifying and removing or mitigating barriers to action. Many argue—and studies have demonstrated—that social marketing can be effective in changing specific conservation behaviors, particularly in the short term (McKenzie-Mohr, 2000). Because social marketing efforts pinpoint singular, directed behaviors, the outcomes can more easily be measured and quantified—either an individual does or does not adopt a particular behavior promoted by the social marketing campaign.

While social marketing may be successful when promoting a specific behavior in a particular setting to a well-defined audience, questions arise as to the continued efficacy or transferability of those behaviors to other situations. This is where discrepancies between social marketing and environmental education models are most evident. Environmental education strives for environmental literacy, or producing lifelong learners with the attitudes, knowledge, and skills to make decisions in an ever-changing world. Environmentally literate citizens are also adept at applying prior learning to new, complex situations. By contrast, social marketing focuses on discrete audiences, well-defined barriers, and context-specific actions with often-positive short-term results. However, because of the specificity, social marketing may not prepare learners with the same flexibility for applying actions in novel situations.

Nevertheless, the potential of social marketing for producing certain behaviors under certain conditions is indisputable. Therefore, approaches that integrate environmental education, when appropriate, with more directed social marketing initiatives may be the most efficacious way to affect behavior changes that are initiated in the short term, but sustained and adapted over the long term.

APPLYING BEHAVIOR CHANGE THEORIES AND STRATEGIES TO FREE-CHOICE LEARNING SETTINGS

While the aforementioned models provide insight into what motivates people to undertake pro-environmental behaviors, a particular challenge arises in light of the length and intensity of many free-choice learning interventions. Free-choice learning tends to be short-term of duration and episodic, representing a small portion of the participant's overall life by contrast to the long-term, sustained "captive" learning, which frequently takes place in formal education settings. In addition, free-choice learning by definition allows "individuals [to] exercise significant choice and control over their learning" (Falk, 2005, p. 270). Consequently, behavioral models that require learners to follow a particular path, practice certain skills, and engage in directed actions are often not appropriate for or applicable to these more fluid learning situations.

Because of the nature of free-choice learning, behavior change models relying upon lengthy and repeated exposure to shift attitudes and values as well as increased knowledge may not be effective in those settings. Storksdieck et al. (2005) observed that, "effecting change is inherently difficult in [free-choice] learning situations, where learning is based on people's personal interests, their motivations, and their needs to know . . . and because longer-lasting profound changes in attitude or understanding . . . takes time" (p. 354).

Assessing the impact of free-choice learning initiatives on behavior is also challenging, thanks again to its short-term and episodic nature. Behavior change, particularly when affected through education, usually takes place over a lengthy period. For example, participating in a conservation-related educational program at a zoo today may not lead to a change in an individual's behavior tomorrow. Rather, education prepares participants to make adaptive decisions over the course of a lifetime. While a learning event may mark a watershed moment in an individual's life, it more likely represents one in a series of cumulative events that may affect knowledge, attitude, and skills, which have the potential to eventually link with changes in behavior. This temporally and spatially distant connection between free-choice learning events and behavior emphasizes the importance of utilizing behavior change models as they may be of value in suggesting short-term indicators predictive of long-term change.

Another necessary consideration is related to the nonprofit classification of many free-choice learning institutions. By definition, these organizations or institutions cannot engage in lobbying. This distinction becomes muddied with conservation organizations, for example, where the mission may be to protect biodiversity; in that case, all organizational activities—including politically related work, as well as marketing and education—are likely to be conducted with an eye toward the conservation mission. Therefore, the fine line between educational activities, which traditionally focus on literacy and skills development, and social marketing activities, which promote specific behaviors, may require attention to ensure that the activities conducted are appropriate in light of the organization's nonprofit status. Concurrently, if it cannot be demonstrated that certain activities are moving the organization toward mission attainment, then their value may be questioned. Education promoting behavior change sits in a precarious position with regard to these challenges.

By contrast, institutions such as zoos, aquariums, and natural history museums often operate under different conditions and expectations. While historically there may have been a reticence to engage in education related to politically charged issues, more free-choice learning institutions in this sector have begun to pursue exhibitions and programming with explicit conservation messages and suggesting particular behaviors.[8] The question still exists, however, as to the appropriateness of employing education to promote specific behaviors versus education to enhance literacy and encourage personal decisions based on the best available information.

A further complication may arise when assessing the efficacy of education as a tool for influencing behavior because the temporal scale may differ substantially from behavior motivated (or required) by legislation. Once a policy is implemented, enforcement begins straightaway, hence changing behavior within an immediate time frame. By contrast, behavior changes influenced by a free-choice learning event may be evidenced only within a much longer time frame. These differences make it difficult for an immediate posttreatment evaluation to detect major shifts in action.[9] Moreover, it is challenging to assess whether the actions were motivated by the free-choice learning activity versus other influences, such as personal or situational factors.

Therefore, in the current conservation climate, which is heavily focused on assessment and measurable short-term outcomes, the effectiveness and efficiency of education for behavior change may be questioned. Environmental education in a free-choice learning setting, with the intention of affecting behaviors, may not be an easily defensible strategy based solely on measuring the impact on large-scale (both temporally and spatially) issues. When using the criteria of biodiversity conservation as the outcome measure, for example, it is challenging to gauge the efficacy of free choice in motivating behavior change.

In many, if not all, mission-driven institutions, assessment has traditionally been and continues to be a focus, helping make critical decisions about guiding scarce funds in ways that impact the bottom line of conservation. With behavior change through education occurring over months or even years, these organizations and institutions may question whether the benefits achieved through education outweigh the opportunity costs of failing to pursue strategies, such as policy changes, which may have more immediate results.

In sum, a number of considerations arise when targeting behavior change through free-choice learning. With institutions that provide opportunities for free-choice learning, encouraging specific conservation behaviors must be seen as part of an equation balancing the organization's overall mission with the ethical complexities inherent in education for literacy versus education for action.

CONCLUSION

In light of today's pressing environmental issues, conservation groups, zoos, aquariums, parks, and other public institutions are eager to engage individuals in productive conservation action. Increasingly, free-choice learning opportunities are developed with the recognition that pro-environmental behaviors are important, and in some situations essential, outcomes. Thus, questions around what motivates people to engage in pro-environmental behaviors, what sustains those behaviors, and how those behaviors impact the bottom line of conservation are of tremendous interest.

This area is ripe for further research to illuminate the processes specific to free-choice environmental learning settings. As described, many behavioral models derive from the health field, where impacts may be more immediate and personal. When an individual's actions may have cumulative impacts that accrue over a larger scale, contributing to massive issues such as climate change, for example, the mechanisms influencing and motivating those behaviors may be drastically different. Research into educational strategies for addressing behaviors with more distant and less personal outcomes will be essential to informing high-quality program design.

Another area requiring attention is that of the foot-in-the-door strategy, or whether taking smaller, simpler behaviors prepares people to take larger behaviors requiring greater sacrifice. Although the belief that small actions pave the way for larger ones is popular, frequently offered as a rationale for encouraging individual-scale pro-environmental behaviors, research has been inconclusive. While there may be some basis to this assumption, the mechanisms by which smaller actions link with larger actions require more study.

A final arena needing further exploration is the ethical element of promoting specific behaviors. It is essential to ask difficult questions, such as which individuals or organizations hold the power to recommend and promote actions; which actions are mutually agreed upon as beneficial; where the line lies between education and advocacy, and when it is appropriate to cross that line; and what standards exist for ensuring age- and developmentally appropriate behaviors are encouraged for the range of audiences involved in free-choice learning. These and other issues must be addressed by organizations and institutions that conduct educational activities, social marketing, and other engagement strategies with the intention not only of enhancing knowledge and teaching skills, but also motivating behavior.

Although many aspects of this topic remain to be studied, there are also strong, well-researched, time-tested theories that can help guide ethical, thoughtful efforts to address pro-environmental behavior. Many behavior change models possess similar elements demonstrated to motivate, sustain, and routinize pro-environmental behaviors. These models suggest that engaging the cognitive, affective, and values-based realms, coupled with a focus on skills and opportunities for action, lay the groundwork for influencing and predicting behavior. Free-choice learning experiences built on these elements display promise for encouraging individual-level behaviors while also helping develop a more environmentally literate citizenry motivated to take action on complex environmental issues. If environmental education aims to create new patterns of behavior, then free-choice learning experiences that leverage behavioral motivators and provide opportunities for action are fundamental to creating an empowered and engaged society that supports and restores the environment, now and well into the future.

NOTES

1. Free-choice learning does not only occur in out-of-school settings. As Falk emphasizes, "What makes [free-choice] learning opportunities different is partially the

physical setting and institutional philosophy, but equally important, and perhaps even more so, are the underlying motivation and interest of the learner" (2005, p. 271).

2. Reflexive behaviors are "mechanical responses . . . that show little variability" and intuitive behaviors are "based on natural reactions and instinctive responses to stimuli" (Heimlich and Ardoin, 2008).

3. See Burger (1999) for a full discussion and literature review of the "foot-in-the-door" strategy.

4. For more on this dilemma and efforts to assess the impact of education on conservation outcomes, see chapter 6 in this volume titled "Tools of Engagement: How Education and Other Social Strategies Can Engage People in Conservation Action."

5. For an example, refer to the Center for a New American Dream's Turn the Tide initiative, described online at www.newdream.org.

6. Several comprehensive literature reviews of behavior theories, within an environmental context, are available. See Heimlich and Ardoin, 2008; Kollmuss and Agyeman, 2002; Stern, 2000; and Vining and Ebreo, 2003.

7. Evaluation of a range of free-choice learning programs in the environmental and health arenas, among others, has contributed to knowledge of how and why these models work, although a thorough discussion of these assessments and their findings is beyond the scope of this chapter.

8. Monterey Bay Aquarium, for example, promotes sustainable seafood choices to visitors (see Quadra Planning Consultants and Galiano Institute, 2004), and the Bronx Zoo's Congo exhibition encourages visitors to actively participate in choosing which conservation activities their entrance fees support (see Conway, 2003).

9. Because of the difficulty of conducting adequately lengthy postexperience assessments, many environmental education evaluations measure intention to act, rather than actual actions. Based on theories such as the theory of planned behavior, intention to act is believed to be a relatively strong predictor of future action (see Armitage and Conner (2001) for a meta-analysis of the predictability of the theory of planned behavior model).

II

INFORMING PRACTICE

5

From Mission to Practice

Tim Merriman and Lisa Brochu

Most agencies and organizations working in the environmental arena have environmental conservation, protection, or preservation as one of their primary goals, usually stated clearly as part, if not all, of the mission statement. Education, interpretation, and outreach components of the organization must be designed to serve this mission. However, many educational programs are driven by the availability of funding and so may move the educational efforts off mission as the organization strives to please individual funding sources. This chapter describes the benefits that accrue to organizations that put "mission into practice" and the liabilities that result when they do not, as well as offering suggestions for how to stay mission focused and avoid "mission drift."

BEING ON A MISSION

Almost all nonprofit organizations and educational institutions claim to be mission driven, yet many cannot articulate their own mission or identify how it guides their operations. When asked about that discrepancy, the response often reveals a lack of clarity about the characteristics and role of a good mission statement. The point of a mission is to clarify the purpose of an organization, thereby providing sideboards for its operations. The critical components of a good mission statement are simple: It should clearly state what the organization does and possibly what or where is its audience.

The Monterey Bay Aquarium in Monterey, California, is a good example with its mission of "inspiring conservation of oceans." In very few words they identify that their mission is worldwide, not limited to the Monterey Bay environment. By not specifying a target audience, they imply that their message is applicable to anyone, and their commitment to reaching multiple audiences is reflected in a wide array of programming and exhibits in multiple languages, learning styles, and readability levels.

The aquarium does not specify that education is a primary focus of its efforts, but like many organizations that identify stewardship of cultural or natural resources in their mission, one of its goals is to increase a learner's knowledge or skills regarding the resource with the intention that such growth will support conservation activities. In essence, such a mission becomes a mandate for learning objectives with behavioral outcomes. Without the efforts of staff and volunteer teachers, educators, or interpreters and supportive nonpersonal media such as signs, exhibits, videos, and maps to empower the learner, the mission becomes almost impossible to achieve.

According to Howard Strauss of Princeton University, all of Disney World's employees—even their IT department—know the business they are in, a good measure of an effective mission statement. Their fifteen-word mission statement is "We create happiness by providing the finest in entertainment to people of all ages, everywhere." Disney World, noted more as an entertainment organization than an educational entity, has been a model for careful planning with its emphasis on a simple mission statement that anyone from the CEO to a seasonal worker can easily commit to memory. The simplicity and clarity of their mission is critical for a large corporation trying to deliver consistent services at all levels. They emphasize the importance of training around this mission during the orientation course required for each newly hired employee.

Keeping the mission statement to a phrase or simple sentence of ten to fifteen words helps in this endeavor. A fifty-word mission or one that includes a run-on sentence filled with redundant or unnecessary modifiers will keep most employees from making the effort to learn it or put it into practice. Tag lines are often used as a way of making a longer mission memorable in addition to serving as a marketing slogan. Disney World's tag line is, "the happiest place on Earth," which is easy for employees and customers to remember and captures the intent of the mission. Such an approach is a reasonable compromise when shortening the mission statement is not an option or when a simple marketing slogan is desired, but a tag line that is so broad that it no longer expresses the purpose of the organization should not be considered a substitute for a good mission statement.

BENEFITS OF MISSION-BASED PERFORMANCE

When asked to state their mission from memory, most employees of learning organizations will say, "It's something about . . ." before trailing off at a loss to find the phrases that constitute their guiding principle. In their defense, they explain that the mission statement consists of several hundred words or several pages or they've never been expected to know it. Often, the "mission statement" is actually a muddle of mission, vision, goals, objectives, and core values, resulting from compromises among stakeholders during a poorly defined or poorly facilitated planning process. The result is a mission that points in so many directions that the organization cannot be strategic in pursuit of long-range goals that lead toward a common vision. Looking at these elements separately can reveal how each can be used to support each other in a planning and operational framework to determine whether an organization is accomplishing what it believes it should.

Vision statements identify the desired impacts if the organization is successful in pursuit of its mission over a specified period of time. In other words, if a mission is what the organization does, the vision expresses what will happen if the organization is successful. For example, Monterey Bay Aquarium states, "we envision a world with healthy oceans that support a diversity of marine life." Their vision suggests the impact they hope to have as they accomplish their mission of inspiring conservation of the world's oceans. Core values provide another sideboard for operations. When stated alone, as opposed to being embedded in the mission statement, they set idealized boundaries for behavior of the organization. The National Association for Interpretation identifies six core values that include:

We value the biodiversity and cultural diversity of the planet.
We connect people with their cultural and natural heritage to promote stewardship of resources.
We believe in responsible business management that supports healthy environmental practices to the greatest extent possible in all aspects of NAI operations.

These identify the core beliefs of the organization and guide daily operations but do not specifically identify how the mission will be accomplished.

It is the goals of the organization that define how the mission will be achieved. Goals tend to be general statements that indicate methods of pursuing the mission and may include verbs like educate, foster, advance, encourage, promote, provide, or attain. They may relate to specific areas of operations: maintenance (goal: to provide safe, accessible, and well-maintained facilities and programs), administrative (goal: to encourage staff development in support of business plan directives), finances (goal: to be a self-funding operation), or program (goal: to educate our region through a variety of methods targeted to specific audiences).

Objectives, on the other hand, are individual measurable actions that will accomplish the goals. Foundations, such as the Kellogg Foundation, encourage the use of logic models as a mechanism for operationalizing objectives, because logic models help an organization clearly define success. Kellogg defines a program logic model as "a picture of how your organization does its work—the theory and assumptions underlying the program." Their "Logic Model Development Guide" describes how results can be better defined through the use of outputs, outcomes, and impacts. These different levels of measurable objectives correlate with those found in most strategic plans, but they express the planned results in more explicit terms.

Most educational and interpretive programs in free-choice learning settings have traditionally planned and reported progress in terms of output objectives. For instance, the visitor center will be open 300 days, trail programs will be conducted for 700 groups, or 1,000 brochures will be given to visitors. Output objectives measure the effort of the organization but reveal little about the effectiveness of what is being done. The use of logic model objectives permits evaluation in a variety of ways. Outcome objectives reveal more about effectiveness because they reflect a desired change in knowledge or behavior. At the outcome level, learning can be measured as cognition (20 percent of the audience will be able to identify the protected bull trout) or as commitment through participation in desired behavior (50 percent of the audience will stay and help clean up the beach after the program). Impact objectives measure the benefit or change in the resource or organization as a result of the outputs and outcomes.

Increased competition for philanthropic funds has brought a greater focus on measurable effectiveness in recent years. The ability to show results that support the mission of an organization is critical to receiving financial support. For that reason, many organizations are now using logic models to project and demonstrate success through continuing evaluation of results. For example, research at Monterey Bay Aquarium supports the idea that a learner's behavior may be influenced by a visit to the aquarium. Further, their studies show that learners who attend programs conducted by staff or docents are more likely to show desired behaviors than those who simply view exhibits.

MISSION-DRIVEN PLANNING LEADS TO MEASURABLE SUCCESS

Interpretive planning for free-choice learning sites begins with a review of mission, vision, core values, goals, and objectives. The mission does little as a standard bearer for the organization if it is not a guidepost in planning and made operational through alignment of goals and objectives. Too often the investment in educational programs and interpretive media is made with little or no discussion of these guiding beliefs and the audiences receiving the experiences. In *Interpretive Planning: The 5-M Model for Successful Planning Projects* (2003), Brochu defines interpretive planning as ". . . the decision-making process that blends management needs and resource considerations with visitor desire and ability to pay to determine the most effective way to communicate the message to targeted markets." (p. 2) Analyzing the relationship among these vital components in the planning process helps identify appropriate objectives that put the mission of an organization into practice. The power of planning resides in making decisions that invest available funds in doing what is most effective in alignment with the organizational mission. Financial resources invested in facilities, programs, or services that do not achieve the objectives of the organization are wasted dollars in the view of managers or governance boards. Facilities that do not tie their activities to core organizational objectives are often the ones closed or who have programs eliminated during budget austerity periods in economic recessions. A more thoughtful approach to planning can keep operations in alignment with the mission, which leads to measurable success instead of financial disasters.

A recent project to build a watershed stewardship center in Cleveland, Ohio, near the Cuyahoga River exemplifies this planning approach. The center will be devoted to demonstrating the sustainable uses of water in this watershed. The stated mission is "To enhance and protect the health of our urban watersheds." The site lies within a small valley that drains to the Cuyahoga River and includes an old landfill embedded in second growth forest, surrounded by homes. It is an appropriate urban test location for involving a community in understanding and contributing to the health of the watershed with both educational and management strategies in mind. The planning team designed logic model objectives to evaluate their progress with learners in the surrounding community along with measurement of the impact on the ecosystem.

The project identified two goals: to show positive change on the ground and to increase the capacity to effect change through citizen participation. In working toward the first goal, management objectives identify success in terms of measurable ecological improvements (impacts) in the stream shed, such as:

• Mean Headwater Macroinvertebrate Field Evaluation Index (HMFEI) score for streams in the West Creek watershed increased by 20 percent, with no more than 25 percent of streams exhibiting a decrease in HMFEI scores.

• Restored and enhanced 1,500 lineal feet of stream within West Creek watershed and the mean HMFEI score within those segments is increased by at least 50 percent.

The second goal requires strategies for engaging the citizen in active learning as citizen scientists. The following objectives illustrate the approach taken in development of these strategies.

Outputs—what the organization will do

    • Develop a neighborhood action program with certified citizen scientists.
    • Design or build a Leadership in Energy and Environmental Design–certified stewardship center as a meeting place and education center for West Creek.
    • Facilitate two on-site programs per month at West Creek Watershed Stewardship Center by 2009.
    • Conduct thirty-five on-site grades K–12 school programs annually.
    • Provide quarterly public seminars on natural resources restoration, enhancement, and protection issues relevant to the West Creek watershed by 2007.
    • Conduct fifteen off-site presentations annually about restoration, enhancement, and protection.
    • Publish an annual West Creek Watershed Grade Card on sustainability (relates directly to impact objectives stated for goal of showing positive change on the ground).
    • Monthly meeting of watershed coordinators to share ongoing progress.

Outcomes—how learners will perform or change if outputs are successful

    • Twenty-five trained volunteers will put in 250 or more hours annually on West Creek watershed projects.
    • Average of twenty-five local citizens will attend monthly best-management practices training/commitment event.
    • Ten West Creek watershed citizen households will participate in a streamside best-management practices demonstration project annually.
    • Five local businesses along West Creek will participate in best-management practices demonstration project.
    • Annual event for citizens, city officials, and scientists to share progress and training toward future objectives.

Impacts—how the organization or resource will benefit if outcomes are successful

- Protect through conservation easement or purchase an additional 250 acres of green space in the West Creek watershed.
- Protect 200 acres of green space in adjacent urban watersheds.

The experience in Cleveland has been that cleaning up the environment encourages people in the community and makes them more likely to protect green space. More than a century of urban sprawl, conflicting resource use, and lax water quality policies is not easily changed through new laws and tighter enforcement. Citizen participation is necessary to getting lasting commitments in a community. Defining the desired mission and aligning it with specific, definable impacts helps achieve success because programming can be tested and improved continually against the benchmark of the objectives.

Engaging citizens in working together to achieve mission-related goals and objectives gives the organization an advocacy network that is lacking if the audience is viewed only as a program user or consumer. This approach is a more sustainable strategy for communities in general because it makes everyone responsible for personal actions that improve or degrade local resources.

The competition for financial resources is a reality of resource management and education that will not go away. Building constituency can help keep organizations afloat in difficult times. Mission statements set a thoughtful focus on how an organization can create advocates while putting their mission into practice. Whether broad in focus such as Monterey Bay or more community based as in Cleveland, engagement of audiences as learners remains a consistent element of success. Logic model objectives define that success and build evaluation measures into the program plan, allowing any organization to see its mission accomplished.

LIABILITIES OF MISSION DRIFT

Nonprofit organizations that rely on grants for some portion of their financial support often are diverted from the organizational mission when the grantor has a specific interest. If the organization needs the money, it will sometimes bend from its mission to accept the funds. The resulting "mission drift" can result in programming, facilities, or exhibits that detract from the overall experience instead of reinforcing it. Grant funds last for a set period of time, and staff hired with them or work done with the funds often cannot be sustained, ultimately draining the organization of operational resources to support an activity that is outside of its mission.

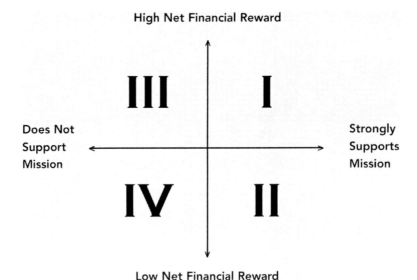

Figure 5.1.   Mission money matrix.

A mission money matrix (Brochu, 2003) can be a useful diagnostic tool in reviewing an organization's activities to detect mission drift. This simple matrix, as shown by Figure 5.1, places a horizontal axis of not mission related to highly mission related against a vertical axis of profit to loss. Sector I is the most desirable place to focus efforts (high mission relationship and reasonable profit). Most nonprofit organizations have several business activities in sector II (losing money but very focused on mission). Sector III is where the pure fund-raising activities with no mission value show up. Sector IV activities lose money and have no mission value. Plotting revenue-based programs on this matrix with an honest analysis of the costs of volunteers and other hidden expenses will create an overview of the organization's commitment to mission and identify activities that may detract from success.

The Internal Revenue Service (IRS) in the United States audits nonprofit organizations as well as for-profit businesses. Alignment of programs with mission is one of the areas of evaluation in an IRS audit. Profit-making activities that do not align with mission may be taxed as unrelated business income. Unrelated business income tax may even apply to some mission-aligned activities such as magazine ads due to case law precedents. These taxes are punitive unless the activities are extremely profitable. In extreme cases the IRS may determine that your organization is no longer eligible to be a nonprofit with tax exemptions due to mission drift.

Financial contributors also evaluate the mission orientation of organizations they support. Foundations have led the way in demanding results-oriented planning and evaluation. Donors and volunteers may lose interest in an organization when it invests financial resources differently than depicted in the campaigns and programs that solicit funds and donated time.

CONCLUSION

The benefits of putting mission into practice through thoughtful planning and operations are significant. Mission-driven organizations are focused and have a greater chance for success through planning the results they expect. A concise mission of fifteen words or fewer helps ensure that the mission will be remembered by all stakeholders and consequently put into practice.

Clarifying the differences between mission, vision, core values, and goals and objectives helps an organization define success. Writing objectives that include impacts and outcomes as well as outputs provides well-defined expectations to help direct the allocation of scarce resources. When results clearly support the organization's mission, donors, volunteers, staff, learners, and other constituencies are more likely to support the organization.

6

Tools of Engagement: How Education and Other Social Strategies Can Engage People in Conservation Action

Judy Braus

There's one thing that all conservation organizations know: Conservation results depend on people. From reducing global warming to improving water quality—it takes people knowing more, caring more, or doing more to create change. So in a world where people have an almost infinite array of choices about what to learn, how to spend their free time, and how they can contribute to society, conservation organizations and agencies have a big challenge—and opportunity—for how to best engage people. They can use all the tools in the "social strategies" toolbox to engage the people and communities they most want to reach in their cause—and do it in a way that is authentic, empowering, and effective. By making conservation relevant to individuals and communities as a whole, conservation-minded organizations and agencies can build stronger constituencies that have the knowledge, attitudes, and skills—and especially the motivation—to create the changes needed to protect the systems and resources that support all life on Earth.

Findings from a study that included surveys of more than 600 conservation professionals and interviews with 15 influential environmental leaders (Heimlich and Ardoin, 2006) indicated that considering a number of important components can help achieve conservation targets more effectively:

- Start by identifying your conservation targets and then pursue a deliberate planning and evaluation process to make sure you have selected the right ones.
- Identify the audiences, approaches, tools, and strategies that will help you achieve your goals, building on the research about what works best.

- Make sure you have representatives from your target audience and from diverse disciplines involved in the planning process so that you get input from an integrated group from the start.

The survey respondents also emphasized the need to build learning into the planning process itself. Selecting an adaptive management strategy that focuses on incorporating learning into all stages of your program, and to make changes as the situation evolves, is critical because it is almost impossible to get everything right from the start.

Many conservation organizations have used education to help build a conservation constituency and move people to take conservation action. This chapter explores an integrated planning process that includes education but goes well beyond, relying on all the social strategies (including education, communication, social marketing, and advocacy) and coordinating with policy and science activities to achieve and sustain conservation results. It also examines how free-choice learning environments—those that foster self-motivation and are defined by the needs and interests of the learner—offer important and exciting opportunities for conservation groups to engage new audiences in conservation and use a deliberate and strategic planning process to achieve and sustain results.

Seabirds in the Gulf of St. Lawrence—*Changing Behaviors*

Between 1955 and 1978, seabird populations along the north shore of the Gulf of St. Lawrence in Canada plummeted. Populations of puffins and razorbills had declined by 85 percent and 76 percent, respectively, mainly due to the illegal harvesting of the seabirds and their eggs. In surveys, it was clear that the majority of people in a nearby community felt that this illegal harvesting was acceptable. The challenge was to change the behavior and provide alternative practices. Over the course of the next twelve years, Kathleen Blanchard, working with her colleagues and the community, achieved amazing results: In 1981, more than 75 percent of the families were harvesting seabirds and eggs, but by 1988 that number had dropped to 27 percent. The population of threatened seabirds nesting on the sanctuary islands roughly doubled during the ten years in which the program was working to change attitudes and behaviors. So how did they do it? It was a combination of strategies, from summer youth conservation programs, school presentations, information (posters, etc.), citizen guides and study tours, and economic incentives that provided alternatives to current practices. The social norms in the community changed, and by the end of the program, the majority of the community felt it was wrong to harvest and eat seabirds and their eggs.

Source: Blanchard (1995).

EDUCATION AND CONSERVATION: A LONG HISTORY

Education has been an integral part of many conservation and environmental organizations and agencies since the birth of the conservation movement. Education was written into the constitution of the National Audubon Society, founded more than 100 years ago. The organization declares its intent "to arouse through education, public recognition of the value of, and the need for, protecting wild birds and other animals, plants, soil and water, as well as of the interdependence of these natural resources" (National Audubon Society, 1997). To this day, education, along with scientific research and public policy work, is a core element of Audubon's conservation work. Education has also been part of the National Wildlife Federation's key strategies since it was formed in 1936, and today the organization promotes education as "the key to creating a world where wildlife thrives" (National Wildlife Federation, 2008). Education and outreach have been mainstays of the U.S. Fish & Wildlife Service, where connecting people with nature to "ensure the future of conservation" is a priority (U.S. Fish & Wildlife Service, 2008). The Association of Zoos and Aquariums considers conservation education a prime directive in efforts to engage people and to conserve biodiversity. Education is part of the U.S. Environmental Protection Agency's strategy for achieving environmental results, part of the strategy that Disney's Animal Kingdom uses to engage visitors in environmentally friendly behaviors, and part of the mission of many local and state departments of natural resources and the environment.

Even organizations that have claimed in the past that they don't "do education" deliver a number of education and outreach programs around the country. The Nature Conservancy, best known for buying and protecting natural places, runs an innovative high school internship program for underserved audiences in New York City (see case study below) and conducts education initiatives in partnership with others on many of its properties. The Wilderness Society, the Sierra Club, Conservation International, and other national and international conservation organizations have a number of educational programs and initiatives, including interactive websites and outreach strategies for teens and adults, advocacy for environmental education legislation, and social marketing campaigns designed to promote environmental action.

Many conservation organizations and federal and state agencies conduct programs in conjunction with the formal school system (working with preschool–12 and university students), as well as teachers and university professors. For example, the Maryland Department of Natural Resources partners with K–12 classrooms and offers free-choice learning opportunities through partnerships with other organizations. The Nature Conservancy partners with

Building Future Conservationists—
Linking Free-Choice Learning and Formal Education

In New York City, high school students are experiencing hands-on conservation and learning life skills at the same time: More than 250 students are taking part in an innovative internship program called the Internship Program for City Youth. The program was launched in 1995 and is a partnership with the Friends of the High School for Environmental Science and the Brooklyn Academy of Science and the Environment. The goal is to link formal activities with free-choice learning opportunities and provide urban students with opportunities to work on nature preserves. It also gives Nature Conservancy staff an opportunity to engage with these students and focus on land management, scientific research, and outdoor activities. The program is designed to provide students with critical life and workplace skills while they are independent of friends and families. They participate in demanding field work; manage time sheets and budgets; and work as a team to cook, clean, and do laundry. When they return to the city in the fall, they share their experiences with their classmates and community.

This example demonstrates that conservation organizations often collaborate with schools to provide opportunities for growth and learning in free-choice learning environments.

Source: The Nature Conservancy (2008).

a high school in New York City to provide free-choice learning opportunities for high school students. The National Audubon Society has a network of more than fifty nature centers, many of which offer programs for educators and students, as well as those that link schools and the community.

In addition to conducting school-based programs, conservation organizations are also expanding free-choice learning opportunities as an effective strategy for engaging constituents. In a more information-based society, with dozens of opportunities for nonschool and nonwork learning, individuals have choices about which issues they want to get engaged in—and how they want to be engaged. In fact, studies have shown that young people and adults spend most of their lives learning outside of the formal school system and the workplace (Falk and Dierking, 2002; Falk, Storksdieck, and Dierking, 2007), and that there are increasing opportunities for doing so. It therefore makes sense for conservation organizations, as well as government agencies and community groups, to reach learners where they are most willing to be reached.

The challenge for organizations and agencies with a conservation mission is how to determine what the most effective strategies might be, in a world where potential partners have innumerable pulls on their emotions, intellects, and money. Different organizations have different methods for deciding

The Conservation Education Dilemma—*Finding Common Ground*

Conservation organizations and agencies around the world have had something of a love–hate relationship with education for years, grappling with what environmental education is, how it can help further the organization's mission, and how to measure its effects.

A review of the literature and a survey of more than 400 conservation and education professionals at a number of mission-driven organizations and agencies reveal that many conservation professionals do not agree on what environmental education is, when to use it, how to use it, and if it makes a difference in achieving conservation results (Fien et al., 1999; Heimlich and Ardoin, 2006). There was also disagreement about the most effective level of intervention (chapter 4 in this book). For example, if your goal is reduced energy use, is it better to target corporations to develop energy efficient products, the individuals who can demand and buy energy efficient products, governmental agencies or legislative bodies, or all three?

In the same conservation education study, we heard over and over again that education is crucial to the mission of many organizations and that education is a fundamental strategy for achieving conservation goals. Respondents described how education has inspired, informed, and moved people to take conservation action. They say it has created new audiences and funding sources, helped people think differently about issues, and created change over time. Interviews also showed how education has opened doors and allowed other conservation activities to take place.

The conclusion? Although conservation professionals do not always agree or even speak the same language, due to differences in training and experiences, almost everyone we talked to emphasized the importance of engaging the right audiences and using proven strategies to accomplish conservation targets.

which programs and strategies make sense and match their mission. In this chapter, I am supporting a process of decision making that starts with the conservation goals—not the strategy. For example, many groups have produced materials (posters, videos, etc.) without knowing how the materials would actually help achieve the conservation or program targets.

EXAMPLES OF EDUCATION, COMMUNICATION, AND OUTREACH STRATEGIES

Conservation-minded organizations and agencies have developed a number of education, communication, and outreach programs to support their conservation missions. Many target free-choice learning environments, given the huge need to engage citizens in conservation. Many others target both formal

---

Windows on the Wild—*Exploring the Diversity of Life on Earth*

Windows on the Wild (WOW) is a biodiversity education program that provides teaching ideas for formal and informal educators. Originally published by World Wildlife Fund,* this series is an example of supplementary curriculum materials for educators to engage young people in environmental education and conservation. The series includes a number of modules with background information for educators, teaching activities, resources, ready-to-copy activity sheets, a conceptual framework, and posters and others materials to use in teaching. As part of Windows on the Wild, WWF created a traveling exhibition, called Biodiversity 911: Saving Life on Earth, that traveled to museums across the country and reached millions of people with biodiversity messages focused on fishing, toxics, global warming, and other issues. *WOW* is just another example of how conservation organizations are getting their messages out in free-choice learning environments.

*WWF recently transferred the copyright of *Windows on the Wild* to the National Audubon Society.

---

and free-choice learning environments. Here's a small sample of the kinds of programs and activities that have been supported by conservation organizations (for additional examples, see Jacobson et al., 2006).

- Supplementary curriculum and activity guides: Developing materials for teachers and educators who work outside the formal school system.
- Conservation information: Among the most common forms of outreach are posters, brochures, CDs, PowerPoint presentations, exhibits, websites, TV, radio, and other materials designed to provide information on conservation issues.
- Training and workshops: General training and professional development for educators, conservation professionals, and others.
- Youth initiatives: Many conservation organizations partner with youth programs, such as Girl Scouts, Boy Scouts, Boys and Girls Clubs, 4-H,

---

State-of-the-Art Training Opportunities

The U.S. Fish & Wildlife Service manages the National Conservation Training Center, which offers dozens of courses focused on various aspects of education, communication, and outreach, including environmental education methods, engaging communities, public participation, developing teacher training, environmental interpretation, leadership training, and education programs for youth. This type of professional development is critical for professionals managing or working in conservation programming. Many of the training opportunities focus on free-choice learning environments.

> **Citizen Scientists—*Volunteers in Action***
>
> Every year, more than 60,000 people take part in the National Audubon Society's Christmas Bird Count (CBC). This program has been taking place since 1900, when ornithologist Frank Chapman proposed a new holiday tradition: counting birds rather than hunting them. What started with twenty-seven birders has blossomed into a citizen science program that contributes to biologists' work in monitoring bird populations, behavior, and conservation efforts. In addition to engaging people around the world, this program allows individuals to see how their efforts contribute to the scientific process. The data from more than forty years are accessible to anyone who wants to know more about trends and issues affecting bird life, including the effects global warming has had on bird populations.

the Student Conservation Association, and others who work with young people outside of school, with a goal of integrating environmental content and education into their programming. In most cases the organizations have their own conservation and environmental education programs, but others, like Boys and Girls Clubs, partner with an organization that can provide training and materials.

- Citizen science programs: Many organizations engage a network of volunteers, many of whom have no science background, to help with conservation research. Activities can vary from monitoring bird populations to monitoring water quality.
- Social marketing campaigns: Many organizations have realized the effectiveness of social marketing campaigns designed to engage people in conservation action. From campaigns to get people to buy wood harvested in sustainable ways to getting chefs to buy sustainably harvested seafood, many conservation organizations are teaming up with media and communications firms to develop programs that focus on specific, targeted actions.

What Do We Mean by Social Strategies?

Instead of focusing on whether organizations "do education" or how people define education (versus communication, social marketing, outreach, capacity building, or advocacy), many conservation professionals prefer to focus on the premise that to achieve conservation results, it is important to use all the tools that we have to engage people: basic information about a topic or issue, two-way communication, social marketing, education and experiential learning, advocacy—whatever makes sense for the situation and context. The best way to choose the most effective strategy is to engage a multidisciplinary team that can identify the conservation targets and threats, which behaviors need to be changed or supported, the audiences who need to be reached (and why), and the tools of engagement that can best deliver results.

It is also important to understand what works to promote learning and action and to build on the best practices that have developed over time. That means looking at the research—from education, communication, social marketing, and other social strategies—on how people learn, what moves people to care, how to build skills that lead to action, how to resolve conflicts, how to launch and sustain social marketing campaigns, how to best recognize people, how to integrate persuasion into campaigns, and so on.

This chapter defines social strategies as the ways that conservation organizations and agencies promote learning and engage people in conservation action. Here is a sample of the disciplines that many in the field include as social strategies:

- Environmental education: "[a process] to develop a world population that is aware of, and concerned about, the environment and its associated problems, and which has the knowledge, skills, attitudes, motivations, and commitment to work individually and collectively toward solutions of current problems and the prevention of new ones" (UNESCO-UNEP, 1976, p. 3).
- Strategic communications: communication efforts that apply the tools of communication, education, and public awareness to getting the right message, through the right media, to the right audience at the right time; includes two-way communication and dialogue, messaging and positioning, campaigns, media relationship, writing and materials development, and other strategies to achieve social change objectives (e.g., Spitfire Strategies, 2007; California Wellness Foundation, 2008).
- Social marketing: a communication and education strategy that focuses on the process of influencing human behavior on a large scale, using marketing principles for the purposes of societal benefit rather than commercial profit (RARE, 2008b).
- Capacity building: a process that focuses on how to strengthen organizations and the social capacity of organizations and partners, including infrastructure, operational effectiveness, individual skill building, and leadership development (World Wildlife Fund, 2008).
- Advocacy: speaking out on issues of concern or the act or process; supporting a cause or proposal. An organization may have advocacy as its mission (or part of its mission) to increase public awareness of a particular issue or set of issues (NP Action, 2008; Merriam-Webster's Online Dictionary, 2008).

Social Marketing Campaigns Build Pride and Protect Species—
The Saint Lucian Parrot

In the mid-1980s, the population of the Saint Lucian parrot had dropped to below 100 birds. Paul Butler, one of the founders of RARE, an international conservation organization, launched a campaign to help the people living on the island of Saint Lucia to learn more about the birds and their plight. The campaign included songs about the birds, posters, billboards, bumper stickers, classroom activities, and community events. Through all these strategies, Butler and his colleagues helped the community learn more about the reasons the parrot was threatened and why it was important to the community—and, most importantly, what the community could do to help protect it. In the wake of Saint Lucian independence in 1979, Butler was able to persuade the new island state that not only did it need its own flag, but also a national bird. The parrot is now officially protected and a source of national pride. Its population has climbed to more than 600.

Today, RARE is working in more than forty countries around the world to build grassroots support for environmental protection by training local conservation leaders in the use of commercial marketing tactics to build awareness, influence attitudes, and create change (RARE, 2008).

- Community outreach: education and communication strategies to engage key stakeholders (individuals, groups, and agencies) that are important to the success of a conservation initiative (U.S. Fish & Wildlife Service, 2008).

Many researchers have looked at relationships among the social strategies, and most have found overlap: Education uses communication tools, advocacy uses education, and so on. In 1999, John Fien and Bill Scott were asked by the World Wildlife Fund (WWF) (International) to conduct a ten-year (1989–1999) external evaluation of the organization's environmental education work (Fien et al., 1999). After talking with dozens of conservation professionals at all levels inside and outside of WWF, they characterized the "social strategies" as the strategies that conservation organizations use to engage people. As Fien et al. point out, the overlap of these strategies often leads to confusion. They outlined a way of thinking about the strategies that focused on the nature of the learning process—creating a nesting that starts with information, followed by communication, education, and capacity building. Their chart, summarized below as Table 6.1, shows the complementary function of these strategies, with each subsumed by the strategy to the right.

In this model, education is an integral component of capacity building. Fien et al. build the case for education being one of the most important tools for empowering individuals and communities to have greater control over their

Table 6.1.   A Continuum of Social Strategies for Conservation

	Information	Communication	Capacity	Education Building
Objectives	To increase awareness and understanding on conservation issues	To establish a dialogue by increasing understanding of the conservation issues that are of most concern and sharing experiences and priorities and planning collaborative projects to promote conservation	To promote knowledge and understanding of conservation principles, an attitude of concern for the environment, and the motivation and capacity to work cooperatively with others in achieving conservation goals	To increase the capacity of civil society to support and work for conservation through training, policy development, and institution strengthening

Source: Fien et al. (1999).

lives and natural resources. They also emphasize that all education has a capacity building function. Further they suggest that the role of education within a conservation organization is to build social capacity that supports effective and sustained participation in conservation initiatives including programs in formal, nonformal, and informal education settings" (Fein et al., 1999).

What differentiates education from other social strategies is the experiential learning process (Braus and Ady, 2007; Simmons, personal communication, 2008) that focuses on taking people through a deliberate process of learning guided by a coherent vision (Fien et al. 1999). The International Union for Conservation of Nature defines education as "communication in an organized and sustained manner, to bring about changes in attitudes, values, practices, or knowledge" (Van Hemert et al., 1995).

Scott, working with his colleague Gough (2004), built on Scott's original work outlining the relationship between information, communication, education, and capacity building—framing how each relates to training and education as well as to learning. In Figure 6.1, mediation is the highest level of intervention needed to engage people in issues that are more complex, controversial, value laden, and/or uncertain.

All the social strategies share the purpose of engaging people in a consideration of issues. In the context of this chapter, an important outcome of engagement is about moving people to take actions that address a conservation threat or issue. There is an enormous diversity of thinking about each social strategy; there are studies about each and about the overlap among

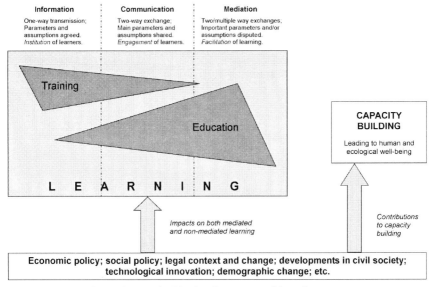

Figure 6.1.   Key issues in sustainable development and learning.

all of them. For example, environmental education (EE) is one key social strategy that we use to engage people. The first internationally agreed-upon definition of EE was developed at the UN conference held in Tbilisi, Georgia, in 1977, which produced the Tbilisi Declaration (UNESCO, 1978). Since then, a body of research has developed around each component of that definition (awareness, knowledge, attitudes, skills, and action) and around the field in general, looking at what works and how EE is related to environmental literacy and citizen action, professional development, strategies, and approaches (Braus and Wood, 1993; Jacobson et al., 2006) and how to evaluate impact. Social marketing has been developing somewhat independently from EE for more forty years (Kotler, 2002; Martinsen, 2002). Unlike many EE programs, social marketing relies on identifying a key conservation target and one or more behaviors that you want people to do or stop doing to achieve your conservation target.

In this chapter I have listed advocacy as one of the social strategies, given the importance of advocacy to conservation initiatives and the link to many of the other social strategies. Many education professionals shy away from advocacy, but the reality is that there are many elements of an advocacy campaign that include education and communication strategies. Helping constituents understand the issues, care about the issues, and know what they can do to help engage in the issues is certainly an educational endeavor. Some people think of advocacy solely in terms of a political or policy agenda—trying to

Restoring a Watershed—*Bringing Back Birds, Shrimp, Plants, and More*

In 1998, concerns about a shrinking riparian habitat in Marin and Sonoma counties, just north of San Francisco, led a group of fourth graders at Brookside School to begin a regionwide restoration program. The students researched the plummeting shrimp populations and publicized their plight, and also partnered with a local rancher and an environmental firm to professionally restore shrimp habitat along Temple Creek in Marin County. The program, originally called the Shrimp Club Project, was later adopted by the Bay Institute and renamed Students and Teachers Restoring a Watershed (STRAW). Students worked side by side with community members to restore the degraded riparian habitat, tackling issues of increased siltation of creek beds, pollution from animal waste, pesticide runoff, loss of creekside vegetation, decreased levels of dissolved oxygen, and higher water temperatures.

Since its start, the STRAW project has involved more than 12,000 students in more than 200 STRAW restoration projects on 38 rural and urban creeks. More than 47,000 hours of volunteer time has been donated, with more than 300 parents and volunteers participating in the restorations every year. The results have been positive for people and conservation, including the side benefit of building leadership skills and promoting community spirit and stewardship. As one third-grade student who participated in STRAW noted: "When you are eight, nobody listens to you. You are just a kid. Nobody thinks you can do anything. But today, I made a difference in the world. We are changing the environment." But this is more than a feel-good program. There have been direct conservation results: Because of the increase in shrimp, there has been an increase in the number of bird species observed. In addition, there has been an increase in woody plant density in riparian corridors that protects the watershed and helps increase shade and decrease water temperatures (Brita Dempsey, personal communication, 2007).

get people to pass or strengthen legislation or affecting policy at the local, state, national, and international level. But helping people advocate for the protection of their own natural resources and community health is connected to all the social strategies. Learning more about civic engagement should be an important component of free-choice learning and formal education.

START WITH THE CONSERVATION GOALS!

So if you are a conservation organization or state or federal agency charged with a conservation mission, how do you decide when and how to use one or more social strategies? As mentioned above, we recommend that conservation organizations do what they do best: thinking about their conservation targets. What are you trying to achieve? Most conservation organizations already do this—and have implemented a number of planning processes. For

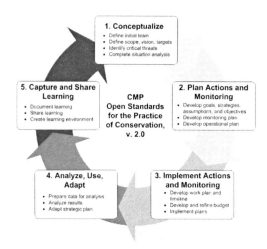

Figure 6.2. Miradi Planning Framework. Conservation Measures Group, 2007, reprinted under the Creative Commons Attribution-Noncommercial-Share Alike 3.0 License of the original document.

example, The Nature Conservancy uses a process called the 5-S Framework that includes a focus on five areas: systems, stresses, sources of stress, strategies, and success measures (The Nature Conservancy, 2000). The WWF has developed an ecoregion conservation strategy that starts with a biological vision and a socioeconomic assessment.

A collaborative group of conservation organizations, the Conservation Measures Group, has developed Miradi (Figure 6.2), an open planning process with standards for the practice of conservation (Conservation Measures Partnership, 2007). Many conservation groups have embraced these standards, including RARE, the WWF, The Nature Conservancy, and the Wildlife Conservation Society.

All of these efforts are focused on a deliberate decision-making process to define and achieve measurable conservation outcomes. They also include an adaptive management strategy that integrates a continuous feedback loop that refines targets, objectives, and strategies.

The Long and the Short of It

Conservation threats are often so pressing that the demands of dealing with current threats can distract us from planning to deal with future ones and thinking about preventative and long-term activities, including education. Some conservationists are engaged in exciting new thinking about how to link short-term (3–5 year) goals with longer-term social strategies that create societal change over time. By planning both short- and long-term strategies, we can address immediate threats while also focusing on sustainable conservation results. The longer-term strategy aims to develop education and outreach initiatives that will help inspire and educate, influence behaviors, develop skills, change social norms, and promote civic engagement in ways that prepare for future conservation action.

A number of organizations, including the U.S. Fish & Wildlife Service, Disney's Animal Kingdom, the National Audubon Society, the Association of Zoos and Aquariums, and the Ohio State University, are developing planning tools that will help conservation organizations use education and other social strategies more effectively in their conservation planning work. With funding from the Environmental Education and Training Partnership, this group has explored how to synthesize the excellent work from a number of organizations (IUCN, Conservation International, RARE, Peace Corps, WWF, etc.) and individuals (Byers, 1996; Jacobson et al., 2006; Wood, 1990) to make it easier for conservation practitioners to think through how to best engage target audiences to help achieve immediate conservation goals, as well as provide a strategy for long-term societal change.

There is a growing consensus among many conservation-minded organizations and agencies that it is critical to lay the proper groundwork for social change—and that individual actions, learning, inspiration, and other factors may be essential in preparing the public to commit to long-term, evolving engagement in conservation issues. Steve Gough, a professor at the University of Bath, reminds us that "No policy objectives can be (or have ever been) sustained over the years in the face of popular indifference or opposition. Education engages learners in terms of their own knowledge, beliefs, and interests and contributes to a social change" (2004).

Honing in on the Right Audience

In a free-choice learning context, it is critical to understand what your target audience values, what prevents them from doing the "right" thing from a conservation perspective, and what will motivate them to take action. When people have a choice about what they learn, how they spend their time, and what matters to them, it's important to understand what moves them, what they care about, what barriers they face, and how to create a will to act and engage.

Conservation issues affect everyone, and every individual affects conservation results. That's why so many organizations develop education programs that target the general public. But in most cases, the smaller and more targeted the audience, the more success you'll have in achieving your goals—especially with a conservation action target. Kristen Grimm, president of Spitfire Strategies, a strategic communication firm headquartered in Washington, D.C., suggests that when considering a campaign, it's useful to think about the smallest number of people you can activate to get what you want (Kristen Grimm, personal communication, 2007). For a social marketing campaign or targeted advocacy campaign, smaller is probably better. For broader awareness and knowledge campaigns, larger audiences may be appropriate. Al Gore's "Inconvenient Truth" movie, slide show, and training program, for example, are aimed at reaching a large audience to increase global warming awareness.

It's also important to think about segmenting the audiences you want to reach and identifying how they relate to the issues, targets, and threats you have identified. When trying to sort out audiences, there are some key questions you might ask:

- Who knows what about the issues?
- Who controls what?
- Who can help to change negative patterns of behavior?
- Who can help protect an area that is not currently threatened, but might be in the future?

Many experts believe that the long-term success and sustainability of conservation efforts depends on how well we understand those we wish to engage. And by assessing and engaging a wide range of stakeholders, we can help focus attention on key issues, audiences, and strategies that will help achieve conservation goals, especially site-based conservation issues.

Stakeholders include people, institutions, and social groups that are involved in, or affected by, decisions made regarding conservation issues. They can include any of the following:

- people directly affecting natural resources (farmers, fishers, builders, consumers, homeowners, etc.)
- people who work with people affecting natural resources
- local leaders and government officials
- influential community members
- subsets of the general public (families, seniors, 18–34-year-olds, etc.)
- specific targets (consumers of seafood, the automotive industry, etc.)
- young people (preschool, elementary, middle, high school, etc.)
- educators (teachers, informal, and others)
- corporations and employees
- other conservation professionals

According to the Spitfire Strategies' *Discovering the Activation Point* (Grimm, 2006a), it is always highly recommended to ask:

- Who do you need to persuade and what do you want them to do?
- Are you trying to build knowledge, build the will to take action, or reinforce action?

- What can you do to build the audience's will to act?
- What barriers need to be overcome and how?
- When is the best time to persuade?
- Once your audience takes action, how do you reinforce that action?

As mentioned above, once you have identified the conservation targets and threats, whom you need to reach, and what you want them to know, feel, and do, you will need to determine the best approach. In most cases, you will be using a variety of strategies and tools from a number of disciplines. For example, you might outline a strategy that includes a social marketing campaign to get a community to stop destructive behaviors that are polluting a local wetland, along with an advocacy plan to influence legislators and engage a grassroots network, and a longer-term education program to help the community understand the value that a wetland provides to the health and tourism of the community.

CONSERVATION SUCCESS: WHAT WORKS?

We still have a lot to learn about how to best integrate the full range of social strategies into conservation planning and how to measure effects. We also have much work to do in getting conservation practitioners from multiple disciplines to have a common understanding of what the research is telling us about what works in moving people to take action—especially the role that free-choice learning can contribute. But we need to make the research accessible so that everyone working in conservation can build programs based on best practices and learning. Many writers have already suggested some directions for designing programs to achieve conservation results:

- Information, social norms, options, and laws and enforcements are the most common and often the most important factors in influencing most kinds of conservation behaviors (Byers, 2003).
- Information and knowledge are seldom the major factors in changing behavior, but in certain cases they can be catalytic factors; information and knowledge often enable other factors to work (Byers, 2003).
- If you want to engage people, it's important to relate any initiative to people's values and comfort zones (Grimm, 2006a).
- Providing recognition for doing the right thing is critical if you want to encourage that behavior and get someone to continue doing the right thing; and when asking people to do something, make sure it's actually something they can do (Spitfire Strategies, 2007).

- The amount of time that children spend outside with a mentor can influence their level of concern for the environment as adults (Chawla, 1998).
- Eliminating the barriers to taking an environmental action is one of the biggest factors in getting someone to try a new behavior. It can also be persuasive to show people how the benefits of a new behavior outweigh the risks (McKenzie-Mohr, 2000).
- In delivering a message, the messenger is critical. If the person or group you are trying to influence doesn't believe the messenger, you won't get support or buy-in (Spitfire Strategies, Smart Chart 3.0, 2008).

Building the capacity of educators and other conservation professionals is also critical in moving people to take conservation action. It's important that there is leadership and commitment to integration at senior levels of the organization—not just of the social strategies, but also integrating the social strategies with science and policy. Other factors that can help conservation-minded organizations or agencies achieve success include:

- Understanding how to assess your audience and understanding how to engage new audiences.
- Creating a culture of learning and evaluation so that you can understand what works and adapt as you go forward; it also helps to have a common understanding of education, how it relates to communication and capacity building, and how all the social strategies can help, directly and indirectly, achieve conservation goals.
- Providing professional development opportunities so that scientists, policy experts, educators, and communicators can better understand the evolving relationships among all the social strategies and conservation action.
- Creating integrated teams that include individuals with social science backgrounds and who understand how to do a stakeholder assessment and lead a participatory process, and who can design, implement, and evaluate education and communication programs that contribute to conservation targets, as well as longer-term engagement strategies.
- Building on research that shows the value of education and other social strategies in helping to achieve and sustain conservation goals.

As our understanding of free-choice learning grows, we will continue to learn more about how to effectively engage audiences outside the formal school system—audiences that are critical for conservation success. A strategic conservation planning process enables organizations and agencies with a

Let's Get the Lead Out—*A Campaign to Save Loons*

During the 1990s, research revealed that the primary cause of death of New England's adult loons was lead poisoning from the ingestion of lead sinkers and jigs. Cooperating conservation organizations realized that anglers needed to be informed of the problem and encouraged to voluntarily switch to nontoxic tackle.

Outreach efforts began in 1997, when the U.S. Fish & Wildlife Service collaborated with the North American Loon Fund and the Loon Preservation Committee to create an easily copied brochure titled "Let's Get the Lead Out." During the following two years, the Service, the New Hampshire Fish and Game Department, the Vermont Agency of Natural Resources, and many other cooperators distributed tens of thousands of brochures. The Service and research cooperators used the charismatic and popular appeal of the loon to their advantage. They invited reporters to accompany researchers capturing and sampling loons, and the news media played a significant role in bringing the issue to light.

When it became clear that the cooperating northeast agencies and organizations were using different approaches regarding sinker outreach, the Service began promoting a coordinated approach to avoid duplication of efforts and focus on a single outreach message. A meeting was held to promote networking and coordinate outreach, and everyone agreed on a slightly expanded message: "You can help stop contaminating our environment and protect waterfowl, especially the common loon, by using nontoxic sinkers." They also developed exchange programs to help encourage anglers to stop using lead tackle and a slide show to help educate a variety of audiences.

Although voluntary cooperation from the angling community was the goal of the outreach effort, several New England states have taken the legislative route, responding to research data and lobbying by nonprofit organizations. This program provides a good example of how outreach and research have been working together to address a serious resource issue, using a variety of outreach tools effectively to achieve a goal. (U.S. Fish & Wildlife Service, 1999; Ady, 2007)

conservation mission to use their resources efficiently to target those audiences who can best achieve results in both the short and the long term and whose actions can create sustainable conservation results. The goal is to design interventions that achieve identified targets in the short term while investing in the longer term to build a stronger conservation constituency with the knowledge, skills, attitudes, and will to act to create a more sustainable future.

7

How Can Participatory Action Research Inform Free-Choice Learning Pedagogy and Research in Environmental Education Contexts?

Michael Brody

THE SITUATION

Both participatory action research (PAR) and free-choice learning have been incorporated into environmental education (EE) in a variety of ways. The EE literature contains a number of references to PAR as a participatory learning model over the past two decades including the use of PAR in education programs directed at ecological and social change such as Project GREEN (Stapp et al., 1996). Much of the previous PAR application in EE has focused on PAR as a pedagogical technique to engage scientists, educators, and learners in community problem-solving studies leading to ecological or social change. This participatory action learning approach is sometimes considered an aspect of critical pedagogy as applied to ecological concerns (Huckle, 1999).

Free-choice learning and the associated contextual learning theory also appear in the EE literature, most notably as the focus of a special edition of the journal *Environmental Education Research* in June 2005. Like PAR in EE the major principals of contextual learning theory in free-choice learning are used to conceptualize environmental curriculum, teaching, and learning in out-of-school or informal education contexts such as nature centers, museums, and aquariums (Falk and Dierking, 2000). Falk (2005) frames the *Environmental Education Research* special edition and emphasizes the contextual learning theory framework for a better understanding of learning, teaching, curriculum, and exhibit design in free-choice informal environmental settings. He explains the four basic principles of the contextual learning theory: experiential base, personal knowledge construction, social knowledge construction, and learning over time. In the same issue, Meyers (2005) suggests the epistemological foundations of free-choice learning in Dewey's pragmatism and Vygotsky's notions of social learning. Emphasis again is on contextual learning theory as a way to understand the pragmatics of EE pedagogy.

Less attention has been directed at how PAR and contextual learning theory in free-choice learning can help us answer research questions about effective environmental teaching and learning outcomes. Both action research (AR) and PAR have also recently been identified as underrepresented research methodologies in the research literature related to assessment of learning outcomes in informal settings (Brody et al., 2007). Emerging paradigms of research in EE suggest that PAR has the potential for contributing to the EE research agenda if researchers consider the intentionality, mutuality, and action orientation of conducting EE research (McKenzie, 2005; Moore, 2005; Varga et al., 2007).

In relation to free-choice learning informing research in EE, Storksdiek et al. (2005) suggest that researchers interested in the outcome of EE in light of free-choice learning should take a number of factors into special consideration. These include assessing incidental, broader, and affirmative learning outcomes. In addition the authors conclude that researchers should take such things as participant prior knowledge, interest, motivation, awareness, and attitudes into consideration; and all of these need to be considered within the context of large informal structures over extended periods of time including lifelong learning. As we shall see, PAR methodologies can take these important issues into consideration.

Expanding the education research agenda in relation to PAR in free-choice learning contexts has been advanced in the science education literature. Leonie et al. (2003) have proposed an agenda for advancing research in out-of-school settings suggesting that researchers expand the variety of methods used to carry out research. However, their focus on data acquisition methods emphasizing naturalistic approaches stops short of opening the dialogue to AR methodologies that are designed for multiple and diverse data acquisition strategies. Feldman and Minstrell (1999) address why AR should be considered for science educators as an effective professional development process focusing on personal practice, reflection, and change.

Although PAR has been associated with EE enterprises for decades, it has not been carried forward specifically as an effective and valid approach to generating research knowledge about free-choice learning in environmental contexts. This chapter proposes that, because of the shared conceptual underpinnings of PAR, contextual learning theory in free-choice learning, and environmental education, PAR is a viable way to enhance research in EE especially as it relates to teaching, learning, and professional development in free-choice settings. PAR is a potential solution to addressing the dilemma of linking research and practice between free-choice learning and EE (Figure 7.1).

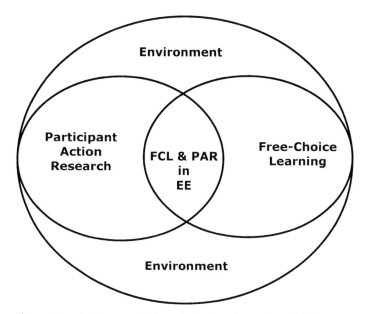

Figure 7.1. Environmental free-choice learning and participatory action research inform environmental education.

PARTICIPATORY ACTION RESEARCH
AS A VARIANT OF ACTION RESEARCH

For the purpose of this chapter, AR is considered to be a family of research methodologies of which PAR is a member. This treatment of AR and PAR is meant to be inclusive of various schools of thought within the field of AR. This is because AR can take different forms but still possess a set of unique shared conceptual characteristics that make it appropriate for better understanding of free-choice learning in environmental settings.

AR as it informs PAR brings to the world of EE research both methodological and epistemological issues. AR and PAR can help bridge the research and practice divide (Ferrance, 2000). Results of AR make a difference in terms of participants making personal and social changes and improvement in established practices. In the case of EE, participation leads to ecological and social changes, often including changes in the physical environment like wetland restoration and social practice such as recycling. AR addresses practical questions in everyday life, environment, workplace, and other informal education settings. AR is a flexible, contextual, and ongoing research process.

Results of AR and PAR are intended to provide feedback directly into practice to make change and ascertain the effects of those changes. The continuous process of this approach explores multiple influences on participant learning and behaviors, interaction of the community of learners, dynamic relationship, and unique contexts of the ecological problem or topics being addressed. AR is a pragmatic approach taking into consideration trade-offs, issues of power, and control and limitations of time, space, and knowledge. All of which are key issues in free-choice learning (Falk, 2005). AR takes advantage of multiple data acquisition methods that are familiar and practical to most educators and typically considered part of their professions' "best practices." AR acknowledges the constraints of personal and social learning, the ecological settings, social contexts, and the real world. AR is embedded in social, cultural, and political milieu that characterizes much of free-choice learning (Somekh, 1995).

In one of the most popular applications of AR in educational research, AR is viewed as effective professional development or professional learning incorporating reflective practice leading to new knowledge about practice. This is true for curriculum developers, teachers, educators, and administrators. This approach is sometimes considered in the context of meaningful professional learning incorporating aspects of cognition, skill, and moral development. As environmental educators strive for meaningful changes in practice, their professional community, and professional development, AR can help lead toward a high-quality intellectual life resulting in both personal and professional identity and liberation from the constraints of current educational oppression. In addition AR leads to new knowledge about educational practice (Whitehead and McNiff, 2006).

AR and PAR can be considered in relation to free-choice learning in informal settings to improve our knowledge of environmental teaching and learning. PAR based in communities of learners with ecological interests are typically found in informal learning settings (Smith, 1996/2001/2007). As such the contextual model of learning proposed by Falk and Dierking (2000) emphasizing the experiential, personal, and social nature of learning across time helps illuminate and bridge the PAR in EE conceptual interface, that is, participatory environmental learning in free-choice settings.

PAR as a variation of AR leads to socially constructed scientific knowledge and environmental change in unique ways and as such is an ideological match to many beliefs about environmental education research and practice. Although PAR has different names and faces, several key characteristics are common; first, participants are completely involved in the research process, the research is committed to personal and group values, projects always embody elements of social learning and lead to change. In some conceptualizations, PAR derives from the work of Paulo Friere and "education outside the schooling system." PAR can also be considered a variant from the Highlander Center's work related to the civil rights movement in the United

States, integrating patterns of new types of relationships based on principles of sharing and equity (Hale, 2005). In these conceptualizations a key factor is knowledge about and for the participants leading to a change in their condition and the evolution of their personal and collective identity. The concept of emerging personal and communal identity is a shared outcome of PAR and free-choice learning. Across a variety of PAR conceptualizations, shared key characteristics are

- The subject of study originates within the setting, environment, individual, community, or workplace (embedded).
- The people in the learning community are involved in determining and controlling the research learning process (embedded).
- Participatory research plays a role in enabling by strengthening people's awareness of their own capabilities and identity (emergent).
- The research goal is to fundamentally improve the lives of those involved through personal, social, and/or structural transformation (change).

PAR is an **embedded** and **emergent** process leading to **change**. Similarly, we can say that contextual learning theory takes into consideration the embedded nature of free-choice learning over space and time, the emergent nature of learning in informal contexts and outcomes leading to cognitive, skill, and dispositional changes in participants. As proposed here, there are many obvious conceptual links between PAR and free-choice learning that can inform EE.

Carr and Kemmis (1986) stress the importance of technical, practical, and critical reasoning and establishing collaborative groups of action researchers who can support themselves in becoming critical. As such, if it is properly organized as a collaborative critical endeavor, it provides an effective means of empowering self and bringing about radical change in society. This essential *reflection and reflexivity* is the basis of critical consciousness and as such plays a pivotal role in PAR, free-choice learning, and EE.

PAR links research and practice in the reflective learning processes about and for people who engage in study of their practice and condition. It is a free-choice learning activity. Like free-choice learning, PAR is intended to improve understanding, skills, and dispositions related to the object of study. Like free-choice learning, PAR is embedded in the community, whether on-line Internet, the local social club, or family. Both cross wide variations in space and time. Concerns, issues, and research questions spontaneously emerging from the social, cultural, political, and environmental conditions of free-choice learning can be systematically studied through PAR. PAR takes time, as does meaningful learning in free-choice environmental settings. McTaggert (1991) emphasizes that the conception of PAR is as a process in which people choose to conduct self-study on aspects of their lives in their own context.

All in all, the characteristics of AR and PAR lend themselves to modern conceptions of the personal, social, and contextual nature of educational research and are thus important to consider in the context of research in EE. However, there are also some concerns. Among these can be an emphasis on working alone and idiosyncratic outcomes that are not communicated to others. In some cases, AR and PAR can foster dependence relationships between facilitators and group members. In terms of professional development AR can be restricted and governed by accreditation standards, administrative control, and government regulations and reform movements dissociating the purpose, process, and outcomes of PAR from the individual or group participant researchers.

PAR AND FREE-CHOICE LEARNING IN EE PEDAGOGY

Integrating PAR and contextual learning theory in free-choice learning can lead to an active, participatory, contextual teaching and learning model suggesting effective pedagogical approaches to improving teaching and learning in environmental settings. However, engaging learners in interdisciplinary, ecological community-based problem solving is not in and of itself PAR as originally proposed as an educational research methodology. In EE, PAR has been predominantly interpreted as a pedagogical model for active participatory teaching and learning. The active participatory learning model that engages teachers and students in iterative processes of research and change does help motivate students and teachers. It is an effective EE pedagogical strategy that has elements of PAR such as context, dialogue, collaboration, and choice embedded in it. The EE active learning model has critical elements of modern learning theory such as the integration of thinking, feeling, and acting. It can also be compared to the contextual learning model popular in the informal education field, taking into consideration four key elements: direct experience, personal learning, social learning, and time (Brody, 2005; Falk and Dierking, 2000).

As an EE active learning model, PAR has been relegated to an alternative active teaching learning process and often evaluated in the context of prescribed educational outcomes. PAR has been used to link EE with educational reform as in promoting standards related to content acquisition, skill development, and positive dispositions (Mordock and Krasny, 2001). PAR may link EE to community development when students research specific environmental concerns and attempt to affect positive ecological outcomes

(O'Donoghue and Russo, 2004). Unfortunately, PAR as an active contextual learning model has not been combined with PAR as an appropriate research methodology generating new knowledge about participation in free-choice learning and EE.

Over the past twenty years the field of EE has adopted some of the key characteristics of PAR and applied them in the limited context of free-choice learning in environmental contexts. The EE literature has been incorporating the ideas of PAR in the context of teaching and learning, often overlooking the conception of PAR as a legitimate research methodology (Reid et al., 2007). EE still tends to confuse the active participatory teaching–learning model with PAR as a research methodology. AR in general is not well represented in the current literature related to learning in informal settings and EE (Brody et al., 2007).

The three journal articles summarized here provide evidence that PAR and contextual learning theory, whether directly stated, suggested, or interpreted, demonstrably contribute to our understanding of effective teaching and learning processes and can contribute scientific evidence of effective EE pedagogical knowledge. The first study from South Africa is presented in the context of PAR as an active pedagogy. The key elements of contextual learning theory underlying the work are isolated and explained. The authors of the second study from British Columbia, Canada, frame their work in the context of free-choice learning. Elements of PAR will again be identified and explained as an unstated conceptual framework for the EE pedagogy congruent with the free-choice learning emphasis. Both projects and studies are set in ecological and social contexts leading to change. Following these two case studies is a clear example of PAR in environmental educational research and a discussion of the strengths and weaknesses of using PAR methodology in free-choice learning and EE.

Case 1: South African Development Community Regional Environmental Education Programme

O'Donoghue and Russo (2004) provide an excellent report of the emerging patterns of practitioners' abstraction and reflective thinking in South African environmental education in their review of materials, methods, and professional development perspectives of the South African Development Community Regional Environmental Education Programme (SADC REEP). The study draws on a number of key PAR principles especially as they have been described in the Global Rivers Environmental Education Network as participatory learning model (Wals, 1994). The authors specifically refer back to the EE literature of the middle 1990s and the emergence of the active learning, community-based, problem-solving approaches in EE. They cite, for example, experiential water ecosystem studies and their "rearticulation" within action research and community problem-solving approaches. The authors emphasize factual information to create awareness of experience, needs, and context. In the article, PAR is appropriated in order to promote trajectories of participatory engagement. However, PAR is not appropriated as a research methodology investigating the participants' engagement.

SADC REEP, although not stated by the authors, is a clear example of free-choice learning in an environmental context and thus is based on critical elements of contextual learning theory. Simply, the four elements of experience, personal, and social learning over time are all present and reported in the study. It is entirely possible that a rethinking in terms of contextual learning theory could add insight into the processes and outcomes of the project.

Although a well-worked and insightful report, the authors selectively use aspects of the PAR paradigm as it was first proposed as an educational research methodology. The conceptualization of an active learning model is certainly justified. The emphasis on developing patterns of inquiry and process in EE curriculum, teaching, and learning is a much needed and valued message. Individual and group choices leading to systematic change over extended periods of time characterize the project. However, key conceptual and methodological elements of PAR have been overlooked. For example, researchers' participation in questions related to personal and group issues is not clearly stated. The researchers also overlook describing personal action and researching the effects of those outcomes. Regardless, a fine conception of active learning framework based on PAR has been proposed and could well be interpreted in light of free-choice learning.

Touching on the value of PAR as a research tool in the conclusions and discussion of the paper, O'Donoghue and Russo make a tentative foray into PAR as research by educators when they describe professional development in changing the social field of the overall SADC REEP project. They suggest that teachers/educators can engage in PAR or AR professional development as a social reflective process that can be driven by the specific interests of the individuals and groups in the project. These processes might result in the construction of new knowledge leading to social transformation, justice, and sustainability of better teaching and learning in that environmental setting. The contextual learning theory in free-choice learning provides the intellectual space for inclusion of the strategies and outcomes of contextual reflexive knowledge and action. Under the right circumstances this aspect of the program study might be conceptualized in the true nature of PAR and contextual learning theory and thus better inform our work in EE pedagogy and research.

Case 2: Eelgrass Stewardship Project

Boyer and Roth (2005) describe a community-based eelgrass mapping and stewardship project in British Columbia as an instance of free-choice learning in the special edition of *Environmental Education Research* devoted to free-choice learning. They used an ethnographic case study research methodology to describe the relationship of individual and group learning and the creation and maintenance of the network supporting the participants. The authors contend that the project experiences are self-directed, voluntary, and guided by the needs and interests of individuals and the group. It is clearly an example of free-choice learning in an environmental setting. The conclusions of the study indicate that the nature of the individual and group are inextricably linked. They describe the relationship as dialectic between individual and collective learning. They also conclude that such dialectical relationships have not been explored in educational research.

It is important to note that the authors contend that their research approach responds to issues and policy put forth by the Ad Hoc Committee on Informal Science Education formed as an outcome of the annual meeting of the National Association of Research in Science Teaching (NARST) in 1999: "Out-of-school learning is strongly socioculturally mediated, so research designs need to offer opportunities to explore social and cultural mediating factors including the role of conversations, social learning networks, cultural dimensions, and the use of groups as well as individuals as the unit of analyses" (Rennie et al., 2003, p. 115). In this case the researchers used a case study methodology.

Although not stated, this study includes several aspects of PAR in its application to critical learning in EE. Among the most obvious PAR characteristics of the study are the role of the individual in producing new understanding and resources in action and as the outcome of collective program activities. Similar to much of the PAR literature, the authors contend that the individual resources expanded the action possibilities of the collective and constituted learning. It is clear from the text that new scientific knowledge is generated. We might assume that, in addition to shared ecological knowledge, idiosyncratic personal and social knowledge was also created but not documented.

Reconceptualization of the work in terms of PAR methodology can add insight into the processes and outcomes of the project. A rethinking of the research in terms of PAR might lead to a more definitive description of appropriate steps to investigate the nature of the author's main conclusion that there remains an unresearched dialectic between individuals and the community. A free-choice setting such as this project requires personal and social participation and leads to action and new knowledge. We know PAR is embedded, emergent, and takes time. It is likely the dialectic is also embedded, emergent, and takes place over time. Considering that the NARST (Dierking, 2003) calls for alternative research methodologies, we can easily see that PAR would address some critical issues for understanding learning in informal settings. If members of the eelgrass project could be included as practitioners/researchers it is possible that the role of individuals, conversations, and social learning in socioculturally mediated contexts could be documented and provide greater depth to the understanding of project outcomes. The emphasis on individual and social groups in PAR would ensure that individual and group analyses would be appropriate. In PAR it is possible that the individuals and groups could have generated that knowledge themselves.

In the eelgrass stewardship project we have a community-based project with emphasis on contextual learning theory in free-choice informal environmental settings to inform teaching and learning. Based on the key characteristics of the project and study, that is, participatory, action, individual and social learning, networks, context, community, and environment, why not match the key characteristics of the project free-choice learning processes and environmental education outcomes to participatory action research methodology?

Case 3: Environment and Schools Initiatives

Varga et al. (2007) report on developing teacher competencies for education for sustainable development (ESD) through reflection in the Environment and School Initiatives in the Department of Biology of Juhasz Gyula Faculty of Teaching of Teacher Training College, University of Szeged, Hungary. Although the title might construe a formal educational setting, the professional learning of the faculty in the department of biology has all the key characteristics of free-choice learning. It is based on experience, individual, community, and occurs over time. It is an example of professional free-choice learning in the context of a university.

The authors' self-study claim that problems of sustainability are wrought with uncertainty and a lack of common understanding and values. They see ESD as a social learning process and AR as a good way to initiate and systematically study social learning processes. The authors used AR as a methodology through which the teachers research their own approaches and geographical, social, and educational contexts to develop case studies of their own practice. They propose that AR could be the starting point for ongoing reorientation of teaching in which the capacity and enthusiasm for self-reflection becomes prerequisite for ESD. Like free-choice learning, we see experience-based and reflexive processes. The results reported indicate that AR can be effectively integrated into teacher professional development, and pedagogical approaches to ESD can be built upon this approach. This report is a clear case of using PAR as a research methodology within the context of EE and ESD. It is not about using AR to teach about environment or sustainability. It is about AR and PAR as professional development including assessment of teaching and learning. The common characteristics of PAR and free-choice learning addressed earlier indicate that EE and ESD work could also be conceptualized in terms of contextual learning theory in free-choice learning, that is experiential, individual, social, and over time.

The authors contend that ESD (similar to EE) is based on change and is change oriented. They go on to say that change can occur only in a meaningful way if it is based on reflective and reflexive processes. Their conclusion is that if we are to teach about environment and the nature of sustainable development, what better place to start than adapting educational processes to a continuously developing world. Then if our teaching and learning is continuously evolving, research on teaching and learning should be changing and cycling as well. The authors as practitioners/researchers are aligning their professional practice with the nature of the subject they want to teach. They then go on to align their research methodology with their practice.

Although not directly stated, we can infer that in this project free-choice learning related to professional development is contextually based, participatory, and environmentally oriented. The study report represents a clear case of alignment among PAR, free-choice learning, and EE in both pedagogy and research. The authors suggest that self-reflection is the starting point of this process leading to the realization that self-reflection is essential to PAR, contextual learning theory in free-choice learning, and EE for sustainable development.

The outcomes of this study lead to conclusions about how international networks contribute to developing the self-reflection at an individual and community level. The authors emphasize that the results contribute to our understanding of systematic, critical, and creative thinking that is seen as a prerequisite for action. In which case, the concept of reflective might be expanded to reflexive to emphasize professional action as outcome. Again, participatory approaches to research that leads to action can help us better understand the role of experience, individual, and social learning over time and in environmental contexts. The challenge to both researchers and practitioners is to incorporate PAR as an embedded, emergent, and long-term process to better understand free-choice learning in environmental contexts.

PAR AND FREE-CHOICE LEARNING IN ENVIRONMENTAL SETTINGS

Participant action research, whether as an individual working on improving his or her professional practice or within a learning community of shared interest in a local environmental problem, is an approach to systematically studying existing conditions, suggesting and implementing ways to change, and then assessing the outcomes of the process. The use of systematic reflective practice in PAR could be critical to a better understanding of contextual learning theory in free-choice settings. Traditional research and evaluation strategies have proven ineffective in elucidating the depth and complexity of learning in informal settings. They do not address the continuum of space and time that characterizes learning in free-choice learning settings. They do not reveal the sociocultural mediating contexts of community-based work. PAR approaches can help reveal both the depth and the complexity of free-choice learning in environmental settings over time (Brody et al., 2007).

PAR is a contextual approach sensitive to local factors and the idiosyncratic nature of informal environmental learning activities. When PAR becomes part of everyday practice, it contributes to our holistic understanding of what, why, and how we pursue environmental education. PAR approaches to practice and research in EE are critical to embedded, informative, and valuable assessment of program outcomes. Rather than looking at prescribed outcomes, experimental treatments, and hypothesis testing, PAR approaches allow practitioners and researchers to assess emergent outcomes both expected and unexpected over extended periods of time. PAR is congruent with the principles of contextual learning theory in its ability to take into consideration the physical, personal, and social construction over knowledge over time.

PAR connects practice and research in the areas of professional development and assessment. Every educator in environmental settings has the ability to systematically study their management, teaching strategies, and learning outcomes. In PAR, practitioners are researchers and researchers are practitioners. PAR bridges the research practice gap. These artificial dichotomies in education can be struck down in favor of blended roles and responsibilities based on cooperation and collaboration.

Table 7.1 indicates some key characteristics of the PAR and their relationship to contextual learning theory in free-choice learning. In each of the cells are a couple key ideas common to PAR and free-choice learning that emphasize the potential for congruence of their ideology, methodology, and epistemology.

PAR can help environmental educators better understand the physical and experiential nature of contextual learning by focusing the participants on the direct experiences of free-choice learning in the environment. Documenting the experiences for both individuals and groups is essential to understanding them. Within the PAR community events such as meetings, presentations, projects, and communication are a vital source of information and should be documented. The physical experience in free-choice learning is often based

Table 7.1. Key Characteristics of PAR and Contextual Learning Theory in Free-Choice Learning

		Participatory Action Research		
		Individual (awareness)	*Community (association)*	*Change (agency)*
Contextual Learning Theory	*Physical*	—direct experience —environment	—meetings —projects	—conditions —problems
	Personal	—reflective —reflexive	—communication —inclusion	—efficacy —abilities
	Social	—group participation —shared meaning	—networks —stakeholders	—solutions —problem solving
	Time	—participation —change	—communication —evolution	—cycles —sustainability

on local conditions, concerns, and problems. These are typically the motivation for PAR activities and as such are part of the documentation of the work. Because the physical experience of free-choice learning is so idiosyncratic, PAR approaches are based on the individual and the personal reporting of the direct experience rather than an outsider's view.

Individual reflectivity is a critical aspect of personal learning that takes place in PAR. In PAR, reflection leads to actions that are based on the reflexive nature and abilities of the participants. Individual members of any learning community are essential to change and must be recognized in terms of their abilities and efficacy. The individual characteristics evolve over time and should be documented. PAR methodology is sensitive to these changes over time and helps provide mechanisms for studying and recording individual learning in free-choice settings. In free-choice learning, individual learning is at the core of the experience. It is based on motivation, personal action, and unique outcomes that are not typically addressed in traditional assessment or evaluation practices. PAR methodology and appropriate data acquisition methods will address these unique individual outcomes.

Group participation in PAR and free-choice learning should be based on meaningful communication and the creation of networks among stakeholders. Fostering group dialogue of problems, problem-solving activities, and solutions is critical. Members of PAR communities must be sensitive to the dynamics, dialogue, and processes within the community as PAR is an embedded and emergent process that depends on the community for its realization. Recent free-choice learning work investigating the roles of groups such as families or civic groups in learning in informal settings indicates the need to better understand the role of social learning. PAR methodology can help reveal the intricacies of this dynamic aspect of free-choice learning.

Both PAR and free-choice learning recognize the importance of engagement over time. This includes participation and change in the individual, communication and evolution of groups and community, cycles of posing questions and seeking solutions, and sustainability of the process. PAR is designed to assess changes over time and through multiple cycles of the process.

ASSESSMENT AND PROFESSIONAL DEVELOPMENT IN EE

There are two very clear ways in which PAR can contribute to EE pedagogy and research in free-choice settings in the immediate future. These are (1) assessment of teaching and learning outcomes and (2) professional development of educators. These two applications of PAR are inextricably linked and we can consider them as part of the same educative processes. Professional development in EE is a matter of improving teaching and learning. Professional development is really a free-choice learning opportunity in the context of PAR.

Informal environmental educators such as natural history museum docents, nature center interpreters, or field study guides are concerned with the effectiveness of their own practice and the educational outcomes of their audiences. It is natural that they would want to systematically study their practice in order to improve teaching and learning outcomes. We can also consider museum or aquarium exhibit designers in this category as they try to improve the effectiveness of their work to engage visitors and help them learn. Environmental educators in informal settings are on a continuous journey of professional development that can be fueled by reflective and reflexive work throughout their careers. In the most positive and meaningful professional development experiences, these activities can be considered free-choice learning opportunities based on contextual learning. They are participatory and action oriented. They occur over long periods of time and in diverse settings. PAR methodologies provide a conceptually congruent and robust framework for studying teaching, learning, and professional development.

PROBLEMATIZING PAR AND FREE-CHOICE LEARNING IN EE

Dillon and Wals (2006) have astutely pointed out that there are prevalent problems in research in EE associated with blurring methods, methodologies, and ideologies. A review of the PAR literature in EE indicates that there is an extreme lack of clarity of methodologies and methods concerning PAR in both EE practice and research. The blurring of research methodology and data acquisition methods into models of critical PAR pedagogy can confound the field of EE research as it pertains to PAR as a research methodology.

What can we agree on about PAR and contextual learning theory applied to free-choice learning in environmental settings?

- PAR challenges the assumptions and status of traditional approaches to educational research. PAR is concerned with process, development, and change in social settings. Contextual learning theory applied to free-choice learning challenges the typical assessment and evaluation strategies in informal settings. Environmental education challenges typical educational outcomes by integrating concepts, skills, and values associated with change in social and ecological conditions.
- In PAR the subject and object of research should be one and the same. In free-choice learning the individual and social group are the unique purveyors of learning, they know best what the experience was and how it evolved for them. Environmental experiences are unique to the individual and group and the setting. Reciprocity and mutual negotiation of meaning and power between the researcher and researched can be addressed in PAR and can be sensitive to the sociocultural mediation of knowledge in free-choice learning. PAR can link research with practice in free-choice EE.
- Triangulation of multiple perceptions in research illuminates different versions of reality and understanding leading to "crystallization" of results and conclusions. In the conception of crystallization (Richardson, 2000) there are more than three sides to the story and crystals grow and change, reflecting out and in and changing light and colors in different directions. The idea of crystallization in research provides a deeper, complex, yet still partial understanding of educative phenomena. In free-choice learning there are more than three sides to the experience, individual, and community and it all extends over extreme variants in time and space. PAR supports multiple data acquisition methods, qualitative and quantitative, as best fits the individual or group questions, resources, and setting. PAR extends to the conception of crystallization of results. In EE we know that everyone sees nature in his or her own way, demanding an elaborate and multifaceted view of assessment over time.
- Free-choice learning as a construct recognizes that all knowledge is situated. Our human and ecological condition is situated in our personal and shared experience. PAR methodology demands the determination of results and drawing of conclusions as situated in community and environment.

What are the problems of PAR and free-choice learning in EE?

- There is the problem of a superficial view of PAR when it is undertaken as cooption and subversion using low-level technical forms of PAR as a means of social engineering, such as AR in teacher professional development dictated by social norms, local administration, or state standards. The demands of government funding of research in free-choice learning can lead to the application of traditional research and evaluation strategies of learning in informal settings in less than appropriate ways. PAR, free-choice learning, and EE are subject to cooption in relation to exclusively promoting student achievement and national education standards.
- There is the problem of time, and longer commitments to research. PAR takes time. It is emergent and embedded. It is cyclical and demands revisiting outcomes and generating new questions. Free-choice learning is a lifelong process and extends over space and time. We are always engaged in environmental contexts and learning to some extent.
- There is the problem of self or identity. PAR is written in first person based on reflection, reflexivity, revelation, reevaluation, individual complexities, and richness of social interaction. PAR is a complex, holistic process interdependent with change. Reflection in PAR and free-choice learning is personal, problematic, and critical. Everyone's experience with environment is unique and complex and with rapidly changing ecological conditions, critical. In PAR and free-choice learning there is the risk of the tendency to become ingrown, idiosyncratic, contentless to the point where learning is incommunicable.
- There is the problem of changing fields and an individual ability to "keep up" with what is relevant and important. In PAR there is the critical need to understand what has been done in relation to identified problems and solutions. There is the need to reconceptualize the situation as you proceed and accept the provisional nature of knowledge as it is generated. In free-choice learning the learner must recognize that personal understanding changes over time and that accepted knowledge changes as well. The environment is always changing, more so now than in any historic time.

DISCUSSION

The one thing that PAR, free-choice learning, and EE may have in common is their integration into a meaningful professional development model with the potential for generating valid and reliable knowledge about teaching and learning. If possible this new integrated conceptualization can lead to more meaningful curriculum, effective teaching strategies, and positive learning outcomes in informal environmental settings. If PAR is driven by educators working in their own best interest, effective professional development will follow. Like PAR, free-choice learning is self-motivated, reflective, and leads to development of identity. That identity can be personal and professional.

PAR, free-choice learning, and EE are experiential, personal, and social and occur over long periods of time. The embedded, emergent nature of free-choice learning as professional development over time should help inform the choice of our research and pedagogical strategies. Just as PAR provides a holistic alternative to traditional research, it also can be an alternative to traditional professional development incorporating assessment and evaluation of teaching and learning in free-choice learning in environmental settings.

PAR and contextual learning theory in free-choice learning settings can and have contributed to EE practice by contributing key ideas related to effective teaching and learning. PAR can also significantly contribute to EE research if we take the key principles of the research methodology seriously. PAR and contextual learning theory as embodied in free-choice learning can help us better understand teaching and learning in environmental settings. PAR and free-choice learning in EE can help bridge the research practitioner divide. It is likely that in most cases, the strengths of this integrated approach will outweigh the constraints. In overcoming the constraints we can enhance our understanding, practice, and outcomes of free-choice learning in environmental settings in meaningful and productive ways.

8

Environmental Literacy through the Lens of Aquarium Ocean Literacy Efforts

Jerry R. Schubel, Corinne Monroe,
Kathryn A. Schubel, and Kerry Bronnenkant

INTRODUCTION

The world ocean covers 71 percent of the Earth's surface. It modulates Earth's climate and controls much of its weather. It supplies over half of the oxygen to the atmosphere, and is a major sink for CO_2. Life originated in the ocean and the ocean was and continues to be a major driving force in the evolution of life on Earth. The world ocean contains a greater diversity of life at the phylum level than do all land areas, including rainforests.

The world ocean is an appropriate lens through which to examine environmental literacy. To be ocean literate is a significant step in becoming environmentally literate. The future of life on Earth as we know it—including humans—may be in jeopardy if public environmental literacy is not improved and if that knowledge is not translated into individual and societal actions. The ocean might have the potential to be a good vehicle for accomplishing this because of the public's inherent interest in the ocean and in marine life.

In this chapter the authors examine the concept of what it means to be an ocean literate person, explore briefly the evolution of the concept of ocean literacy and the ocean literacy principles, describe a portfolio of strategies for enhancing public ocean literacy, and make some recommendations. Our pedagogical focus is on free-choice learning institutions. Our geographic focus is on the United States because that is what we are most familiar with and because we believe free-choice learning models are transferable, and not because we believe that similar concerns and efforts are not occurring in other parts of the world. We know they are. There is only one ocean—the World Ocean—and efforts to rehabilitate and conserve it must be global in their reach.

The American Association for the Advancement of Science (2004) commissioned a survey of 2,400 American adults to assess their attitudes and opinions on marine issues. Some highlights of what that survey revealed are:

- Nearly 80 percent of those surveyed indicated they felt that human-made stresses are endangering coastal regions and oceans and these stresses may lead to long-term damage and serious problems.
- Only 21 percent believed the oceans are so vast and healthy that they can withstand human-made stresses.
- Only 31 percent thought their personal actions have a lot of influence on the health of oceans and coastal regions.
- No significant differences in perceived threat or personal influence were noted by sex.
- Adults in the northeast United States were significantly more likely than adults in other parts of the country to believe human-made stresses are leading to long-term damage and serious problems.
- Adults in the West and South central sections of the United States were more likely than people from the Northeast or North central regions to believe their personal actions have a lot of influence on the health of oceans and coastal regions.

Although surveys such as this measure awareness and not literacy or understanding, the level of awareness they provide is a reasonably good indicator of the respondent's understanding of scientific issues (Krosnick, 2007). While this survey used a relatively crude instrument, the finding that only 31 percent of those surveyed thought their personal actions had a great deal of influence on the health of oceans and coastal regions is troublesome. Everything we know about the world ocean, and particularly the coastal ocean, indicates very clearly that most coastal and ocean problems have their origins on land as a result of the collective of individual human activities. It is clear that we have a major challenge in enhancing public ocean literacy. It also is clear that we must focus efforts on adults and the general public, as well as children in both school and nonschool settings, if we are to effect change on the temporal and spatial scales called for by the Pew Oceans Commission (2003) and the U.S. Commission on Ocean Policy (2004). This argues for an important role for free-choice learning.

One possible way to make these concerns more concrete would be to utilize the guidelines laid out by the Ocean Literacy Network (2005) (Table 8.1).

According to this group, an ocean literate person is characterized as one who understands the seven essential principles and fundamental concepts at some level, can communicate them in a meaningful way, and is able to make informed and responsible decisions regarding the oceans and its resources.

Table 8.1.   Essential Principles of Ocean Sciences

1. Earth has one big ocean with many features.

2. The ocean and life in the ocean shape the features of Earth.

3. The ocean is a major influence on weather and climate.

4. The ocean makes Earth habitable.

5. The ocean supports a great diversity of life and ecosystems.

6. The ocean and humans are inextricably linked.

7. The ocean is largely unexplored.

Although the ocean literacy principles were developed almost exclusively with K–12 students and teachers in mind, we believe they could also be relevant within the free-choice learning domain. How they are packaged and delivered in a free-choice learning context would of course be different than how they would be delivered for formal education settings.

OCEAN LITERACY FROM THE AQUARIUM CONTEXT

Free-choice learning institutions such as aquariums, museums, and science centers use many modalities communicating with the public such as storytelling, visit experiences, films, improvisational theater, and field trips. Successful informal learning environments and experiences require a level of design and orchestration even more sophisticated than formal classroom programs because participation in free-choice learning is "by choice." In free-choice learning all the theories of learning come into play, and context and perspective take on added value, particularly given the heterogeneous nature of the groups in terms of age, existing knowledge, education levels, experience, motivation, socioeconomic status, and background, to name a few. Personal relevance is a key to success in free-choice learning (Koster and Schubel, 2007). The challenge is to recapture the curiosity of the learner and the thrill and challenge of exploration and discovery without the fear of "failure" that can stifle learning and creativity.

The publication resulting from the national conference on "The Coming Revolution in Earth and Space Science Education," *Informal [Earth and Space Science] Education and Outreach* (Morrow et al., 2002), identified four ways in which free-choice learning could "help promote the revolution in Earth and Space Science Education":

- Collaborating with formal education. The authors view informal, free-choice education as a precursor and extension of formal learning experiences that can stimulate curiosity that prepares the individual to learn in a formal setting.

- Motivating a love of science. The authors note that many scientists trace the origin of their fascination with science to experiences as youngsters in free-choice learning institutions that captured their imaginations.
- Creating a scientifically informed citizenry. Citizens of the twenty-first century will confront waves of scientific and environmental issues that will continue long after they leave formal schooling. Free-choice learning should strive to create mechanisms to engage citizens in lifelong learning by providing them with opportunities to learn the science necessary to understand topics important in their daily lives.
- Generating new ideas in learning. Free-choice learning institutions can serve as important laboratories for prototyping and testing new pedagogical approaches because they offer flexible opportunities to experiment with and evaluate how students learn.

This chapter provides an important validation of the roles free-choice science learning institutions can and sometimes do play in (1) stimulating an interest in and a love of science, (2) in promoting lifelong learning, and (3) nurturing environmental and ocean literacy. The authors believe that the unrealized potential in fulfilling these roles is huge, and that partnerships will be critical in seizing this potential. Partnerships include those with K–12 schools; colleges and universities with marine science programs; governmental agencies that have ocean mandates; and nontraditional partnerships that can add new modalities of learning, such as art museums, nature centers, and libraries. Partnerships of free-choice learning institutions with formal K–12 schools often are best served if there is also a partnership with a college or university that can provide additional subject matter depth and access to the latest scientific findings. The free-choice learning organizations in turn can provide valuable services in the translation and packaging of current science into forms interesting and engaging to youngsters and to the general public. Some free-choice organizations also can provide the locations for education and training for both teachers and their own educators on what is new in environmental and ocean sciences.

ON THE IMPORTANCE OF CONNECTING PEOPLE WITH NATURE

Perhaps no single factor relative to enhancing environmental and ocean literacy is more important than connecting people with nature—not necessarily to expansive areas of unspoiled wilderness, although that is desirable related to age and scale—but to nature near the places where they live, work, and play. Richard Louv (2005) makes a compelling case for the importance of getting youngsters out into nature in his book, *Last Child in the Woods: Saving Our Children from Nature-Deficit Disorder.* The benefits go far beyond developing an appreciation and affection for nature and extend to fitness and socialization. Louv's "Leave No Child Inside" (Louv, 2007) initiative is a growing movement to reconnect children and nature and appears likely to be supported by new national laws in the coming years that will mandate states to enact guidelines for achieving this goal (No Child Left Inside Act, HR-3036 and S-1981). According to Louv, it is a movement that all who believe in environmental literacy should get behind. Those committed to enhancing ocean literacy in this country and worldwide need to develop and nurture strategies to connect people with nature. These connections must be deep and visceral if they are to inspire people to transform knowledge into wisdom—the ability and inspiration to take action on things they have learned. And connections with nature are just as important for adults as for children.

While more than 50 percent of the world's population lives within fifty miles of a coast, this leaves a lot of people who live more than fifty miles from the ocean. The surprising fact is that there are large numbers of people living in coastal cities throughout the world who have never visited an ocean beach or even seen the ocean, even though it may be only a few miles from where they live. People in economically disadvantaged neighborhoods of coastal cities globally may live their entire lives without walking along a beach or exploring a wetland or tidal pool—i.e., without interacting with the ocean. Given the increasing urbanization of the coast, particularly in the developing world, connecting residents with the environment and the ocean takes on added importance and poses a major challenge. And this is not a problem only in the developing world.

For example, there are people in less affluent sections of Long Beach, California, who made their first trip to the ocean because of an invitation and free admission provided by the Aquarium of the Pacific. This was also true in many other U.S. cities where aquariums and other informal education organizations have created similar opportunities. The disconnect from the ocean makes it difficult for residents to understand that their actions affect the ocean and that the ocean affects their lives. The ocean connections and relevance to their lives have simply never been established. Add to this the large number of people who live hundreds or thousands of miles from the closest ocean vista and it should not be surprising that levels of ocean literacy are so low or that it is so difficult to convey the concept that *no matter where you live, you have a personal connection with the ocean.* It also suggests that ocean and environmental issues such as global climate change, coral bleaching, overfishing, and overfertilization of coastal waters need to be framed not as narrow environmental issues, but in the context of larger societal issues such as poverty, health care, access to clean drinking water, and social justice—issues with which a large fraction of the world's population are intimately familiar.

Special Opportunities for Aquariums

Aquariums have impressive opportunities to connect people with the ocean because of their live animal collections and realistic looking habitats. People come to aquariums with a predisposition to be interested in the ocean, or at least in marine animals (Adelman et al., 2000). In general, aquariums do a very good job of connecting their visitors with the ocean animals in their collections and with their exhibit habitats. They do a less effective job of connecting people with ocean ecosystems and ocean issues, and in promoting ocean literacy as defined by the *Essential Principles and Fundamental Concepts of Ocean Sciences* (Ocean Literacy Network, 2005). These additional dimensions offer aquariums opportunities to expand the learning domain from aquatic animals in captivity and their well-protected aquarium homes to their relatives in the wild and to the habitats and ecosystems they depend upon for their survival. This more expansive approach can capture the biological, physical, chemical, and geological processes that are at the heart of the ocean literacy principles and are key to understanding land–ocean connections and human–ocean interactions. Until we integrate the role of humans as part of nature into our exploration of ocean ecosystems, it will be impossible to achieve an ocean literate public. Humans are not only a part of ocean ecosystems, they dominate many of them.

Most aquariums have programs that get people out into nature offering whale watching cruises, field trips, beach walks, stream or beach clean-ups, and other off-site activities. Many aquariums also take a little piece of the ocean out to communities to broaden the delivery of ocean literacy messages to the general public. As one example, the Aquarium of the Pacific takes its Mobile Community Outreach Exhibit to diverse venues including science teacher conferences, family events, children's events, environmental and cultural festivals and fairs, beach and street clean-ups, seafood and diver shows, and community parades. The community events in which various aquariums participate allow them to introduce the public to their exhibits and programs and to educate the public about the ocean, its inhabitants and ecosystems, and its health. Using biofacts, pictures, props and maps, and personal interactions to foster ocean literacy, a dominant goal is to help the public make emotional and intellectual connections to the ocean, inspiring people to become ocean stewards. A variation on this is the use of modified trailers or vans to take live animals to classrooms and public events to promote ocean literacy.

Direct experiences with the ocean and with ocean animals in the wild and in aquariums are important, but they leave the vast majority of the ocean and ocean life unaccounted for. Direct interaction with most parts of the ocean simply is usually not possible except for researchers and a limited number of the general public who have participated in research programs such as those offered by EarthWatch Institute and other ecotourism organizations. It is ironic that more humans have walked on the moon than have been to the deepest part of the world ocean. And animals exhibited in aquariums are restricted largely to those that occupy the upper ocean and the coastal fringes. To extend public experiences to the entire ocean, to the full spectrum of ocean life, and to the full range of oceanic processes and phenomena would require a combination of direct experiences and virtual experiences such as those through TV nature programs, environmental films, animated films, video, interactive experiences, and on-line learning communities. Combinations of direct and virtual experiences can go a long way in enhancing ocean literacy.

ENHANCING OCEAN LITERACY:
A PORTFOLIO OF POTENTIAL STRATEGIES

A portfolio of some of the pedagogical strategies that have been proven to be effective in engaging people in learning in free-choice environments is addressed in this section. Methodologies that address both cognitive and affective learning are necessary. The best free-choice learning is experiential rather than didactic. The formal lecture still has a place in the free-choice learning domain, but not as the primary teaching and learning modality. Some proven strategies are listed in Table 8.2. Many of these that have proven to be effective in engaging people are discussed. While the emphasis of some of them has been on K–12 students and teachers, all have relevance to the general public.

Information on most of the specific programs is available on-line. The purpose in presenting this list is to demonstrate the myriad powerful tools available to educators to further ocean, and indeed environmental, literacy through free-choice learning.

Using Existing Networks of Institutions to Develop and Deliver Common Ocean Messages

We are convinced that the strategy with the greatest potential for enhancing public ocean literacy—particularly if combined with mass media and social media—is to energize existing networks of free-choice learning institutions

Table 8.2.   Strategies for Enhancing Ocean Literacy

Signage	Restaurants	More complex strategies
Website	—Messages on menus	—Partnerships
—Podcasts	and placemats	—"Thank You Ocean"
—Blogs	—Sustainable seafood	Campaign
—Breaking news	selections	—The JASON Project
—Conservation page with	**Gift shops**	—The Immersion Network
links to external URLs	—Sustainable products	—NOAA Ocean Explorer
—Fact sheets with	—Recycled paper bags	—NOAA BWET
conservation messages	**Cultural festivals with**	—LabVenture
—Virtual reality	**conservation stories**	—NOAA's "Science
On-site	**Forum discussion groups**	on a Sphere"
—Floor presenters and	**Lecture series**	—Magic Planet™
interpreters	**Getting out into nature**	—Energizing existing
—Behind the scenes tours	—Birding	networks of institutions
—Sleepovers	—Whale watching trips	such as members of
—Camps	—Tidepool exploration	AZA, Coastal America's
Programs for seniors and	—Beach and watershed	Coastal Ecosystem
for preschoolers	clean-ups	Learning Centers, etc.
Mobile single subject carts	**Films and video productions**	
Off-site	**PSAs and radio programs**	
—Mobile exhibits	**Exhibits, on-site**	
—Traveling classrooms	**and traveling**	
—Street banners	**Bumper stickers**	
—Speakers bureau	**Visitor greetings**	
	and goodbyes	

in partnership with associations of scientific organizations to develop and deliver uniform, engaging, and educational messages about the ocean. This should be a common-sense approach, but institutional inertia, existing reward structures, and other factors make it a challenge.

There are numerous associations of institutions that share an interest in the ocean. These include Coastal America's Coastal Ecosystem Learning Centers (CELC); Centers for Ocean Sciences Education Excellence (COSEE); Natural Association of Marine Laboratories (NAML); Integrated Ocean Observing System's (IOOS) Regional Observing Programs; Sea Grant; Association of Zoos and Aquariums (AZA); Association of Science-Technology Centers (ASTC); and the Ocean Project. In addition, there are professional associations of individuals such as the National Marine Educators Association (NMEA) that work to promote ocean literacy, particularly in the classroom. Although associations of institutions often describe themselves as networks, the term "network" implies interactivity among member institutions as an entire set or as subsets of the members in collaborative ventures. To date, in the United States there has been relatively little interaction within any of these "networks" to develop and deliver shared messages about the ocean.

At the 2008 Ocean Sciences meeting in Orlando, Florida, Louis Legendre (personal communication, May 3, 2008) described the EUR-OCEANS program that brings together ocean scientists in the European Union with a network of European aquariums to develop and deliver important ocean messages to the general public visiting those aquariums. It certainly appears to be a model worth replicating. The organizations that are in early stages of development such as the One Ocean Forum for the Pacific, the Marine Educators Society of Australasia (MESA), and South Africa's Marine and Coastal Educators' Network mostly focus on networks of individuals rather than networks of institutions.

Small Beginnings

The U.S. National Conference on Ocean Literacy (CoOL) held in Washington, D.C., in June 2006 (Conference on Ocean Literacy, 2006) brought together senior government officials, experts in formal and free-choice education, nongovernmental organizations, and industry representatives to help lay the groundwork for development of a national strategy for creating an ocean literate society. Among the recommendations most relevant to the theme of this paper was the need for free-choice learning institutions to work together to create and deliver unified global and national ocean messages supplemented by each institution incorporating regional and local stories. Recognizing the challenges of getting and sustaining true collaborative efforts, it was suggested that a group of six to ten members of the Coastal America Coastal Ecosystem Learning Center (CELC) network might initiate the effort, and once established, open membership to other CELCs. One such effort is five aquariums (Aquarium of the Pacific, National Aquarium, National Mississippi River Museum and Aquarium, J. L. Scott Marine Education Center and Aquarium, and Shedd Aquarium), working collaboratively with Coastal America and the Smithsonian Institution to receive daily the information displayed on the master "Ocean in the News" kiosk in the Smithsonian's Ocean Hall. In turn, the CELC participants have the opportunity to supplement the national feed with regional and local stories that may be more relevant to each CELC's own visitors and to send their own stories to Ocean Hall. The CoOL report also recommended that individual associations of institutions create linkages to other associations of institutions to create meta-networks. As already discussed, the number of potential partners is large. To date there has been limited success in energizing individual networks with common messages or collaborative programs, let alone collaborations across networks, but the landscape appears to be changing. To reach the large numbers of people necessary to have an impact on the world ocean, there will need to be far more collaborative, and more assertive and creative use of web-based communications vehicles such as blogs and podcasts that have become part of the public's portfolio of preferred communication strategies.

In response to the U.S. Commission on Ocean Policy report, the Bush administration developed the U.S. Ocean Action Plan (2004) and established an administrative structure to implement the recommendations of that plan. The Interagency Committee on Ocean Science and Resource Management Integration (ICOSRMI), one of the key committees for promoting ocean literacy, established the Interagency Working Group on Ocean Education (IWGOE), which was charged with reviewing all federal agency programs in ocean education and making recommendations to strengthen these efforts.

IWGOE's recommendations included (2008): increasing coordination and promoting collaboration, developing a coordinated ocean education and outreach message, ensuring data from ocean and earth observing systems are translated for usable forms for various audiences, and ensuring a well-prepared ocean workforce.

Clearly, greater cooperation and collaboration and the use of existing networks to develop and deliver common ocean messages are recurrent themes. Implementing them is another story. Fostering and maintaining collaboration among federal agencies is no less challenging than collaborations among nonprofit institutions or for-profit institutions. Agency cultures and reward structures do not encourage cross-agency collaborations, and the present climate of accountability under the Government Performance Results Act focuses on individual agency performance and short-term measures of success. While institutional mechanisms are critically important in leveraging ocean literacy initiatives, the role of the individual educator should not be underestimated.

EDUCATORS ARE THE KEY

Educators—both free-choice educators in informal settings and teachers in formal classroom settings—are the key to making science come alive and in enhancing environmental and ocean literacy. An interaction with a knowledgeable and skillful educator is still one the best learning experiences in any environment. Unfortunately not all educators in museums and aquariums, and not all teachers, particularly those teaching at the lower grade levels, have extensive scientific backgrounds in environmental subjects such as oceanography and marine science. A much broader familiarity and grasp of physical, chemical, geological, and biological oceanographic processes and of human–ocean interactions are at the core of ocean literacy, and of physical, chemical, life, geological, biological and ecological sciences, and other disciplines such as economics, psychology, communications, history, and civics, which are also components of environmental literacy. Free-choice learning institutions have the opportunity to provide this education for their own educators and for teachers in neighboring school districts in appealing, low-risk settings. Appropriate partnerships with colleges, universities, oceanographic institutions, and governmental agencies with strong expertise in ocean sciences and ocean issues can strengthen such programs by adding content and the most recent advances in scientific understanding.

A recent program—"Communicating Ocean Sciences to Informal Audiences" (COSIA)—was funded by the National Science Foundation to develop partnerships between universities and informal science institutions. The goal of the program is to help the next generation of ocean scientists become more effective communicators with the general public about their research and their passion for ocean sciences (Halverson and Strang, 2007). COSIA is a project of partnering aquariums or science centers with universities. Other academy–practitioner relationships include such things as aquariums providing platforms in which young university scholars are able to interact with the public and university faculty being located within free-choice learning settings to facilitate transfer of information.

Another need for educator education is to enhance the ocean or environmental literacy value of exhibits. To do this, it is important to provide opportunities for staff to gain a better grasp of the science behind new programs, new information, or new exhibits.

A Special Category of Educators: Teenaged Docents or Volunteers

One tool for helping foster environmental or ocean literacy is through docent programs, and in particular teenaged docents or volunteers. There are a number of advantages in having teenagers as docents. Two of the most obvious are (1) some visitors find it easier to relate to younger docents and (2) this is an age group that often loses interest in aquariums and other free-choice learning institutions, so volunteering can provide a hook to keep them involved. By keeping them involved, a continued interest in science, in lifelong learning, and in personal stewardship is promoted. As one example, the New York Aquarium Docent Program–Teen Conservation Program, which has been in existence since 1969, has 200 docents recruited from New York City high schools. The docents reach the multicultural population of visitors to the facility in the summer, conduct visitor programs, and engage in a wetland habitat restoration project at Coney Island Creek (K. Acevedo, personal communication, June 14, 2008).

Another example is the Aquarium of the Pacific's VolunTEEN Program that is designed for youth ages 14–16. After training, each participant agrees to a commitment of eighty hours of service, where they provide hands-on educational opportunities for guests in all of the Aquarium's galleries (S. Penna, personal communication, February 25, 2008). Zoos, nature centers, and many nongovernmental organizations all have similar opportunities for youth that are designed to serve the needs of the organization, increase the effectiveness of messaging to visitors and the public, and help provide potential career experiences to interested youth, all of which serve ocean or environmental literacy in meaningful ways.

EXPLOITING THE MEDIA TO PROMOTE OCEAN LITERACY

Since the release of the various reports cited at the beginning of this chapter, it has become clear that it is important to reach the broadest spectrum of the general public; to accomplish this we must also incorporate mass media and social media into any comprehensive ocean or environmental literacy campaign. Traditional mass media often are defined as print, television, and radio. These media focus on the general public of readers, watchers, and listeners. Mass media have the ability and the potential to reach large numbers of people simultaneously by using technology to transmit the information. Mass media communication is mostly one way, and often individual outlets have a particular point of view. Because the number of outlets is large, the public has a great deal of choice, but they often need to be selective to achieve accurate, balanced reporting. Aquariums, museums, and science centers have been identified as a major and trusted source from which the public acquires knowledge about the ocean and its inhabitants, and the need for conservation of its resources enjoys the trust of the public in presenting balanced and accurate information on important environmental issues (Coyle, 2005).

Various studies have examined the impact of news media (particularly newspapers) on public knowledge of some disciplines (e.g., government) and some have focused on environmental topics and issues (e.g., Pierce et al., 1992; Steel et al., 1992; Steel, 1997; Steel et al., 2005). The news media provides a key source of environmental information for the general public (e.g., National Science Board, 2006; Boyes and Stanisstreet, 1997; Lehmann, 1999; Ostman and Parker, 1986) with, until very recently, television being by far the most important source of science information for U.S. residents (National Science Board, 2006; Wilson, 2002). Relatively little is known about how news providers perceive the importance of coverage of environmental topics and issues or how their reports influence public understanding of, interest in, and/or attitudes about the environment (Storksdieck et al., 2007; Ostman and Parker, 1987). The power of the media in the environmental domain has been demonstrated clearly on the issues surrounding global climate change. Over the past several years there has been a significant increase in public awareness of the multiple dimensions of global warming and global climate change, a growing concern, and a much better grasp of the issues (Krosnick, 2007). Part of the power was derived from the deep involvement of Vice President Al Gore as a highly visible spokesperson, but the reasons go well beyond one person's involvement (Krosnick, 2007).

There are a number of good examples of regularly scheduled television and radio programs that deal with the environment and often cover ocean issues. These include the Discovery Channel, the National Geographic Channel, the Catalina Conservancy's National Public Radio program called "Isla Earth," and many others. These are important, but may not reach as broad a cross section of the general public as one would like to believe.

The Growing Importance of Social Media

With the rapid development of new tools and technologies for communicating messages, social media are rapidly changing the information access landscape. Social media constitute the on-line technologies and practices that people use to share content, opinions, insights, experiences, and perspectives. These media take many different forms, including text, images, audio, and video. The social media sites typically use tools such as message boards, forums, podcasts, bookmarks, communities, wikis, and web logs. The iPhone increases the power of such networks because now one can be "connected" anywhere, anytime.

By enabling rapid access to and exchange of information, these technologies have already revolutionized communication and have the potential to revolutionize many aspects of education if certain safeguards are put in place (e.g., Barrie and Presti, 1996). They can be an appropriate and important component of a comprehensive environmental literacy campaign because they provide convenient access to timely information on rapidly developing environmental issues at local, regional, and global levels. They also give educators and learners opportunities to explore their interests independently, on a real-time basis with researchers and explorers, and to contribute to information sources as well as benefit from them. However, there is a danger. Blogs generally represent the personality and opinion of the authors. Personal opinions are not the same as expert knowledge, and validation of accuracy and balance of many social media outlets can be problematic. Partnerships of trusted sources of scientific information with social media have the potential of providing access by large numbers of people to accurate and balanced information.

It is estimated that close to 70 percent of Americans use the Internet (Miniwatts Marketing Group, 2007), which is lower than most countries in the developed world. Given this statistic and the fact that we live in a very mobile society that has the ability to access websites and news media from virtually anywhere in the United States, and in the world for that matter, this form of media should not be overlooked for its power in promoting ocean or environmental literacy. A Pew/Internet report (Horrigan, 2006) showed that the Internet has replaced broadcast media as the primary science information resource for most Americans.

With proper safeguards, the combination of trusted sources of environmental information such as aquariums and science centers with mass media and social media can raise public awareness of environmental and ocean issues, and deepen public understanding—both critical factors in developing an ocean literate society. Since there is no reason to believe that we will abandon these new ways of communicating and interacting, we would do well to concentrate on learning how to use this new world to achieve important societal goals. Enhancing environmental and ocean literacy and stewardship are among them.

CONCLUDING COMMENTS

Given the continued and accelerated deterioration of our planet's ecosystems, including the world ocean, it is clear that installation of a new Earth ethic in large numbers of people across the world is needed if this trend is to be slowed, stopped, and finally reversed. This has been pointed out in the two most recent comprehensive reviews of the condition of the world ocean (Pew Oceans Commission and the U.S. Commission on Ocean Policy). Deeper understanding and greater awareness are keys to changing attitudes and behaviors, but they are no guarantee. Also needed are ways to help the public make emotional connections to the ocean and to the environmental legacy that will be left to future generations.

The authors believe that the nation's and world's networks of aquariums, science centers, and natural history museums combined with traditional mass media and social media using web-based programs have huge unrealized potential to contribute more to the goal of a literate public. Ocean literacy is a good lens for thinking about and implementing environmental literacy and stewardship efforts, and a number of strategies have been identified that have proven to be effective—at least at some level—in free-choice learning institutions and in partnerships of free-choice learning and formal educational institutions. The number and kinds of partnerships need to be expanded and strengthened. Greater involvement of scholars in defining the content of scientific and environmental messages that can then be packaged and distributed by free-choice learning institutions to a large number of people can enhance quality. These efforts need to be combined with mass media and the new modes of social communication that are sweeping the Earth—the twenty-first-century's blogs, YouTube, Wikipedia, social networking websites, and others. To the extent possible, virtual experiences should be grounded in direct experiences with nature. Finally, most of the evidence of the impacts of free-choice learning programs and partnerships on science education and environmental and ocean literacy remain anecdotal rather than empirically determined. The impacts of these programs need to be rigorously evaluated.

III

ENVISIONING THE FUTURE

9

Free-Choice Environmental Learning in Practice: Research to Inform Environmental Education Practice

Elaine Andrews

The future of a free-choice environmental learning model depends on its perceived usefulness to practitioners and on the extent that the vision for free-choice learning is integrated into related education or outreach disciplines. Application depends on its appeal to professionals who could put the theory into practice, on its clear links to user needs and user skills. These requirements could then serve as criteria for whether we have successfully integrated free-choice learning and environmental education theories. This chapter highlights current efforts to identify best practices in environmental education and suggests guidelines for how these could be integrated with best-practice standards for free-choice learning. A community-based environmental education model is proposed as one example where free-choice learning and environmental education are integrated. New guidelines provide a foundation that practitioners can use to envision scenarios for potential application.

BACKGROUND AND THEORY

This initiative to discover how free-choice learning could enhance education for the environment parallels efforts among several groups looking for ways to improve the effectiveness of education for conservation and stewardship behavior. The North American Association for Environmental Education (NAAEE) pioneered this exploration with an extensive effort to compile components of environmental education theory. This new text, *Excellence in Environmental Education: Guidelines for Learning,* identified four strands basic to learning about the environment: questioning and analysis skills, knowledge of environmental processes and systems, skills for understanding and addressing environmental issues, and personal and civic responsibility (1999). This text, developed for broad use but primarily for application with school-based youth, provided clarity and inspiration for work in this field. It fell short, however, of satisfying educator interest in addressing learning and behavior change in everyday life for learners of diverse ages across multiple settings, in addressing the use of specific natural resources, and in facilitating participation to guide government policy development. This is not an indication of lack of value for this seminal work, but more a demand to amplify how these principles might apply in people's lives at home, at work, and in the community.

In response or in parallel, several professional groups launched efforts to identify best practices and provide training for techniques that educators can use to create environmental understanding and to encourage stewardship behaviors (see, for example, Andrews et al., 2002; Andrews, 2007; Dixon et al., 1995; Fedler, 2001; Holsman, 2001; NAAEE 2004; Stevens and Andrews, 2006; Tetra Tech, 2003). This work can inform ideas about applications of free-choice learning theory, although only some are intended as formulations that can be applied outside of the formal classroom.

This section briefly summarizes new initiatives to apply environmental education for particular purposes and demonstrates potential links between environmental education theory and best practices, and free-choice learning theory. Linking the two theories is most likely to focus on three context factors (personal, sociocultural, and physical) that the free-choice learning model describes as contributing to and influencing interactions and experiences that people have when engaging in learning by choice (Falk and Dierking, 2000).

NAAEE Guidelines for Learning

In the 1990s and early 2000s, members of NAAEE promoted and supported the idea of developing tools to facilitate the expansion of an environmentally literate citizenry. New NAAEE resources recognize that environmental literacy is not a goal that is reached easily. But they support educators who can aid individuals to go beyond the fact-by-fact, piece-by-piece examination of our environment, and begin to understand and think in terms of systems. The goal is to develop a sophisticated set of skills that allow citizens to solve novel environmental problems and determine the best set of actions. Strategies support individuals to become thoughtful, skillful, and active citizens in a democracy (NAAEE, 1999, pp. 2–4; see Archie, 1998, for background).

A follow-up effort provided general planning principles for integrating environmental education into nonformal, or out-of-classroom, efforts, but did not expand environmental education principles to consider the perspective of the individual invited to participate in the free-choice event (NAAEE, 2004). Guidelines for both NAAEE resources acknowledge the personal, social, and cultural context of learners, but they do not provide advice for how to address these factors in the broader environmental education effort. Conversely, attention to context factors gains meaning when applied in support of NAAEE's environmental learning recommendations.

Recreational Boating and Fishing Foundation

Beginning in the late 1990s, the Recreational Boating and Fishing Foundation (RBFF) Education Task Force worked to develop research-based guidelines for boating and fishing education. The task force asked, "Which processes provide the best experiences for conveying knowledge, developing skills, and changing attitudes and behaviors?" Experts summarized research and made recommendations (Fedler, 2001).

The RBFF Education Task Force defined "best practice" as a program or practice that has been clearly defined, refined through repeated delivery, and supported by a substantial body of research. The group outlined components of effective programs as well as specific opportunities to enhance programs. According to RBFF findings, themes for best-practice address guiding principles for boating, fishing, and aquatic stewardship education [these are context-sensitive principles]; program development and implementation; professional development; program evaluation; and research.

RBFF implemented the task force's recommendations by developing a leader training resource (Seng and Rushton, 2003). A best-practices workbook includes additional chapters with guidance on specific needs (i.e., programming to serve ethnic minorities or persons with disabilities, boating programs, fishing programs, and aquatic stewardship education). RBFF guiding principles and best practices identify quality practices that assure that stewardship education will be learner centered and reflect attention to the personal, sociocultural, and physical context recommendations referenced in free-choice learning theory.

U.S. Fish& Wildlife Service—Documenting Practices for Aquatic Resource Education

In a parallel effort, Holsman (2001) conducted a literature review to discover research-based advice about aquatic resource education on behalf of the U.S. Fish & Wildlife Service. Holsman's process discovered best practices for teacher training, residential outdoor camps, field trips, guided discovery, citizen issue investigation and action, and angler education. Many findings validate the power of attention to the learner's context, focusing on the benefits of experiential learning techniques. Holsman (2001) does not, however, provide a system or guidance for how to apply these findings.

> The literature supports many current practices like field trips (if integrated into a classroom unit), guided discovery methods, cooperative learning, construction of mental models (e.g. drawing habitat zones for a wetland), visual aids, personal investigation, role-playing, and investigation and evaluation modules and community action research where students have the opportunity to exercise citizen action skills. The literature suggests several methods that are less effective: lectures, the use of field trips in isolation, outcome based experiments (activities where the focus is on successfully completing a series of steps in order to arrive at "the answer") and values clarification or moral reasoning as a way to teach ethics. (p. 7)

U.S. Department of Agriculture (USDA) Water Outreach Initiative

The USDA Water Outreach Project identifies best education practices (BEPs) that relate to water and stewardship education. The project created a website with a searchable library of research-based BEPs (University of Wisconsin, 2004). The website also provides information to facilitate professional development and application of BEPs.

The water outreach website presents BEPs in two ways, according to theory and as a summary of research. In "Essential BEPs," which are derived from education theory, BEPs are grouped according to typical ways that the educators think about learners: for work with individuals, groups, communities, or units beyond the size of a single community. Essential BEPs summarize education theory (such as provided by the American Psychological Association, 1997) and incorporate key findings from other summative initiatives such as the RBFF initiative described above, work by Holsman (2001), and studies to analyze what makes youth nonformal or informal education successful (Horton and Hutchinson, 1997).

Target audience BEPs are derived from research and are grouped according to the purpose of the education practice under investigation. The practice could relate to the audience, message content, message delivery, outreach design, outreach implementation, public participation, or evaluation. Study-specific recommendations for fourteen audiences are reported on the water outreach website (Stevens and Andrews, 2006). Additional audience recommendations are derived from a national symposium to further analyze what we know about audiences of strategic interest to water educators (Reilly and Andrews, 2006). Recommendations provided either as essential BEPs or target audience research results confirm the benefit of focusing on the learner and on learning contexts.

American Fisheries Society Stewardship Initiative

Aquatic educators are uniquely positioned to apply much of the best advice generated through free-choice learning studies. Because of the hands-on, real-life, and outdoor nature of aquatic subject matter, educators can provide youth and adults with opportunities to be curious, have a direct experience with aquatic resources, address authentic problems, develop solutions to problems, and have fun while doing so (Andrews, 2007). The American Fisheries Society also sought to build a national consensus on best practices in a 2005 symposium bringing together fifteen national leaders in this area of thought.

Building toward this effort, Knuth and Siemer (2004) summarized research about instilling aquatic stewardship behaviors that has led to important conclusions about what to emphasize. Their recommendations are built on the findings of numerous researchers and refer to models developed by others who have also analyzed multiple studies (e.g. Hines et al., 1987; Hungerford and Volk, 1990). In their summary Knuth and Siemer (2004) suggest that aquatic stewardship programs that often occur in a free-choice setting could focus on (1) awareness and knowledge of aquatic systems and their importance to overall ecosystem functions, (2) knowledge among individuals of the consequences of their specific behaviors related to the aquatic environment, and (3) knowledge and skills needed to implement aquatic stewardship behaviors. They suggest that implementation practices are more likely to lead to successful efforts if they are learner-centered, engaging, and cognizant of the cultural and environmental contexts of those engaged.

Andrews (2007) proposed a model for integrating environmental education and aquatic stewardship education in a book summarizing the 2005 symposium findings. That model may also help provide a structure for integrating context-focused learning theory with environmental education and conservation education theory. The model is adapted for more general use later in this chapter.

U.S. Environmental Protection Agency (EPA) Getting in Step Resource

Educators striving to assist communities to adopt specific conservation practices, such as reduction of pollution in storm water runoff, needed to find a communication method that reliably led to preferred outcomes. Behavior change research summarized by social psychologists identified specific techniques that might produce the consistent result policy makers demanded. While a number of researchers have ably summarized behavior change research, Douglas McKenzie-Mohr effectively packaged results into the framework of a relatively new field, community-based social marketing (McKenzie-Mohr and Smith, 1999).

U.S. EPA funded Tetra Tech to adapt the research into a guidebook for educators seeking to apply findings to watershed outreach campaigns (Tetra Tech, 2003). This publication along with training sessions offered by McKenzie-Mohr catapulted the benefits of this theory into widespread use. Tetra Tech's *Getting in Step* (2003) and similar resources highlight the importance of researching and crafting a communication message to speak directly to the interests and needs of the targeted audience. This emphasis is building educator understanding of the importance of investigating and working with a specific audience in order to make change in environmental practices. This is one context where free-choice learning theory can be successfully positioned to encourage adoption by educators.

INFORMING PRACTICE

Findings from these outstanding national initiatives and studies can be coupled with context-sensitive theories to encourage a lifetime of quality environmental learning. Conservation education is evolving just as is our understanding of effective free-choice learning. Free-choice learning does not substitute for these and other initiatives, but can enrich their application. In order to apply context-focused learning effectively, these other initiatives also need to perfect their art. Free-Choice Learning and the Environment Conference participant recommendations and understandings about community-based environmental education provide direction for a proposed synthesis (Institute for Learning Innovation, 2005).

Free-Choice Learning and the Environment Conference Participant Findings

A 2005 conference organized by the Institute for Learning Innovation and funded by several federal agencies and professional organizations examined the juxtaposition of free-choice learning and the environment. Conference planners identified several potential themes relevant to the application of free-choice learning theory with environmental topics. Other themes addressed research needs, which are also seminal to future efforts but are not addressed in this chapter. Conference participants expanded each theme allowing a more nuanced discussion of how the theme might apply. Selected findings from theme and associated discussions can be merged to establish guidelines for imagining future uses of free-choice learning in practice. Elements identified as requiring research can and should be compared to recommendations for application so that each approach can validate the one recommended by the other.

Conference discussion identified several guiding parameters and questions for considering future application opportunities (Institute for Learning Innovation, 2005):

About learning:

- Learning is cumulative; it occurs over time and space (pp. 25, 51).
- Learning occurs in a personal context, but takes place within a community (pp. 25, 51).
- Learning is more likely to be successful when derived from a broad variety of experiences (p. 26).

About communities:

- Recognize that communities are comprised of natural, cultural, social, political, financial, and built capital (or assets) (p. 33).
- Recognize that a community has knowledge and values related to the environment. Identify or develop program design model(s) that focus on assets recognized by the audience (pp. 25, 26).
- Environmental education efforts are more likely to be effective if placed in the context of a community of experiences (p. 25).
- Leverage emerging technologies to address the changing definition of community and virtual communities (p. 47).

About application:

- Build an infrastructure that connects school and community environments to support learning (p. 30).
- Free-choice learning applied in communities could be an effective means for environmental education as it works with what people already know and what they care about (p. 35).
- Free-choice learning could shift the emphasis of conservation action education by emphasizing community rather than individual actions and what concerns the community rather than what concerns the conservation educator (pp. 47, 49).

About educator preparation:

- To identify learning context needs for environmental topics, educators also need to be competent with understanding and describing their audience; communication techniques, identifying and strengthening infrastructure and networks; empowering and mobilizing people to action; and cross-discipline approaches to community-based learning such as adaptive management, conservation biology, community-based conservation, community development, environmental education, participatory action research, and asset-based community development (p. 34).
- Professionals who could or want to apply free-choice learning concepts may benefit from support of a learning society or community of practice (p. 52).

Establishing a Learning Continuum: The Goal

Themes identified by 2005 conference participants suggest a promising perspective for improving the practice, evaluation, and future research for free-choice learning as it relates to the education about the environment. Recommendations place the *learning experience* in the context of a person's life—as an individual and as part of society. They suggest that educators are likely to be more successful at enhancing learning when they can engage in or at least recognize a partnership between formal and free-choice learning opportunities.

About Learning and Communities

A community-based environmental education (CBEE) model developed by Andrews (1998) integrates learning theory with activities that take place in the community context and can serve as a model for how educators can apply free-choice learning when teaching about the environment.

CBEE differs from traditional education in that the educational activities not only build individual knowledge and skills, but also help to build an infrastructure for change that is sustainable, equitable, and empowering. But in CBEE, the educator has an unconventional role. The community-based model emphasizes selection of the education strategy in a way that also *builds local skills* and *supports voluntary actions*. Practitioners work in collaboration with the community to choose a strategy, to consider how and when the strategy could be used, and to guide whether the strategy is applied alone or in combination with others (Andrews, 1998).

The "community" in the CBEE model may be a community of *place*, a community of *identity*, or a community of *interest*.[1] In each situation, the intent is to build the skills of citizens to gather, analyze, and apply information for the purpose of making environmental management decisions. Successful application of CBEE contributes to the "environmental policy capacity" of the community (Andrews et al., 2002).

CBEE goals are designed to be responsive to the reality of the community economic, political, and social context. CBEE incorporates public participation, social marketing, environmental education, and right-to-know strategies. CBEE integrates information dissemination, traditional education, participatory decision making, and other tools used in communication/diffusion approaches. Measures that contribute to the effectiveness of volunteer activities are also encompassed in this model.

About Application and Educator Preparation

In a community-based education model, a community (Table 9.1; Andrews, 1998):

- has or establishes a vision and goals;
- inspires an instigator who, stimulated by these goals, enlists or gathers a group or coalition to start an initiative and to keep it going;
- supports group activities to gather and analyze information; and finally,
- through the group, engages the larger community in carrying out what it has learned through policy changes, new regulations, and/or education.

We call this community-based model an *education* model for several reasons. CBEE's community context and process approach exemplifies the ideal application of learning theory, which maintains that individuals are not motivated to learn unless the information is *relevant to their lives* and they have a *sense of control* about the learning process (Carlson and Maxa, 1997; Heimlich and Norland, 1994).

From this point of view, education is regarded as a process that relies on the existence of a body of knowledge, but its power is in the fact that the knowledge is not only *transferred* to the individual, but is instrumental in *transforming* the individual. For education to take place, the individual has to actively receive the knowledge and know what to do with it (Bloom, 1956; Whitehead, 1929; Weintraub, 1995). The educator's job is to provide the education in a way or at a time when the individual is receptive, and to assure that the individual knows what to do with specific knowledge, which ". . . requires some analysis or understanding of the new situation; it requires a background of knowledge or methods which can be readily utilized; and it also requires some facility in discerning the appropriate relations between previous experience and the new situation" (Bloom, 1956, p. 38).

Table 9.1. Organizing Principles for Community-Based Education about the Environment

Community Education about the Environment

Is Locally Based
- Responds to a locally identified/initiated issue or concern.
- Takes advantage of opportunities (such as a new law or current event) and community assets.
- Works in or with representative groups, including targeted audience (i.e., the people who collaborate represent all the interests associated with the issue).
- Works toward a positive outcome to a specific concern.

Works with a Coalition or Group
- Identifies someone who takes responsibility for managing or leading the process.
- Attends to process objectives and product objectives.

    Process objectives = group building, leadership development, capacity building, conflict management.
    Product objective = successfully addressing a substantive issue.

- Relies on systematic planning procedures.
- Uses expert facilitation.
- Uses consensus decision making.
- Develops linkages to enhance the group's effectiveness.

    To other communities or regions; to other partners; to resources: technology, experts, agencies, funds.

- Communicates broadly using multiple venues (newsletters, town meetings, TV, festivals, etc.).
- Provides recognition and rewards.
- Is flexible—both to process and to conditions; adopts a "learning organization" perspective.

Takes Action Based on Information
- Relates actions to long-term community vision and goals.
- Takes into consideration the community as a whole.

    Evaluates context; considers sociopolitical, economic, historical, cultural influences; looks to the future.

- Generates and makes use of data about the local condition.
- Involves citizens in gathering and analyzing data.
- Builds on locally existing skills and resources and scales actions appropriately to community resources and skills.
- Respects, encourages, and rewards local initiative.
- Evaluates and reports accomplishments.

Practices Quality Education with Broader Groups
- Uses social marketing techniques.

    Identifies and addresses *individual barriers* to preferred behavior; identifies and addresses *social or structural barriers* to preferred behavior.

- Uses training to support the community-based initiative. For example, provides training to

    improve planning process skills, generate and refine implementation ideas, improve data gathering and analysis by citizens, increase access to resources by group/ coalition, teach skills that group has identified as needed to accomplish goals.

- Implements an education strategy that

    presents all points of view; relates to a specific audience and their needs; presents behaviors that (a) provide immediate, observable consequences, (b) are similar to what people already do, (c) do not require a lot of steps or training, (d) are relatively low cost in terms of time, energy, money, materials; provides target audience with opportunities for self-assessment and for practicing or applying new skills; uses creative approaches, e.g., a town treasure hunt for valued places.

Source: Andrews (1998).

An education program, if it is going to accomplish transformation, or even if it is merely to result in the adoption of a target behavior, must include communication, skill development, and application. The CBEE model creates the transformation opportunity, while stressing the importance of a careful match among the person who will learn, the situation where learning will take place, and the choice of education process (Andrews et al., 2002).

Education programs developed based on the CBEE model rely, primarily, on *free-choice learning*—learning through activities that occur primarily outside formal educational settings and that are characterized as voluntary, as opposed to required for school credit. Just as in formal education, however, free-choice learning experiences can be structured to meet a stated set of objectives and can be designed to influence attitudes, convey information, and/or change behavior (Crane et al., 1994). Equally, CBEE activities may be supported by formal education opportunities. For example, drinking water quality described by the Consumer Confidence Reports found in homeowner water bills might be studied in the high school chemistry class (Andrews et al., 2002).

For groups or coalitions, the CBEE model demonstrates where education fits in a community process for making change. For educators, the CBEE model provides guidelines for developing education activities that are relevant to society's needs; and it provides a context for applying quality education practices because the model requires higher-order learning skills and integrates education into real-life experiences (Bloom, 1956; Horton and Hutchinson, 1997; Joplin, 1995; Knox, 1993; Westwater and Wolfe, 2000; Andrews et al., 2002). Application of CBEE embodies the partnership between groups or agencies that affects a person's life and educators who strive to facilitate learning in a variety of situations.

ENVISIONING THE FUTURE

This section proposes a model for linking free-choice learning, conservation education, environmental education, and community-based education efforts described in this chapter (Table 9.2, modified from Andrews, 2007). This model provides a foundation that educators can use to test their ideas about how to employ free-choice learning as they design and deliver an opportunity that helps communities make sustainable changes that they desire.

Monroe et al. (2007) identify key points about the implementation of environmental education that underlie the proposed model as well:

- Formal and nonformal or informal education are often unnecessarily segregated and use similar but not identical methods to accomplish the same goal.
- Environmental education is a complex and broad umbrella that incorporates a variety of strategies and content from natural science to social science and top-down to bottom-up with little to great audience participation.
- To help people function and engage in decisions in an uncertain world, environmental education must include collaborative strategies of community education, mediation, social learning, and adaptive management.

An additional perspective important to effective application of free-choice learning derives from extensive work by social psychologists to describe variables that have been shown through research to affect a person's likelihood of adopting environmentally significant behaviors. These can be grouped according to attitudinal variables, personal capabilities, contextual factors, and habit and routine (Stern, 2000). Stern's perspective along with free-choice learning theory and best-practice initiatives summarized for this chapter suggest themes that, if applied, can result in programs or activities that have potential to build stewardship and community motivation.

A proposed structure for integrating free-choice learning theory with environmental education and conservation education theory focuses on instruction content; learner needs; learner self-confidence; and program purpose, development process, quality, and context. Table 9.2 lists key parameters for each theme. These themes are already familiar to educators. What is less familiar to educators is the integration of factors that influence the experiences that people have when engaging in free-choice learning activities.

For example, identifying "learner self-confidence" as a parameter of equal importance to instruction content and program purpose presents a change in

Table 9.2. Best Practices for Free-Choice Learning and the Environment

Theme	Parameters
Instruction content	• Provide a program or experience or opportunity that addresses community or local interests at a depth appropriate to the individual's previous experience; address environmental education skills where possible and appropriate: o questioning, analysis, and interpretation skills; o knowledge of environmental processes and systems; o skills for understanding and addressing environmental issues; o personal and civic responsibility.
Learner needs	• Investigate and provide programs or experiences that address social and personal qualities about the target audience including: o attitudinal variables, o personal capabilities, o contextual factors, o habits and routines. • Provide a program or experience that is o learner-centered (skills, abilities, motivation and expectations; interest; prior knowledge and experience); o engaging; o cognizant of and builds on the cultural and environmental contexts of those engaged; o able to provide choice and learner-control. • Implement other best practices for enhancing learning, as educator training and outreach opportunity permit.
Learner self-confidence	• Provide opportunities for the learner to develop self-confidence in applying skills and in encouraging a commitment to try the new skill. • Offer education or outreach initiatives that are part of a repeated opportunity and provide long-term reinforcement for appropriate application of skills. • Attend to sociocultural context factors: o within group sociocultural mediation; o facilitated mediation by others; o culture—previous learning by the individual and by the society in which they live; o physical context factors.
Program purpose	Select an intervention strategy based on what the initiative hopes to accomplish (Monroe et al., 2007): • convey information, • build understanding, • improve skills, • enable sustainable actions.

(*continues*)

Table 9.2. (*continued*)

Theme	Parameters
Program development	• Attend to building local or group support for the new process behaviors, especially as they relate to community expectations and practices. o Are the goals of the activity determined by a bottom-up process, or a top-down process? o Is the intervention targeted narrowly to a specific audience or broadly to whole populations? o Is the locus of control in the hands of individuals or community groups, or with marketing agents? o Is the interest group actively involved in creating information and targeting research; or is the interest group a passive consumer of information? o Does the intervention build sustainability for its impacts by engaging people at different *levels of responsibility* within the community (such as property owners, political leaders, and the agency that has jurisdiction)?
Program quality	• Rely on instructors trained in best-education practices. • Use effective program planning, especially to engage the target audience in the planning process; to pilot test outreach strategies; and to revise efforts based on evaluations.
Program context	• Attend to the physical context for the learning experience, including entry and exit experiences. o advance preparation, o setting is comfortable and has the "right feel," o design that capitalizes on elements of the real world, o subsequent reinforcing events and experiences. • Provide learning experiences in the setting where stewardship behaviors will be applied.

traditional educator emphasis. Conscientious application of this feature alone could have a huge impact on the effectiveness of learning about the environment in free-choice learning settings. In another example, educators give "lip service" to attending to learner needs, but often attention is superficial. Authentic attention to the learner requires substantial investigation of learner qualities and evaluation of applications from that perspective. Finally, educators are less comfortable with the program development process as envisaged in this model, especially in applying practices that focus on building local and group support for an education initiative. Many, especially environmental educators, wonder if this is appropriate work for an educator. Attention to the learner's sociocultural context requires educator comfort with addressing this component on a routine basis.

Ultimately the future of free-choice environmental learning depends on its perceived usefulness to practitioners and on the extent that the vision for free-choice learning is integrated into related education or outreach disciplines. The model outlined in Table 9.2 could provide a foundation for developing a vision and for building user skills in integrating free-choice learning factors with environmental education and natural resources conservation goals. Because free-choice learning is a relatively new perspective for educators, a model proposing key categories for consideration can help educators make the choice to apply this technique. Educator acceptance of and comfort with free-choice learning perspectives could result in a broader application of environmental education in society and a more productive result in terms of increasing environmental literacy.

NOTE

1. "*Community* refers to the topic or situation under discussion. In fact, *community of interest* is a useful characterization of the term. *Community*, as used here, implies more than merely a physical place, although it can, and often does, include a geographic element. It may reference a discrete collection of persons about which a common interest is shared, yet they may be located in different places and not necessarily even mutually aware of their shared interest. The community of interest also need not be made up of similar perspectives. Indeed, it often is made up of diverse perspectives surrounding a common issue." (Wise, 1998)

10

Future Directions for Research in Free-Choice Environmental Learning

Roy Ballantyne and Jan Packer

Research is the means by which a discipline or field of study grows and develops its underpinning theory and guiding principles. In the field of free-choice environmental learning, this may involve developing a better understanding of visitors' needs, motivations, learning processes, and learning outcomes. Research can also be applied to solve practical problems, improve practice, develop new products or procedures, and evaluate program effectiveness. Through research, we build an empirically supported body of knowledge on which we can base decisions about best practice. Research advances by building incrementally on previous theories and research findings.

Research in free-choice environmental learning is informed by a range of disciplines, including education, psychology, sociology, geography, and tourism, as well as the broader field of free-choice learning. Falk and Dierking's (2000) contextual model of learning is widely accepted as a theoretical framework for understanding and investigating free-choice learning. This model conceptualizes learning as being constructed over time, as the process and product of the interactions between three overlapping contexts—the personal, the sociocultural, and the physical (Falk and Dierking, 2000). The model recognizes that free-choice learners have a range of prior experiences and motivations for learning that influence the way they experience the learning environment, and that learning is a cumulative process drawing from a wide variety of sources over long periods of time. The contextual model of learning is consistent with recent educational theories such as constructivism (Hein, 1996, 1998) and sociocultural theories (Schauble et al., 1997) that view learning as an active process of meaning-making that emerges as individuals interact with phenomena and information in a social context.

In the following sections, we discuss the ways in which free-choice environmental learning research differs from other kinds of free-choice learning research, focusing on both theoretical and methodological issues. We then present a number of challenges that we believe free-choice environmental learning research needs to address in order to advance theory and practice in the field.

THEORETICAL ISSUES IN FREE-CHOICE ENVIRONMENTAL LEARNING RESEARCH

The issues that distinguish free-choice *environmental* learning from free-choice learning in general relate to the special characteristics of environmental learning, as well as the theoretical and philosophical concerns inherent in the field of environmental education. Arguments regarding the nature and purpose of environmental education abound and there is considerable debate regarding its aims, and the ways in which it is, and should be, implemented. For example, Scott and Gough (2003) identify nine different "categories of interest" that encapsulate a range of different focuses, objectives, and assumptions held by those who espouse environmental learning. These range from a focus on the individual learner, to a focus on the social context, from a realist view of nature to a metaphorical one. The interests include "sharing the joy and fulfilment derived from nature"; "understanding the processes of nature"; "using environmental, conservation and/or sustainability issues as contexts for the development of skills and knowledge related to the exercise of democratic social change"; and "promoting nature as a metaphor for a preferred social order" (Scott and Gough, 2003, p. 54). All of these perspectives have something to contribute to our understanding of the breadth and depth of what might be termed environmental learning, but all require very different research questions and approaches. This is a highly contested issue in environmental education. Arguably, much of the work on environmental learning in formal education contexts has involved academics and practitioners debating the nature of the subject and arguing from different paradigms, rather than undertaking research that leads to practical improvements in environmental learning, however this is defined. For the purposes of this chapter, therefore, we focus on a particular view of environmental learning, to which we believe the mainstream of environmental educators, particularly those working within free-choice learning settings, ascribe. In this way, we hope to provide some positive suggestions for future research directions in free-choice environmental learning, without becoming immobilized by debates regarding aims and approaches to facilitating environmental learning.

The perspective we take in this chapter is based on the United Nations Educational, Scientific and Cultural Organization–United Nations Environmental Programme (UNESCO-UNEP) description of environmental education from the Tbilisi Declaration of 1977 (UNESCO, 1977). This description "has received wide and enduring acceptance internationally and provides a useful foundation for continued action" (Environment Australia, 1999). It holds that the goals of environmental education are

- to foster clear awareness of, and concern about, economic, social, political, and ecological interdependence in urban and rural areas;
- to provide every person with opportunities to acquire the knowledge, values, attitudes, commitment, and skills needed to protect and improve the environment; and
- to create new patterns of behavior of individuals, groups, and society as a whole toward the environment. (UNESCO, 1977, p. 26)

Thus environmental education should not only extend students' knowledge about the environment, but should also challenge the attitudes and behaviors that form the basis of environmental citizenship (Ballantyne and Packer, 1996). According to Tilbury (1995), the decision to participate in environmental improvement is more likely to be stimulated by affective factors such as personal motivation and a sense of responsibility than by cognitive factors. Free-choice environmental learning, then, must also adopt a broad definition of learning that incorporates affective as well as cognitive aspects.

Some of the major theoretical issues underpinning free-choice environmental learning research arise from a focus on the affective aspects of learning and include the following in relation to (1) learning outcomes, (2) learning processes, (3) learning strategies, and (4) the gap between learning and action.

Environmental Learning Outcomes Can Include Aspects of Knowledge, Attitudes, and Behavior

Attempts to define the nature and scope of environmental education often promote, as its ultimate aim, the development of responsible environmental behavior (Howe and Disinger, 1991; Hungerford and Volk, 1990). Effective environmental learning thus involves not only a change or growth in understanding, but also a willingness to depart from previously held attitudes and beliefs and make commitments to new ways of interacting with the world (Ballantyne and Packer, 1996). Research in free-choice environmental learning must therefore find ways of measuring not only changes in knowledge and understanding, but also changes in attitudes, beliefs, motivation, and behavior, and the interrelationships among these. For example, learning outcomes may include changes in the way people feel about particular species or the environment in general; changes in awareness, appreciation, and concern for wildlife; the development of empathy; an increase in motivation or commitment; lifestyle changes; willingness to talk to others about environmental issues; joining volunteer programs; or donating to environmental organizations (Ballantyne and Packer, 2005).

Affective Factors May be More Important than Cognitive Factors in Bringing about Free-Choice Environmental Learning

Recent theories of learning have started to take greater account of the role of emotion in learning, especially as a motivational force, influencing our selection of what we attend to, and what seems important to explore (Boler, 1999; Eich and Schooler, 2000). Emotion also plays a major role in moral judgment and attitude development (Breckler, 1993; Kaplan, 1991; Yob, 1997). Kals et al. (1999) contend that rational decision-making processes are not sufficient to explain engagement in environmentally responsible behaviors, and that the power of emotions such as guilt, fear, or empathy must also be taken into account. Our research (Ballantyne et al., 2001a, 2001b; Ballantyne and Packer, 2002) has consistently found that the empathy and emotional engagement with wildlife experienced by school students on field trips to natural areas, and by participants in nature-based tourism experiences, are the most powerful factors contributing to the achievement of environmental education and sustainability goals.

Theories of Attitude and Behavior Change Can Inform the Development of Free-Choice Environmental Learning Strategies

If the aim of free-choice environmental learning is to encourage people to question and change their attitudes and behavior, as well as develop their knowledge and understanding, then the strategies and techniques used to present and interpret experiences need to be informed by theories of attitude and behavior change. One particularly influential theory in this regard has been Ajzen's (1985) theory of planned behavior. The theory posits that behavior is a function of three categories of salient beliefs: behavioral beliefs (beliefs about the outcomes and consequences of particular behavior); normative beliefs (beliefs relating to social pressures to perform or not perform the behavior); and control beliefs (beliefs about our ability, knowledge, skill, resources, and opportunity to perform the behavior). Free-choice learning experiences that target the specific beliefs that people hold in relation to an environmental action are likely to be more effective in influencing people to adopt (or refrain from) that action (Ham and Krumpe, 1996). Community-based social marketing theory (McKenzie-Mohr and Smith, 1999), which is an extension of the theory of planned behavior, is similarly based on identifying and targeting the barriers and benefits associated with the adoption of conservation activities. Drawing from these and other theories of attitude and behavior change, free-choice environmental learning research needs to investigate the beliefs, barriers, and benefits typically associated with different environmental behaviors. Such research will be valuable in informing the types of messages that need to be presented in order to facilitate effective environmental learning.

Motivation Theories Can Inform Our Understanding of the Gap between Environmental Learning and Environmental Action

Maehr and Braskamp (1986) define motivation in terms of the extent to which individuals invest themselves (their time, talents, and effort) in a given activity. Education researchers have long recognized the importance of motivation in our understanding of human learning. The concept is particularly relevant to environmental learning, especially if we accept that the aim of such learning is to bring about responsible environmental behavior. Adding the *free-choice* component further multiplies the importance of motivation, as participants can freely choose the extent to which they attend to, take heed of, and enact the messages presented in free-choice learning contexts. The concept of motivation incorporates cognitive, affective, behavioral, and biological aspects, but it cannot simply be regarded as an individual characteristic. The situational context in which an activity is embedded is also conceived as a major constituent of motivation (Turner, 2001). Motivation is seen to impact on the selective *direction* of behavior (why one behavior is chosen over another); the selective *energization* of behavior (how much effort is devoted to it); and the selective *regulation* of behavior (whether a particular behavior is maintained, altered, or terminated) (Ford, 1992; Locke and Latham, 1994; Pintrich et al., 1993). Clearly these factors are relevant to an individual's choice to act in an environmentally responsible manner, to devote effort and energy to such actions, and to persist in these actions in the face of barriers and obstacles. Motivation theories thus have great potential to inform research in free-choice environmental learning. Some attempts have been made to understand the motivational factors that influence participation in, and learning through, free-choice learning experiences (e.g., Falk, 2006; Hood, 1983; Packer and Ballantyne, 2002). These need to be extended to inform our understanding of factors that influence the uptake of environmental actions in response to a free-choice learning experience. Perhaps, for example, different visitor groups will be more open to different types of environmental messages, and knowing this will enable these messages to be more accurately targeted (Dierking et al., 2004; Falk et al., 2008).

METHODOLOGICAL ISSUES IN FREE-CHOICE ENVIRONMENTAL LEARNING RESEARCH

Some of the methodological issues faced by free-choice environmental learning research relate to (1) difficulties in measuring behavioral impacts, (2) the need for follow-up measures beyond the site, (3) the limitations of a purely quantitative approach, and (4) the diversity of contexts in which free-choice learning occurs.

Difficulties in Measuring Behavioral Impacts

The impact of free-choice learning experiences on participants' environmental learning is notoriously difficult to measure, especially in relation to long-term behavioral changes. While it is possible, and indeed valuable, to observe the impact of a free-choice learning experience on visitors' behavior at the actual site of the experience, it is much more difficult to measure long-term changes to everyday environmentally responsible activities, using anything other than self-report measures. People don't always behave the way they say they behave, and so it is difficult to establish the validity of purely self-report measures. To further complicate the issue, research has demonstrated that different environmental actions appear to be relatively independent (Ebreo and Vining, 2001; Granzin and Olsen, 1991; Oskamp et al., 1991), and so changes in relation to one environmental action do not necessarily imply or predict changes in others. Free-choice environmental learning research must therefore employ multiple measures in order to assess a range of possible learning outcomes and environmental behaviors and attempt to establish validity through triangulation.

The Need for Follow-Up Measures Beyond the Site

If the aim of free-choice environmental learning experiences is to develop environmentally responsible behavior in everyday life, there is a clear need for measures of learning outcomes that extend beyond the site itself. An often-used shortcut has been to measure the impact of a learning experience on participants' behavioral intentions as they leave the site, but clearly, there are many factors that might influence the extent to which intentions are converted into actions. Utilizing follow-up measures some weeks or months after the experience provides a more realistic assessment of the behavioral impact of a free-choice environmental learning experience; however, it then becomes difficult to isolate the impact of the free-choice learning experience itself from a range of other influences. Researchers need to accept that learning is a complex process that occurs incrementally, and it is neither possible nor desirable to dissect the experience into discrete events. It will often be necessary to take a more holistic view, which recognizes the synergies between multiple experiences.

The Limitations of a Purely Quantitative Approach

One of the key difficulties of assessing the educational impact of free-choice learning experiences in general is that visitors differ greatly in their previsit experiences, knowledge, attitudes, interests, and motivations. Learners in free-choice contexts are a more heterogeneous group than is typically the case in formal education settings (Falk and Dierking, 2000). Free-choice learning experiences are also more self-directed and personalized than formal education experiences. As a consequence of these two factors, it is often very difficult to predict the learning outcomes that may be expected from a free-choice learning experience. Quantitative measures of learning that rely on responses to a predetermined set of items can often, therefore, miss the mark and/or fail to detect small but important changes in awareness, understanding, attitudes, and behavior. However, reliable and valid quantitative data that can be collected from large numbers of respondents are clearly necessary in order for research to progress from the exploratory stage into more rigorous hypothesis testing and multivariate analysis. For this reason, researchers have often found it necessary to use a hybrid measurement system that entails quantification of qualitative data. Personal meaning-mapping (Falk, 2003) is a good example of this. This method is designed to measure how a learning experience uniquely affects each individual's understanding or meaning-making process. It does not assume that all learners enter with comparable knowledge and experience, nor does it require an individual to produce a specific "correct" answer in order to demonstrate learning. The procedure involves participants providing multiple responses to a "prompt" word or phrase, which are then scored on four dimensions—the extent of knowledge, the breadth of conceptual understanding, the depth or richness of understanding, and level of mastery. In our own research we have also used a method for dealing quantitatively with qualitative data. We use a set of open-ended questions designed to elicit extended qualitative responses regarding changes in understanding, attitudes, and behaviors that participants attribute to the free-choice environmental learning experience. Responses in each of three categories (knowledge, attitude, and behavior) are then coded on a four-point scale from no change through to a definitive statement of new knowledge, a changed attitude, or a new behavior that has been adopted as a result of the experience. The disadvantage of these hybrid methods, however, is their reliance on participants' insights into and ability to verbally describe their learning experience. These measures may thus be difficult to use with children or with those who are responding in a nonpreferred language.

The Diversity of Contexts in Which Free-Choice Learning Occurs

Free-choice environmental learning may occur in a range of contexts, from a fleeting glance at a television news report, to an intensive, immersive ecotourism or educational tourism experience. Thus not only do visitors differ greatly in what they bring to the experience, but also free-choice environmental learning experiences themselves are highly variable, in their duration, their aims, their intensity, and their educational impact. For example, in the context of ecotourism, Weaver (2005) identifies two types of experience: the minimalist, which emphasizes superficial learning opportunities and aims only to maintain the particular site or property on which the experience is based; and the comprehensive, which aims to foster deep understanding and transformation of visitors' behavior. The minimalist approach tends to be associated with the "soft" ecotourism market, i.e., larger numbers of participants making relatively short and physically comfortable visits, while the comprehensive approach tends to be associated with "hard" ecotourism, i.e., relatively long, specialized trips that are physically and mentally challenging. According to Weaver (2005), more effort is needed to devise strategies and techniques that enable transformative outcomes to be generated through mass (or soft) ecotourism experiences. A similar challenge faces the providers of free-choice environmental learning experiences in other contexts—to devise strategies that enable even very brief free-choice learning encounters to have a transformative effect on visitors and their subsequent actions. Research is thus needed in a range of free-choice learning contexts in order to establish the generalizability of the results obtained in specific settings.

CHALLENGES FOR FUTURE RESEARCH IN FREE-CHOICE ENVIRONMENTAL LEARNING

The following challenges that face the field of free-choice environmental learning provide ample opportunities for research.

Advancing Theory in Free-Choice Environmental Learning

Pure, theory-based research is needed in order to establish and advance our understanding of the processes and outcomes of free-choice environmental learning. For example, further research is needed to explore the links among environmental knowledge, attitudes, motivations, intentions, and behaviors in the context of free-choice learning settings. Research in free-choice environmental learning needs to go beyond the cognitive domain of learning. The role of emotion in free-choice environmental learning, attitude change, and behavioral decision making needs to be further explored, particularly in relation to the intensity of responses and their persistence over time. The salient elements within free-choice learning experiences that facilitate and support visitors' adoption of environmentally sustainable practices need to be identified. An understanding of the ways in which visitors approach and respond to different experiences is necessary in order to inform the development of strategies that maximize the effectiveness of free-choice environmental learning experiences.

Developing Research Methodologies

Instruments and procedures for measuring all aspects of environmental learning outcomes need to be developed. As discussed above, measures of learning outcomes need to extend beyond the learning site, in both space and time; behavioral measures need to be validated using triangulation procedures and if possible direct observation measures; and techniques should ideally incorporate both quantitative and qualitative aspects. Researchers working in different contexts and different locations need to share both their research methods and their findings in order to build a comprehensive database that will support meta-analysis.

Integrating the Cognitive, Affective, and Behavioral Elements of Free-Choice Environmental Learning

In the context of formal environmental education programs, we have previously argued the importance of a holistic approach that recognizes the interrelatedness of environmental knowledge, attitudes/values, and behaviors (Ballantyne and Packer, 1996). Such an approach is perhaps even more important in free-choice learning settings. Research is thus needed to inform the development of free-choice environmental learning experiences that integrate the cognitive, affective, and behavioral elements of environmental learning. For example, research by Ballantyne and colleagues (2001a; 2001b) led to the recommendation that for maximum effect, environmental learning experiences should focus on the *evidence* of an environmental problem (particularly in relation to human impact and mismanagement), the *effects* of the problem (particularly in relation to wildlife and wildlife habitats), and the *efforts* needed to alleviate the problem (practical steps the learner can take). Free-choice learning experiences are in an ideal position to apply this approach, which clearly incorporates and integrates cognitive, affective, and behavioral aspects. Further research is needed to establish the long-term impact of such an approach upon visitor environmental learning in free-choice settings and to identify other strategies that are likely to be effective in this regard.

Balancing the Needs and Purposes of Different Stakeholders

As many free-choice environmental learning experiences are provided by profit-making enterprises, research is needed to understand the sometimes contradictory agendas of different stakeholder groups. For example, providers want to make a profit, visitors want to be entertained, protected area management agencies want to ensure that the site and/or wildlife are properly managed and protected, and the wider society wants venues for education in sustainability. Information from a variety of different perspectives will be required if these divergent needs and purposes are to be addressed. Researchers from a range of disciplines, including business, tourism, psychology, education, and ecology, will need to work together in this regard. A further challenge lies in the dilemma that increased visitation to nature-based free-choice learning experiences may contribute to the destruction of the site or habitat on which the experience depends. Providing effective visitor experiences can thus be counterproductive, unless appropriate management plans and visitor infrastructures are in place. Further research into the role of interpretation and education in controlling visitors' on-site behavior may be helpful in this regard.

Balancing Professional Responsibilities

Much of the research into influencing visitors' behavior through environmental free-choice learning experiences has been based on theories of persuasive communication or social marketing. For some, this may raise questions about the ethical issues involved in "indoctrination" and "behavior modification." In interpreting controversial issues, museums and other free-choice learning sites often prefer to take a "balanced approach" that seeks to present a number of differing interpretations of events and issues in order to encourage visitors to engage with different viewpoints and meanings (Ballantyne and Uzzell,

1999). Such an approach avoids the accusation of bias and is consistent with a postmodern view of meaning-making where different perspectives are equally valued. In relation to environmental issues, however, there may be a case for the active promotion of pro-environmental messages. Uzzell and Ballantyne (1998) argue that interpreters should play a positive role in leading and shaping public opinion. They argue that taking a neutral approach in response to an emotive or contentious issue is also a form of value judgment. Thus free-choice environmental learning experiences need to find a balance between their professional responsibility to present a balanced or unbiased interpretation and their social responsibility to bring about positive societal change. Uzzell and Ballantyne (1998) argue that visitors should be encouraged to reflect on contentious issues, question their own values and beliefs, and appreciate and understand differing viewpoints, attitudes, and behavior. Research is needed to explore the most appropriate and ethical ways of bringing about positive and long-lasting behavioral changes. It may be, for example, that approaches that target emotional or behavioral responses alone, without addressing associated components of knowledge, values, beliefs, and attitudes, are short lived in their effectiveness.

Interpreting Human Impacts

There has often been a perception that visitors to free-choice environmental learning experiences such as zoos and aquariums are there to be entertained, and so may not be open to receiving confronting or challenging messages about environmental issues. Our own research suggests otherwise. Responses from 839 visitors to an aquarium, a marine park, and marine ecotourism experiences indicate that 89–94 percent of visitors at each site endorsed the statement that "Experiences like this should give people information about conservation issues" (Ballantyne, Packer, and Hughes, 2008). Comparable data were collected in a large study of 1,555 visitors to four zoos and aquariums (Falk et al., 2008). Free-choice learning experiences that involve any sort of contact with live animals provide optimal conditions for presenting an effective environmental message. Our research suggests that a powerful way of doing this is to make visitors aware of the impact of human actions on the animals they are observing. For example, an aquarium exhibit showing the effects on a whale of ingesting a plastic bag (mistaken for a jellyfish) provides an excellent opportunity for interpretation designed to not only raise awareness and convey information, but also to change visitors' everyday behavior. Further research is needed to document the long-term impacts of this form of interpretation. Preliminary evidence from our own research suggests that this approach has the potential to motivate visitors to not only change their own behavior, but also to promote responsible environmental behavior with others, thus multiplying the impact of the visit.

Overcoming Action Paralysis

The recent media attention given to global issues such as climate change may exacerbate the "action paralysis" identified by Uzzell and Rutland (1993). Visitors may be so overwhelmed by the enormity of the environmental issues facing the world that they are unable to take any action at all. It is therefore vitally important that free-choice environmental learning experiences provide positive messages that demonstrate to visitors that their actions *can* have an influence on environmental problems. They need to provide practical examples of everyday actions that visitors can take to reduce their "ecological footprint."

Extending the Focus from Site-Specific to Global Issues

Visitors to free-choice environmental learning experiences consistently report that such experiences impact on their general knowledge of, interest in, and concern for the well-being of the particular animals they see in their visit (Ballantyne et al., 2007). They report less of an impact on their knowledge and understanding of conservation issues and their concern for the well-being of wildlife in general. This suggests that if free-choice environmental learning experiences are to have a general impact on conservation attitudes and actions, more efforts are needed to help visitors generalize the impact of the experience beyond the specific animals they have observed. This provides a challenge for interpreters and educators, who have often been taught to focus their interpretation on the unique qualities of the animal or environment they are presenting. Research is needed to support the development of interpretation techniques that maintain this emphasis on what is special, while also extending the vision beyond the specific example, and conveying the interconnectedness of all aspects of life.

Supporting and Maintaining Long-Term Behavioral Impacts

Falk and Dierking's (2000) contextual model of learning makes it clear that free-choice learning experiences do not stand alone. They are influenced by the preexisting learning dispositions that individuals bring with them to the experience, as well as by the reinforcing learning events that occur after the experience. Until recently, most site-based free-choice learning research (for example, in museums, zoos, and aquariums) has focused on the experience

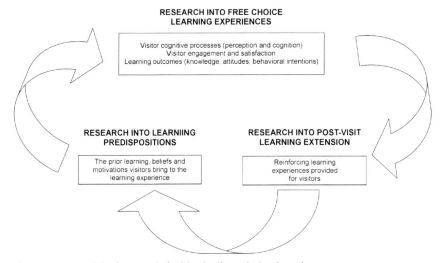

Figure 10.1. Model of research foci in the free-choice learning process.

itself, the learning predispositions that influence and interact with the experience, and the immediate learning outcomes. Very little research has taken place with regard to what happens after the visit. Research is needed at all three points in this process, as illustrated in Figure 10.1.

Further research is needed in the area of postexperience events that reinforce and extend the new knowledge, attitudes, or behavioral intentions developed during a visit. Existing research at the National Aquarium in Baltimore suggests that visitors' immediate postvisit enthusiasm to become involved in conservation activities gradually dwindles to previsit levels (Adelman et al., 2000; Dierking et al., 2002). Similarly, our own research at an ecotourism site found that only a small proportion of visitors actually translated their increased awareness of, and interest in, wildlife into real actions (Ballantyne et al., 2007).

By providing postvisit "action resources" that reinforce on-site conservation messages and provide practical examples of environmentally sustainable actions that visitors can take in their everyday home and work environments, free-choice learning experiences can extend their impact beyond the immediate space and time of the visit. Action resources are learning materials designed to reinforce tourists' on-site learning and motivate them to adopt postvisit environmentally sustainable behavior. Such materials should build on and extend on-site conservation learning and sustainability messages and link these with postvisit behavioral responses. Action resources can be delivered through handouts given to tourists on exiting from the free-choice on-site learning experience or by accessing learning materials through the Internet when they return home. Research is needed to explore the effectiveness of such materials in motivating and empowering visitors' uptake of environmental action.

CONCLUSION

The suggestions for future research outlined in this chapter are designed to support the development of new ways through which free-choice environmental learning experiences might promote visitors' conservation awareness and sustainable behavior. Such research will also contribute to extending our theoretical frameworks and conceptual models for understanding the nature and impact of free-choice environmental learning experiences. In this way, research can contribute to developing the important role that free-choice learning experiences play in helping the global community develop a greater capacity to respond to the challenging environmental issues facing society today.

11

The Federal Government and Free-Choice Learning

Janet Ady and Ginger Potter

All who have meditated on the art of governing mankind have been convinced that the fate of empires depends on the education of the youth.

—Aristotle

A popular government without popular information, or the means of acquiring it, is but a prologue to a farce or a tragedy, or perhaps both.

—James Madison

INTRODUCTION

The previous chapters of this book have discussed the definition of free-
choice learning and the benefits this approach can have on enhanced environmental quality by educating all sectors of society about the environment. The
purpose of this chapter is to explore free-choice learning within the context
of the U.S. federal government system.

The federal government has long been involved in informing and educating
Americans about environmental issues, beginning in the nineteenth century
with conservation education and continuing into the twenty-first century with
free-choice learning and education for sustainability. This chapter explores
why and how the federal government should not only continue, but substantially increase the use of education as a tool for environmental protection.
Benefits to the federal government of being involved specifically in free-
choice learning will be discussed. In addition, this chapter explores which
agencies should become involved in free-choice learning in the future.

PROTECTING THE ENVIRONMENT *IS* THE GOVERNMENT'S JOB

In 1962, Rachel Carson's *Silent Spring* was published, attacking the indiscriminate use of pesticides, launching the modern environmental movement. Eight years later, the Nixon administration brought together those federal offices tasked with various aspects of environmental protection and created the U.S. Environmental Protection Agency (EPA). Also in 1970, the first piece of legislation on environmental policy—the National Environmental Policy Act (NEPA)—was passed into law. The aim of NEPA was "to declare a national policy which will encourage productive and enjoyable harmony between man and his environment; to promote efforts which will prevent or eliminate damage to the environment and biosphere and stimulate the health and welfare of man; and to enrich our understanding of the ecological systems and natural resources important to the Nation" (Lewis, 1985). The public demand for environmental protection grew exponentially from that point on. Highly visible point-source pollution from factories and businesses gave the public a large, visible target at which to aim when demanding safe water, clean air, and the protection of natural resources. Business and industry were seen by the public as the primary source of pollution and primarily responsible for the deteriorating environment and thus were the primary early targets of federal regulatory activities.

Responsibility for protecting human health and the environment has been assigned by the American people primarily to the federal government; this is true not just at the federal level, but at the local and state levels as well. The EPA and many other federal agencies have shouldered the burden of implementing legislation designed to protect the country's natural resources. Clearly public expectation was for government to develop and vigorously enforce regulations aimed at protecting American neighborhoods from environmental polluters.

The dominate approach used by government agencies to ensure environmental and human health protection has been "command and control"—developing sets of rules, regulations, and standards focused mainly on changing the behaviors of the business and industry sectors. Gardner and Stern (1996) note that the defining characteristic of this approach to dictating pro-environmental behavior is that it encourages companies to behave in the public interest. But as successful as the command and control policy has been in reducing the levels of point-source pollution, many believe that the limits of what that type of environmental policy can achieve have been reached (Rejeski and Salzman, 2002).

In the past twenty years, federal agencies have also been looking toward market-based approaches that allow those industries targeted by a particular environmental policy the freedom to decide how they can best economically reduce their pollution stream. An agency decides the appropriate level of pollutant emission, then issues permits for that set level. Permits can be bought and sold in the market; firms that are good at reducing their emissions can profit from their efforts to prevent pollution (Dietz and Stern, 2002). Again, many believe that these approaches may have also reached the limits of what can be accomplished by focusing most federal dollars on point-source pollution. These major point sources of pollution were indeed major contributors to air and water pollution, but as they have been cleaned up, other, more insidious sources of pollution have been revealed.

American citizens still rely heavily on government at all levels to enforce regulations on business and industry, not realizing that the public's own actions are now responsible for the majority of pollution problems in this country. Regulation and enforcement have been successful enough to shift the major sources of pollution in this country to individuals, the household and small- and medium-sized industries, businesses, and farms. Regulation of these amorphous, nonpoint sources of pollution turns out to be extremely difficult and costly. As the National Research Council noted in 2002, education, information, and voluntary compliance programs should now be viewed as the new tools for environmental protection (in addition to, and complementary to, regulation and enforcement) and show the most promise toward mitigating the effects of the actions of individuals as they affect health and the environment. In fact, the Department of Interior, under Secretary Gale Norton, embraced a cooperative conservation approach. Cooperative conservation is defined as actions that relate to use, enhancement, and enjoyment of natural resources, protection of the environment, or both, and that involve collaborative activity among federal, state, local, and tribal governments, private for-profit and nonprofit institutions, other nongovernmental entities, and individuals. Through cooperative conservation, citizens play a central and substantive role in the stewardship and governance of their environments.

An executive order was issued by President George W. Bush to facilitate the implementation of cooperative conservation and to ensure that the departments of the Interior, Agriculture, Commerce, and Defense and the EPA implement laws relating to the environment and natural resources in a manner that promotes cooperative conservation. An emphasis was placed on appropriate inclusion of local participation in federal decision making, in accordance with their respective agency missions, policies, and regulations.

An interagency team was formed in 2005 within the Department of the Interior to increase capacity and competencies in partnerships. Training courses and resources were developed and provided for employees to better establish collaborative community relationships for achieving conservation goals. Key to this collaborative approach is providing information and educating community partners about natural resource management issues, so that they can be informed and able to participate fully in the decision-making process. However, federal employees must always proceed in their education efforts with some caution, lest they be viewed as lobbying in favor of a specific special interest, an activity that is expressly forbidden for federal employees.

PROTECTING THE ENVIRONMENT IS *EVERYONE'S* JOB

Protecting the environment is a complex and long-term process that requires the participation of all sectors of society. Educating society about its role in protecting human health and the environment has been an important part of the federal response to the various aspects of environmental protection mandates for many federal agencies today, including the departments of Agriculture, Commerce, Defense, Energy, Health and Human Services, Homeland Security, Interior, Transportation, and several small and independent agencies such as the EPA, NASA, and the National Science Foundation (NSF). However, federal agencies tend to target particular audiences with their education programs, depending upon the mission of the agency.

The Cooperative State Research, Education and Extension Service (CSREES) of the U.S. Department of Agriculture public education programs include educating landowners about current agriculture research and economic analysis; educating homemakers about nutrition, food safety, and health issues; and educating children through 4-H youth development programs. CSREES free-choice learning programs focus on local community residents and operate at the county level through extension agents. Many exemplary conservation education programs have been developed through this program in cooperation with land and sea grant universities, and they are all accessed by "volunteer" learners. CSREES programs are very successful free-choice learning programs that tie directly to the mission of the agency.

The National Park Service and other public land management agencies have educational and interpretive programs that target the visiting public, primarily families and adults. Many agencies that do not have a land base or visitor destinations must reach their publics via mass media or in partnership with educational institutions, according to their enabling legislations and mandates. Educational videos, publications, and products are produced and distributed at fairs, on public television, and on the Internet.

The mission of the NSF includes support for science and engineering education, from pre-K through graduate school and beyond. The scientific research funded through NSF is thoroughly integrated with education to help ensure that there will always be plenty of skilled people available to work in new and emerging scientific, engineering, and technological fields and capable teachers to educate the next generation. Lifelong science and mathematics learning has become an increasing emphasis at NSF with significant monies earmarked specifically for funding innovation and research in the area of free-choice learning. Over the past several years, a number of major projects have been funded by the NSF that relate directly to the area of free-choice environmental education.

However, public education is a difficult task, made even more difficult due to low levels of funding and support found within most federal agencies. Additionally, many federal agencies are now investing in public information programs that focus on public media and website outreach campaigns; these campaigns are viewed by the agencies as "educating the public" although more accurately they are merely just "informing the public." Professional environmental educators know that providing information or making it accessible is only the beginning of the education process. Information alone will not create an environmentally literate public with the knowledge and skills needed to make important environmental decisions within their own communities. The process of becoming environmentally literate starts with being "aware" of the issues; acquiring "knowledge" of the natural and built systems; embracing an "attitude" of appreciation of and concern for the environment; developing critical thinking, problem-solving, and decision-making "skills"; and finally, committing to civic participation and taking personal and collective action in order to preserve and protect the environment. Informational booklets and media campaigns will never be enough to create an environmentally literate citizenry. The federal government needs to make a concerted commitment to foster environmental literacy and encourage stewardship, to the same extent it has committed to regulation and enforcement. The most appropriate tools must be used, those with the highest level of impact on current major sources of pollution and habitat degradation at the state, local, and national levels. When approaching environmental issues, government agencies need to integrate education, especially free-choice learning opportunities, into the planning process, along with the traditional tools, accounting for the current level of awareness and propensity for positive action of the key constituents and stakeholders involved.

BUILDING THE CASE FOR FEDERAL SUPPORT OF LIFELONG, FREE-CHOICE LEARNING

In 1990, the U.S. Congress passed the National Environmental Education Act (P.L. 101-619) in response to a growing need to provide all citizens with the knowledge and skills necessary to become active participants in the protection of human health and the environment. A similar piece of legislation was passed in 1970 giving the Department of Health, Education and Welfare (before moving it to the Department of Education in 1979) responsibility for public education about the environment, but no monies were ever appropriated to implement the mandates of that law and the law terminated in 1981. The 1990 National Environmental Education Act, implemented by the EPA, once again notes the "growing evidence of international environmental problems such as global warming, ocean problems and declines in species that pose a serious threat to human health and the environment" including quality of life and economic vitality. In 1990, the authors of this legislation recognized that federal programs designed to inform and educate the public about the natural and built environment were woefully inadequate. However, the Congress has never appropriated more than $10 million a year to educate the public on environmental issues since the law was enacted. Nor was the legislation reauthorized when it expired in 1996.

Now, nearly twenty years later, the federal government's financial commitment to public education is flat at best and focused heavily in the formal school system. Considering the magnitude of the environmental problems we face that are having a profound effect on both quality of life and economic prosperity in this country, educating Americans to become more active stewards of the county's natural resources remains not only necessary, but more urgent than ever before.

However, even if the National Environmental Education Act is reauthorized, many believe that it is "inadequate in both design and funding" (Elder, 2003, p. 70) to have any real effect on the field of environmental education or to increase and improve environmental literacy in this country. Additionally, the focus of the Act has been on K–12 education in both the formal and the nonformal sectors, where most agency funding is directed. The general adult public is reached primarily through media campaigns and information pamphlets, not by well-designed education efforts.

Another example of federal legislation that encourages free-choice learning and education is an amendment to the Fish and Wildlife Act of 1956, approved in 1998. The amendment promotes volunteer programs and community partnerships for the benefit of national wildlife refuges. The law enables the U.S. Fish & Wildlife Service to implement volunteer programs, authorizes establishment of a Senior Volunteer Corps, and provides authority for refuge managers to organize and collaborate with partner organizations. The law also requires the Secretary of the Interior to develop refuge education programs to provide outdoor classroom opportunities for students to promote understanding of the National Wildlife Refuge System and to improve scientific literacy in conjunction with both formal and informal education programs.

In order to effectively achieve its environmental protection and natural resource conservation responsibilities for the American people, the federal government needs significant funding increases to improve environmental literacy and education, and needs to broaden the scope of these efforts to include all sectors of society. In addition, the National Academy of Science's National Research Council (2002) makes a sound case for the federal government as an active participant in informing and educating the public, particularly related to becoming active participants in the protection of local community environments. Free-choice learning offers all federal government agencies an opportunity to reach all sectors of society to improve environmental literacy through education programs that are focused on the learner and targeted to address specific environmental protection and conservation issues.

Also important to a national environmental literacy program is the need for rigorous evaluation of the programs themselves and the results of such programs. The question of whether education programs are leading to improved environmental literacy is essential. The question of whether these programs are also leading to improvements in human heath and the environment are essential as well.

The federal government can provide the necessary large investment of resources to build a national vision and strategy for educating the public by providing the tools to improve environmental literacy for all citizens. There are many important reasons for the government to invest in free-choice learning. The federal government cannot achieve environmental protection goals alone; the help and commitment of all citizens to stewardship is needed. The trend is for less government and cheaper government. The ultimate goal is less dependence on the government for answers and actions, and more involvement and decision making at the local community levels. A well-educated and informed public can help implement policies.

As the role of government changes, many question whether government regulation can lead to achieving the goals of environmental protection given the shifting sources of pollution in this country. Education is believed to increase the efficiency of consumers' and producers' responses to economic signals of the need to change behavior to reduce environmental costs (National Research Council, 2002). Many argue that the federal role in education in the formal school system should be diminished. Free-choice learning allows the government to further the goals of stewardship by focusing on the informal education setting, because more environmental learning is acquired outside of the formal school system.

Education about the environment is more of an approach than a discipline and is, therefore, hard to fit into the rigid discipline approach to formal education (Falk, 2005). Free-choice learning takes advantage of a learner's interests—issues they may have learned about in school but wish to learn more about at their own pace. The wide variety, diversity, and complexity of environmental issues requires a broader approach to improving environmental literacy than the formal school system approach; free choice learning targets all sectors of society, not just those of school age. To sustain any improvements in environmental literacy rates and increases in environmental stewardship requires embracing the philosophy of lifelong learning; free-choice learning is lifelong learning.

There are many examples of successful use of education and free-choice learning to address natural resource management goals. In a report prepared for the U.S. Fish & Wildlife Service National Conservation Training Center's Division of Education Outreach (Byers, 2003), sixteen cases were analyzed in which education, communication, and outreach were employed to influence human behaviors that affected conservation targets, such as threatened and endangered species, migratory birds, and critical habitats. The case studies demonstrated that such interventions produced measurable changes in actions, choices, and behaviors that threaten wildlife, and improved the status of threatened species and habitats. The cases also demonstrated, however, that simply providing information alone, although necessary in all cases, was not sufficient in itself to improve conservation-related behaviors. Careful, upfront assessment of stakeholders, target audiences, the ecological impact of behavior, and the factors that motivate it are needed. Designing interventions and free-choice learning opportunities with this in mind can affect the relevant factors, with a good probability that harmful behaviors can be reduced. Programs that provide information and knowledge, influence social norms, create options, and also include laws and enforcement can be quite successful at changing behavior, even in complex situations. The need for expensive law enforcement can be reduced by using information, developing options and skills, and changing social norms, which reduce the number of incidents requiring enforcement action.

The key to success in each of the sixteen cases analyzed was that the education programs were tied directly to the mission of the organization and the conservation goals the organization was attempting to achieve. In this way, the free-choice learning opportunities were viewed as essential, instead of as public relations or "nice to do," but not necessary, activities. Clearly, free-choice learning can be a critical factor in designing and implementing environmental public policy.

THE ROLE OF THE FEDERAL GOVERNMENT IN IMPROVING ENVIRONMENTAL LITERACY THROUGH FREE-CHOICE LEARNING

To take on the role of providing a national investment in free-choice learning, the federal government needs to make some changes in its management and support of education programs. Education programs should tie directly into an agency's mission and its strategic goals. For example, the EPA has five strategic goals: clean air and global climate change, clean and safe water, land preservation and restoration, healthy communities and ecosystems, and compliance and environmental stewardship.

In order to achieve these goals, the agency has developed seven cross goal strategies: partnerships, information, innovation, human capital, science, homeland security, and economic and policy analysis.

Educating the public is an implied strategy for achieving environmental stewardship; it is not specifically targeted as an approach to achieving either that or the other agency goals. If education is not listed as a specific approach to achieving an agency's goals, it will never receive the attention and funding that is necessary to meet the goals of clean air, clean water, land preservation, healthy communities and ecosystems, and stewardship with the full engagement of an environmentally literate public.

Environmental education programs and initiatives are fragmented and uncoordinated both inside federal agencies as well as between federal agencies. No one agency serves as a focal point for environmental education efforts across the federal government, although the EPA has attempted to take on that role within its existing resources and legislative authority. A large-scale effort to support improving environmental literacy nationally would require a high-level coordinating body to provide strategic vision and coordination of all education activities in all agencies tasked with any aspect of environmental protection—an entity that sits outside of any one federal agency that could represent the interests of all agencies involved. This could be similar to the Coastal America partnership between EPA and the National Oceanic and Atmospheric Administration and could have responsibility for coordinating all federal education efforts to improve environmental literacy. This coordinating body could also give grants to nonprofit organizations and education entities to provide resources for free-choice learning initiatives and to support formal school initiatives. Adequate, consistent funding would ensure continued success, with the majority of that funding going toward grants.

Even should such a governing body exist to focus education efforts (and especially in its absence), individual federal agencies must make a specific commitment to target and recognize education as a cross-cutting strategy for reaching its goals. Federal decision makers charged with managing natural resources must be trained to include public education into their management strategies. Public education, including free-choice learning opportunities, must be as integral to environmental protection as monitoring populations, testing water quality, and enforcing laws. A certain percentage of the project budget should be targeted for educational activities. These activities should be separated from information and outreach activities—where education is often lumped, and elevated as viable management tools, along with research, monitoring, and all other recognized and valued tools.

Combined with formal K–12 environmental education, lifelong, free-choice learning can create the environmentally literate, informed society we now need to deal with imminent challenges of climate change, endangered species, habitat loss and fragmentation, and natural resource depletion. Proven methods exist, are easily available and implemented, and are at an affordable cost. In fact, the cost of not embracing the power of free-choice learning to implement environmental policies will ultimately be much greater. Nongovernmental organizations, educational institutions, and community organizations must all encourage and work with policy makers and agencies to strengthen educational programs and institutionalize these approaches. It is imperative to the quality of life, health, and well-being of our nation and our future generations.

Federal agencies would be best served by thoroughly analyzing their objectives in light of all the tools available to them: legislation and regulation; land management; law enforcement; as well as communication, education, information, voluntary compliance programs, and social marketing strategies. Such an analysis may reveal powerful social strategies as the most cost-effective and impactful options for achieving environmental protection goals.

The future of environmental and health protection lies in each individual embracing their responsibility for their own actions and behaviors—becoming stewards of their local environment in their communities. And stewardship begins with education. As citizens we are all engaging in free-choice learning all the time. The federal government has a tremendous opportunity to impact the quality of the environment by investing in free-choice learning programs on a much greater level than it is currently spending. It is an investment in the future of the country and its citizens.

References

Adelman, L. M., Falk, J. H., and James, S. (2000). Impact of National Aquarium in Baltimore on visitors' conservation attitudes, behavior, and knowledge. *Curator, 43*(1), 33–61.

Ady, J. (2007) Conservation education and outreach techniques: An indispensable guide for creating effective conservation education programs. *Ecology 88*(6): 1607–8.

Ajzen, I. (1985). *From intentions to actions: A theory of planned behavior.* Heidelberg, Germany: Springer.

Ajzen, I., and Fishbein, M. (1980). *Understanding attitudes and predicting social behavior.* Englewood Cliffs, NJ: Prentice Hall.

American Association for the Advancement of Science. (2004). *Marine issues survey.* Retrieved September 20, 2007 from www.aaas.org/news/releases/2004/aaas_survey_report.pdf.

American Association of Museums. (2007). *Museums FAQ.* Retrieved September 4, 2007 from www.aam-us.org/aboutmuseums/abc.cfm#visitors.

American Psychological Association, Board of Educational Affairs. (1997). *Learner-centered psychological principles: A framework for school redesign and reform (K–12).* Retrieved June 21, 2008 from www.apa.org/ed/lcp2/lcp14.html.

Anderson, C., and Keltner, D. (2002). The role of empathy in the formation and maintenance of social bonds. *Behavioral and Brain Sciences, 25*(1), 21–22.

Andrews, E. (1998). *An EPA/USDA partnership to support community-based education: A discussion paper.* EPA 910-R-98-008. Retrieved June 21, 2008 from www.csrees.usda.gov/nea/nre/pdfs/discussion_paper.pdf.

Andrews, E. (2007). Fostering aquatic stewardship with the help of best education practices. In B. A. Knuth and W. F. Siemer (Eds.), *Aquatic stewardship education in theory and practice* (Symposium 55) (pp. 25–32). Bethesda, MD: American Fisheries Society.

Andrews, E., Stevens, M., and Wise, G. (2002). A model of community-based environmental education. In T. Dietz and P. C. Stern (Eds.), *New tools for environmental protection: Education, information, and voluntary measures* (pp. 161–182). Washington, DC: National Academy Press.

Archie, M. (Ed.). (1998). *Environmental education in the United States—Past, present, and future: Collected papers of the 1996 National Environmental Education Summit, Burlingame, CA.* Washington, DC: North American Association for Environmental Education.

Armitage, C., and Conner, M. (2001). Efficacy of the Theory of Planned Behavior: A meta-analytic review. *British Journal of Social Psychology, 40,* 471–499.

Association of Zoos and Aquariums. (2007). *Background.* Retrieved September 4, 2007 from www.aza.org/AboutAZA/AZA_Background/.

Azevedo, F. S. (2004). *Serious play: A comparative study of learning and engagement in hobby practices.* Unpublished doctoral dissertation. University of California, Berkeley.

Badri, M. A., (1991). Mass communication and the challenge on global environmental protection. *The Journal of Development Communication, 2,* 1–16.

Ballantyne, R., and Packer, J. (1996). Teaching and learning in environmental education: Developing environmental conceptions. *Journal of Environmental Education, 27*(2), 25–32.

Ballantyne, R., and Packer, J. (2002). Nature-based excursions: School students' perceptions of learning in natural environments. *International Research in Geographical and Environmental Education, 12*(1), 1–19.

Ballantyne, R., and Packer, J. (2005). Promoting environmentally sustainable attitudes and behaviour through free-choice learning experiences: What's the state of the game? *Environmental Education Research, 11*(3), 281–295.

Ballantyne, R., and Uzzell, D. (1999). International trends in heritage and environmental interpretation: Future directions for Australian research and practice. *Journal of Interpretation Research, 4*(1), 59–75.

Ballantyne, R., Fien, J., and Packer, J. (2001a). Programme effectiveness in facilitating intergenerational influence in environmental education: Lessons from the field. *Journal of Environmental Education, 32*(4), 8–15.

Ballantyne, R., Fien, J., and Packer, J. (2001b). School environmental education programme impacts upon student and family learning: A case study analysis. *Environmental Education Research, 7*(1), 23–37.

Ballantyne, R., Packer, J., and Bond, N. (2007 February). *The impact of a wildlife tourism experience on visitors' conservation knowledge, attitudes and behaviour: Preliminary results from Mon Repos Turtle Rookery, Queensland.* Paper presented at CAUTHE Conference, Sydney.

Ballantyne, R., Packer, J., and Hughes, K. (in press). Tourists' support for conservation messages and sustainable management practices in wildlife tourish experience. *Tourisn Management.*

Balling, J. D., and Falk, J. H. (1982). Development of visual preference for natural environments. *Environment and Behavior, 14,* 5–28.

Bandura, A. (1977). Self-efficacy: Toward a unifying theory of behavior change. *Psychological Review, 84*(2), 191–215.

Bandura, A. (1986). *Social foundations of thought and action: A social cognitive theory.* Englewood Cliffs, NJ: Prentice Hall.

Bandura, A. (2001). Social Cognitive Theory: An agentic perspective. *Annual Review of Psychology, 52,* 1–26.

Bandura, A. (2002). Reflexive empathy: On predicting more than has ever been observed. *Behavioral and Brain Sciences, 25,* 24–25.

Barkow, J., Cosmides, L., and Tooby, J. (1992). *The adapted mind: Evolutionary psychology and the generation of culture.* New York: Oxford University Press.

Barrie, J. M., and Presti, D. E. (1996). The World Wide Web as an instructional tool. *Science, 274,* 371–372.

Baumeister, R. F. (1999). The nature and structure of the self: An overview. In R. F. Baumeister (Ed.), *The self in social psychology* (pp. 1–20). London: Psychology Press.

Beer, V. (1987). Visitor learning at the Chicago Historical Center. *Curator, 20*(3), 206–215.

Belden Russonello & Stewart, and American Viewpoint. (1999). *Communicating about oceans: Results of a national survey.* Retrieved February 20, 2008 from www.brspoll.com/Reports/Oceans%20summary.pdf.

Bem, D. J. (1972). Self-perception theory. In L. Berkowitz (Ed.), *Advances in experimental social psychology, Vol. 6* (pp. 1–62). New York: Academic Press.

Ben-Ze´ev, A. (2000). *The subtlety of emotions.* Cambridge, MA: Massachusetts Institute of Technology Press.

Bexell, S. M. (2006). Effect of a wildlife conservation camp experience in China on student knowledge of animals, care, propensity for environmental stewardship, and compassionate behavior toward animals. Unpublished Doctoral Dissertation, Georgia State University.

Bixler, R. D., and Floyd, M. F. (1997). Nature is scary, disgusting, and uncomfortable. *Environment and Behavior, 29*(4), 443–467.

Bixler, R. D., Floyd, M. F., and Hammitt, W. E. (2002). Environmental socialization: Quantitative tests of the childhood play hypothesis. *Environment and Behavior, 34*(6), 795–818.

Bjornavold, J. (2000). *Making learning visible: Identification, assessment and recognition of non-formal learning in Europe.* Thessaloniki, Greece: European Centre for the Development of Vocational Training.

Blanchard, K. A. (1995). Reversing population declines in seabirds on the north shore of the Gulf of St. Lawrence. In Susan K. Jacobson (Ed.). *Conserving Wildlife: International Education and Communication.* New York: Columbia University Press.

Bloom, B. S. (Ed.). (1956). *Taxonomy of educational objectives. Handbook 1: Cognitive domain.* New York: David McKay Company, Inc.

Bloom, B. S. (1976). *Human characteristics and school learning.* New York: McGraw-Hill.

Bodger, D. (1998). Leisure, learning, and travel. *The Journal of Physical Education, Recreation and Dance, 69*(4), 2–5.

Boler, M. (1999). *Feeling power: Emotions and education.* New York: Routledge.

Borman, S. C. (1978). Communication accuracy in magazine science reporting. *Journalism Quarterly, 55*(2), 345–46.

Boyer, L., and Roth, W. M. (2005). Individual collective dialectic of free-choice learning in a community-based mapping project. *Environmental Education Research, 11*(3), 335–51.

Boyes, E., and Stanisstreet, M. (1997). Children's models of understanding of two major global environmental issues (ozone layer and greenhouse effect). *Research in Science and Technological Education, 15*(1), 19–28.

Braus, J., and Ady, J. (2007). "The Tools of Engagement." NAAEE Conference, Virginia Beach, VA.

Braus, J., and Wood, D. (1993). *Environmental education in the schools: Creating a program that works!* Washington, DC: Peace Corps Information and Exchange Program.

Breckler, S. J. (1993). Emotion and attitude change. In M. Lewis and J. M. Haviland (Eds.), *Handbook of emotions* (pp. 461–473). New York: The Guildford Press.

Brochu, L. (2003). Interpretive planning: The 5-M model for successful planning projects. Fort Collins, CO: InterPress.

Brody, M. (2005). Learning in nature. *Environmental Education Research, 11*(5), 603–21.

Brody, M., Bangert, A., and Dillon, J. (2007). *Assessing the outcomes of informal science learning.* Washington, DC: National Research Council Science Learning in Informal Environments Committee. Retrieved April 8, 2008 from www.informalscience.org/knowledge/citation_view.php?refID=5491.

Bronfenbrenner, U. (1979). *The ecology of human development.* Cambridge, MA: Harvard University Press.

Brothers, C. C., Fortner, R. W., and Mayer, V. J. (1991). The impact of television news on public environmental knowledge. *Journal of Environmental Education, 22*(4), 22–29.

Bruner, J. S. (1973). *Beyond the information given: Studies in the psychology of knowing.* New York: Norton.

Bruner, J., and Kalmar, D. A. (1998). Narrative and meta-narrative in the construction of self. In M. Ferrari and R. J. Sternberg (Eds.), *Self-Awareness: Its nature and development* (pp. 308–31). New York: The Guildford Press.

Burger, J. (1999). The foot-in-the-door compliance procedure: A multiple-process analysis and review. *Personality and Social Psychology Review, 3*(4), 303–25.

Burghardt, G. (1992). Human-bear bonding in research on black bear behavior. In H. Davis and D. Balfour (Eds.), *The inevitable bond* (pp. 365–82). Cambridge, UK: Cambridge University.

Byers, B. A. (1996). *Understanding and influencing behaviors in conservation and natural resources management.* Washington, DC: Biodiversity Support Program.

Byers, B. A. (2003). *Education, Communication and Outreach (ECO) success stories: Solving conservation problems by changing behavior.* A report prepared for the U.S. Fish and Wildlife Service National Conservation Training Center Division of Education Outreach, Shepherdstown, WV.

California Wellness Foundation. (2003). What we mean by "Strategic Communications." Retrieved June 20, 2008 from www.tcwf.org/pub_reflections/2003/feb/pages/what_we_mean.htm.

Cantor, N., Mischel, W., and Schwartz, J. C. (1982). A prototype analysis of psychological situations. *Cognitive Psychology, 14*, 45–77.

Carlsen, M. B. (1988). *Meaning-making: Therapeutic processes in adult development.* New York: W.W. Norton and Company.

Carlson, S., and Maxa, S. (1997). *Science guidelines for nonformal education*. St. Paul, MN: University of Minnesota, Center for 4-H Youth Development.

Carr, W., and Kemmis, S. (1986). *Becoming critical: Education, knowledge and action research*. London: Falmer.

Carson, R. (1962). *Silent spring*. New York: Fawcett Crest.

Chawla, L. (1998). Significant life experiences revisited: A review of research on sources of environmental sensitivity. *Journal of Environmental Education, 29*(3), 11–21.

Chien, C. J. (1996). *Comparison of U.S. science and environmental reporters' perceptual differences regarding factors affecting the quality of environmental stories*. Unpublished master's thesis, The Ohio State University, Columbus.

Clayton, S., Fraser, J., and Saunders, C. (2006, October). Interpreting animals at the zoo: Visitor-to-visitor communication about animal exhibits. Paper presented at the 14th International Conference of the Society for Human Ecology, Bar Harbor, ME.

Cleveland, M., Kalamas, M., and Laroche, M. (2005). Shades of green: Linking environmental local of control and pro-environmental behaviors. *Journal of Consumer Marketing, 22*(4), 198–212.

Conference on Ocean Literacy Report. (2006). Retrieved September 21, 2007 from http://nmsfocean.org/chow2006/pdfs/cool2006.pdf.

Conservation Measures Partnership. (2007). *Open standards for the practice of conservation*. Retrieved April 10, 2008 from www.fosonline.org/CMP/Library/CMP_Open_Standards_v1.0.pdf.

Conway, W. (2003). The role of zoos in the 21st century. *International Zoo Yearbook, 38*(1), 7–13.

Coombs, P. H. 1989. Formal and nonformal education: Future strategies. In E. J. Titmus (Ed.). *Lifelong education for adults: An international handbook* (pp. 57–60). New York: Pergamon.

Cooper, C. R. (1999). Multiple selves, multiple worlds: Cultural perspectives on individuality and connectedness in adolescence development. In A. Masten (Ed.), *Minnesota symposium on child psychology: Cultural processes in development* (pp. 25–57). Mahwah, NJ: Lawrence Erlbaum Associates.

Courtenay-Hall, P., and Rogers, L. (2002). Gaps in mind: Problems in environmental knowledge-behaviour modeling research. *Environmental Education Research, 8*(3), 283–97.

Covington, M. V. (1992). *Making the grade: A self-worth perspective on motivation and school reform*. Cambridge, UK: Cambridge University Press.

Coyle, K. (2005). *Environmental literacy in America*. Washington, DC: National Environmental Education and Training Foundation (NEETF).

Crane, V., Chen, M., Bitgood, S., Serrell, B., Thompson, D., Nicholson, H., Weiss, F., and Campbell, P. (1994). *Informal science learning: What the research says about television, science museums, and community-based projects*. Dedham, MA: Research Communications, Ltd.

Csikszentmihalyi, M. (1990a). *Flow: The psychology of optimal experience*. New York: Harper Perennial.

Csikszentmihalyi, M. (1990b). Literacy and intrinsic motivation. *Daedalus, 119*(2), 115–40.

Csikszentmihalyi, M., and Hermanson, K. (1995). Intrinsic motivation in museums: Why does one want to learn? In J. H. Falk and L. D. Dierking (Eds.), *Public institutions for personal learning* (pp. 67–77). Washington, DC: American Association of Museums.

Curry, A., and Stanier, R. (2002, July). *Filling the disappointment gap.* Paper presented at the Arts Marketing Association Annual Conference, Glasgow, Scotland.

Cyr, A. V. (1999). *Overview of theories and principles relating to characteristics of adult learners: 1970s–1999.* Clearwater, Florida: Cyr Consultant Services.

Davidson, R. J. (2005). Well-being and affective style: Neural substrates and biobehavioral correlates. In F. Huppert, N. Baylis, and B. Keverne (Eds.), *The science of well-being* (pp. 107–39). New York: Oxford University Press.

Decety, J., and Chaminade, T. (2003). When the self represents the other: A new cognitive neuroscience view of psychological identification. *Consciousness and Cognition, 12,* 577–96.

Deci, E. L. (1992). The relation of interest to the motivation of behavior: A self-determination theory perspective. In K. A. Renninger, S. Hidi, and A. Krapp (Eds.), *The role of interest in learning and development* (pp. 43–70). Hillsdale, NJ: Lawrence Erlbaum Associates.

Deci, E. L., and Ryan, R. M. (1985). *Intrinsic motivation and self-determination in human behavior.* New York: Plenum.

Deci, E. L., Schwartz, A. J., Sheinman, L., and Ryan, R. M. (1981). An instrument to assess adults' orientations toward control versus autonomy with children: Reflections on intrinsic motivation and perceived competence. *Journal of Educational Psychology, 73,* 642–50.

Deiner, C. I., and Dweck, C. S. (1980). An analysis of learned helplessness: The process of success. *Journal of Personality and Social Psychology, 31,* 674–85.

DeMares, R. (2000). Human peak experience triggered by encounters with Cetaceans. *Anthrozoös, 13*(2), 89–103.

Denham, S. A. (1998). *Emotional development in young children.* New York: Guilford.

Denison, J. (1996). *Behavior change: A summary of four major theories.* Family Health International. Retrieved August 15, 2007 from ww2.fhi.org/en/aids/aidscap/aidspubs/behres/bcr4theo.html.

Dewey, J. (1913). *Interest and effort in education.* Boston: Riverside Press.

Dewey, J. (1970). *Experience and education.* New York: Macmillan. (Original work published in 1938).

Dewey, J. (1997). *How we think.* Mineola, NY: Dover Publications. (Original work published in 1910).

Dewey, J. (2003). *Democracy and education.* Boston: IndyPublish.com (Original work published in 1916).

DeYoung, R. (2000). Expanding and evaluating motives for environmentally responsible behavior. *Journal of Social Issues, 56*(3), 509–26.

Dierking, L. D. (1987). *Parent-child interactions in a free choice learning setting: An examination of attention-directing behaviors.* Unpublished doctoral dissertation, University of Florida, Gainesville.

Dierking, L. D. (2003). Policy statement of the "informal science education" ad hoc committee. *Journal of Research in Science Teaching, 40*(2), 108.

Dierking, L. D., Burtnyk, K., Buchner, K. S., and Falk, J. H. (2002). *Visitor learning in zoos and aquariums: A literature review.* Silver Spring, MD: American Zoo and Aquarium Association.

Dierking, L. D., Adelman, L. M., Ogden, J., Lehnhardt, K., Miller, L., and Mellen, J. D. (2004). Using a behavior change model to document the impact of visits to Disney's Animal Kingdom: A study investigating intended conservation action. *Curator, 47*(3), 322–43.

Dietz, T., and Stern, P. C. (2002). Exploring new tools for environmental protection. In T. Dietz and P. C. Stern (Eds.), *New tools for environmental protection: Education, information, and voluntary measures* (pp. 3–16). Washington, DC: National Academy Press.

Dillon, J., and Wals, A. (2006). On the dangers of blurring methods, methodologies and ideologies in environmental education research. *Environmental Education Research, 12*(3–4), 549–58.

Dixon, D. O., Siemer, W. F., and Knuth, B. A. (1995). *Stewardship of the Great Lakes environment: A review of literature.* Ithaca, NY: Cornell University, Department of Natural Resources, NYS College of Agriculture and Life Sciences. HDRU Publishing 95-5.

Doering, Z. D., and Pekarik, A. J. (1996). Questioning the entrance narrative. *Journal of Museum Education, 21*(3), 20–25.

Dweck, C.S. (1986). Motivational processes affecting learning. *American Psychologist, 41*, 1040–48.

Ebreo, A., and Vining, J. (2001). How similar are recycling and waste reduction? Future orientation and reasons for reducing waste as predictors of self-reported behaviour. *Environment and Behavior, 33*(3), 424–48.

Eich, E., and Schooler, J. W. (2000). Cognition/emotion interactions. In E. Eich, J. F. Kihlstrom, G. H. Bower, J. P. Forgas, and P. M. Niedenthal (Eds.), *Cognition and emotion* (pp. 3–29). Oxford, UK: Oxford University Press.

Eisenberg, N., Fabes, R. A., Murphy, B., Karbon, M., Maszk, P., Smith, M., O'Boyle, C., and Suh, K. (1994). The relations of emotionality and regulation to dispositional and situational empathy-related responding. *Journal of Personality and Social Psychology, 66*, 776–97.

Eisenberg, N., Spinrad, T. L., and Sadovsky, A. (2006). Empathy-related responding in children. In M. Killen and J. G. Smetana (Eds.), *Handbook of moral development* (pp. 517–49). Mahwah, NJ: Lawrence Erlbaum.

Elder, J. L. (2003). *A field guide to environmental literacy: Making strategic investments in environmental education.* Manchester, MA: The Environmental Education Coalition.

Ellenbogen, K. M. (2003). *From dioramas to the dinner table: An ethnographic case study of the role of science museums in family life.* Dissertation Abstracts International, *64*(03), 846A (University Microfilms No. AAT30-85758).

Environment Australia. (1999). *Today shapes tomorrow: Environmental education for a sustainable future: A discussion paper.* Retrieved January 4, 2008 from www .environment.gov.au/education/publications/discpaper/app2.html.

EPA Strategic Plan (2003–2008): Direction for the Future. Pub # EPA-190-R-03-003

Falk, J. H. (1993). *Leisure decisions influencing African American use of museums.* Washington, DC: American Association of Museums.

Falk, J. H. (1998). Visitors: Who does, who doesn't, and why. *Museum News, 77*(2), 38–43.

Falk, J. H. (2003). Personal meaning mapping. In G. Caban, C. Scott, J. Falk, and L. Dierking (Eds.), *Museums and creativity: A study into the role of museums in design education.* Sydney, AU: Powerhouse Publishing.

Falk, J. H. (2005). Free-choice environmental learning: Framing the discussion. *Environmental Education Research, 11*(3), 265–80.

Falk, J. H. (2006). An identity-centered approach to understanding museum learning. *Curator, 49*(2), 151–66.

Falk, J. H. (in press). *Museums and Identity.* Walnut Creek, CA: Left Coast Press.

Falk, J. H., and Adelman, L. (2003). Investigating the impact of prior knowledge, experience and interest on aquarium visitor learning. *Journal of Research in Science Teaching, 40*(2), 163–76.

Falk, J. H., and Balling, J. D. (1982). The field trip milieu: Learning and behavior as a function of contextual events. *Journal of Educational Research, 76*(1), 22–28.

Falk, J. H., and Dierking, L. D. (1992). *The museum experience.* Washington, DC: Whalesback Books.

Falk, J. H., and Dierking, L. D. (1998). Free-choice learning: An alternative term to informal learning? *Informal Learning Environments Research Newsletter,* July, 2.

Falk, J. H., and Dierking, L. D. (2000). *Learning from museums: Visitor experiences and the making of meaning.* Walnut Creek, CA: AltaMira Press.

Falk, J. H., and Dierking, L. D. (2002). *Lessons without limit: How free-choice learning is transforming education.* Walnut Creek, CA: AltaMira Press.

Falk, J. H., and Sheppard, B. (2006). *Thriving in the knowledge age.* Lanham, MD: AltaMira Press.

Falk, J. H., and Storksdieck, M. (2004). *Understanding the long-term impacts of a science center visit: Final report to the National Science Foundation, Grant #0125545.* Annapolis, MD: Institute for Learning Innovation.

Falk, J. H., and Storksdieck, M. (2005). Using the contextual model of learning to understand visitor learning from a science center exhibition. *Science Education, 89*(5), 744–78.

Falk, J. H., and Storksdieck, M. (in press). Leisure science learning. Journal of Research in Science Teaching.

Falk, J. H., Koke, J., and Dierking, L. D. (2005). *The role of identity in utilization of an urban library.* Technical report. Annapolis, MD: Institute for Learning Innovation.

Falk, J. H., Reinhard, E., Vernon, C., Bronnenkant, K., Heimlich, J., and Deans, N. (2007). *Why zoos and aquariums matter: Assessing the impact of a visit to a zoo or aquarium.* Silver Spring, MD: Association of Zoos and Aquariums.

Falk, J. H., Storksdieck, M., and Dierking, L. D. (2007). Investigating public science interest and understanding. Evidence for the importance of free-choice learning. *Public Understanding of Science 16*(4): 455–69.

Falk, J. H., Heimlich, J. E., and Bronnenkant, K. (2008). Identity-related motivations of zoo and aquarium visitors. *Curator, 51*(1), 55–80.

Fedler, A. J. (2001). Fishing, boating, and aquatic stewardship education: Framework and best practices recommendations. In A. J. Fedler (Ed.), *Defining best practices in boating, fishing, and stewardship education* (pp. 4–17). Alexandria, VA: The Recreational Boating and Fishing Foundation.

Feldman, A., and Minstrell, J. (1999). Action research as a research methodology for the study of the teaching and learning of science. In A. E. Kelly and R. Lesh (Eds.), *Handbook of research design in mathematics and science education* (pp. 429–55). Mahwah, NJ: Lawrence Erlbaum Associates.

Ferrance, E. (2000). *Action research.* Providence, RI: Northeast and Islands Regional Educational Laboratory at Brown University.

Fiedeldey, A. (1994). Wild animals in a wilderness setting: An ecosystemic experience? *Anthrozoös, 7*(2), 113–23.

Fien, J., Scott, W., and Tilbury, D. (1999). *Education & conservation: An evaluation of the contributions of educational programmes to conservation within the WWF network.* WWF, Gland, Switzerland and Washington, D.C.

Fiol, C. M., and Lyles, M. A. (1985). Organizational learning. *Academy of Management Review, 10*(4), 803–13.

Fishman, M. (1982). News and non-news: Making the visible invisible. In J. S. Ettenan and D. C. Whitney (Eds.), *Individuals in mass media organizations, creativity and constraint* (pp. 219–40). Newbury Park, CA: Sage.

Ford, M. E. (1992). *Motivating humans: Goals, emotions and personal agency beliefs.* Newbury Park, CA: Sage.

Forist, B. E. (2003). *A report on visitors to the National Park system.* Visitor Use and Evaluation of Interpretive Media Series. Harpers Ferry, WV: National Park Service.

Fortner, R. W. (1988). *The role of the media in public perception of Lake Erie.* Columbus: The Ohio State University.

Fortner, R. W., and Mayer, V. J. (1983). Ohio students' knowledge and attitudes about the oceans and Great Lakes. *The Ohio Journal of Science, 83*(5), 218–24.

Fortner, R. W., and Teates, T. G. (1980). Baseline studies for marine education: Experiences related to marine knowledge and attitudes. *The Journal of Environmental Education, 11*(4), 11–19.

Friedman, S. M., Dunwoody, S., and Rogers, C. L. (Eds.). (1999). *Communicating uncertainty: Media coverage of new and controversial science.* Mahwah, NJ: Lawrence Erlbaum Assoc.

Frumkin, H. (2001). Beyond toxicity: Human health and the natural environment. *American Journal of Preventative Medicine, 20*(3), 234–40.

Frumkin, H. (2004). White coats, green plants: Clinical epidemiology meets horticulture. *Acta Horticulturae, 639*, 15–26.

Fuller, R. A., Irvine, K. N., Devine-Wright, P., Warren, P. H., and Gaston, K. J. (2007). Psychological benefits of greenspace increase with biodiversity. *Biology Letters, 3*(4), 390–94.

Fung, H. (2006). Affect and early moral socialization: Some insights and contributions from indigenous psychological studies in Taiwan. In U. Kim, K. Yang, and

K. Hwang (Eds.), *Indigenous and cultural psychology: Understanding people in context*. New York: Springer.

Gardner, G. T., and Stern, P. C. (1996). *Environmental problems and human behavior*. Needham Heights, MA: Allyn and Bacon.

Garrison, T. (2007). Ocean literacy: An in-depth top ten. *Oceanography, 20*(1), 198–99.

Gaziano E., and Gaziano, C. (1999). Social control, social change, and the knowledge gap hypothesis. In D. Demers and K. Viswanath (Eds.), *Mass media, social control, and social change: A macrosocial perspective* (pp. 117–36). Ames: Iowa State University Press.

Gilligan, C., and Wiggins, G. (1987). The origins of morality in early childhood relationships. In J. Kagan and S. Lamb (Eds.), *The emergence of morality in young children* (pp. 277–305). Chicago: University of Chicago Press.

Godbey, G. (2005). The use of time and space in assessing the potential of free choice learning. In J. H. Falk (Ed.), *Free-choice science education: How people learn outside of school* (pp. 64–76). New York: Teachers College Press.

Gough, S. (2004). Quote from a presentation to World Wildlife Fund, as part of a meta-analysis of *Windows on the Wild*.

Granzin, K. L., and Olsen, J. E. (1991). Characterizing participants in activities protecting the environment: A focus on donating, recycling and conservation behaviours. *Journal of Public Policy and Marketing, 10*(2), 1–27.

Griffin, J. (2004). Research on students and museums: Looking more closely at the students in school groups. *Science Education, 88*, S59–70.

Grimm, K. (2006a). *Discovering the activation point: Smart strategies to make people act*. Washington, DC: Spitfire Strategies.

Grimm, K. (2006b). *Communicational leadership institute, Spitfire Strategies*. Conference proceedings. Washington, DC.

Groff, A., Lockhart, D., Ogden, J., and Dierking, L. (2005). An exploratory investigation of the effect of working in an environmentally themed facility on the conservation-related knowledge, attitudes, and behavior of staff. *Environmental Education Research, 11*(3), 371–87.

Gross, H., and Lane, N. (2007). Landscapes of the lifespan: Exploring accounts of own gardens and gardening. *Journal of Environmental Psychology, 27*(3), 225–41.

Guenther, M. (1988). Animals in Bushman thought, myth and art. In T. Ingold and J. Woodburn (Eds.), *Hunters and gatherers 2: Property, power and ideology* (pp. 192–202). Oxford, UK: Berg.

Gulf of Maine Research Institute. (2005). *LabVenture! at the Sam L. Cohen Center for interactive learning*. Retrieved September 24, 2007 from http://mystery.gmri.org/about/default.aspx.

Haggard, L. M., and Williams, D. R. (1992). Identity affirmation through leisure activities: Leisure symbols of the self. *Journal of Leisure Research, 24*(1), 1–18.

Hale, J. (2005). On the origins of participatory action research. *ARexpeditions: An online action research journal for teachers*. Retrieved April 7, 2008 from www.montana.edu/arexpeditions/articleviewer.php?AID=101.

Halverson, C., and Strang, C. (2007). Communicating ocean science to informal audiences. Retrieved September 23, 2007 from www.lawrencehallofscience.org/cosia/.

Ham, S. H., and Krumpe, E. E. (1996). Identifying audiences and messages for non-formal environmental education: A theoretical framework for interpreters. *Journal of Interpretation Research, 1*(1), 11–23.

Han, K. T. (2007). Responses to six major terrestrial biomes in terms of scenic beauty, preference and restorativeness. *Environment and Behavior, 39*(4), 529–56.

Hansman, C. A. (2001). Context-based adult learning. In S. B. Merriam (Ed.), *New directions for adult and continuing education, vol. 89: The new update on adult learning theory* (pp. 43–52). San Francisco: Jossey-Bass.

Harter, S. (1999). *The construction of the self: A developmental perspective.* New York: The Guildford Press.

Havitz, M. E., and Mannell, R. C. (2005). Enduring involvement, situational involvement and flow in leisure and non-leisure activities. *Journal of Leisure Research, 37*, 152–77.

Heath, C., and Heath, D. (2007). *Made to stick: Why some ideas survive and others die.* New York: Random House.

Hechinger, F. M. (1992). *Fateful Choices: Health youth for the 21st Century.* New York: Hill and Wang.

Heimlich, J. E. (1993). *Nonformal environmental education: Toward a working definition.* Columbus, OH: ERIC Clearinghouse for Science, Mathematics, and Environmental Education.

Heimlich, J. E. (Ed.). (2005). Free-choice learning and the environment [Special issue]. Environmental Education Research, *11*(3).

Heimlich, J. E., and Ardoin, N. (2006). Preliminary findings: Conservation educators' and practitioners' perceptions of conservation education. Report to EETAP. Washington, DC: National Audubon Society.

Heimlich, J. E., and Ardoin, N. (2008). Understanding behavior to understand behavior change: A literature review. *Environmental Education Research 14*(3): 215–37.

Heimlich, J. E., and Norland, E. (1994). *Developing teaching style in adult education.* San Francisco: Jossey-Bass.

Heimlich, J. E., and Storksdieck, M. (2007). Changing thinking about learning for a changing world. *Southern African Journal of Environmental Education, 24*, 63–75.

Heimlich, J. E., Falk, J. H., Bronnenkant, K., and Barlage, J. (2004). *Phase 1 report: Measuring the learning outcomes of adult visitors to zoos and aquariums for the American Zoo and Aquarium Association.* Annapolis, MD: Institute for Learning Innovation.

Heimlich, J. E, Falk, J. H., Bronnenkant, K., and Barlage, J. (2005). *Measuring the learning outcomes of adult visitors to zoos and aquariums.* Annapolis, MD: Institute for Learning Innovation.

Hein, G. E. (1996). Constructivist learning theory. In G. Durbin (Ed.), *Developing museum exhibitions for life-long learning* (pp. 30–34). London: The Stationery Office.

Hein, G. E. (1998). *Learning in the museum.* London: Routledge.

Hidi, S., and Renninger, K. A. (2006). The four-phase model of interest development. *Educational Psychologist, 41*(2), 111–127.

Hilton, S. C. (1999). *Significant life experiences and career paths of National Park Service educators and interpreters.* Unpublished master's thesis, The Ohio State University, Columbus.

Hilton, S. C. (2002). *Cultural factors of visitors' understanding of U.S. National Park Service natural resource messages.* Ph.D. dissertation. Columbus: The Ohio State University.

Hines, J. M., Hungerford, H., and Tomera, A. (1987). Analysis and synthesis of research on responsible environmental behavior: A meta-analysis. *Journal of Environmental Education, 18*(2), 1–8.

Hoffman, M. (2000). *Empathy and moral development.* New York: Cambridge University Press.

Hoffman, M., and Barstow, D. (2007). *Revolutionizing earth system science education for the 21st century: Report and recommendations from a 50-state analysis of earth science education standards.* Cambridge, MA: TERC.

Holland, D., Lachicotte, W., Jr., Skinner, D., and Cain, C. (1998). *Identity and agency in cultural worlds.* Cambridge, MA: Harvard University Press.

Holsman, R. N. (2001). The politics of environmental education. *The Journal of Environmental Education, 32*(2), 4–7.

Hood, M. G. (1983). Staying away: Why people choose not to visit museums. *Museum News, 61,* 50–56.

Hood, M. G., and Roberts, L. C. (1994). Neither too young nor too old: A comparison of visitor characteristics. *Curator, 37*(1), 36–45.

Horrigan, J. (2006). *The internet as a resource for news and information about science.* Retrieved March 30, 2008 from www.pewinternet.org/pdfs/PIP_Exploratorium_Science.pdf.

Horton, R. L., and Hutchinson, S. (1997). *Nurturing scientific literacy among youth through experientially based curriculum materials.* Columbus: The Ohio State University.

Houle, C. O. (1961). *The inquiring mind.* Madison: University of Wisconsin Press.

Howe, R., and Disinger, J. F. (1991). Environmental education research news. *The Environmentalist, 11*(1), 5–8.

Huckle, J. (1999). Locating environmental education between modern capitalism and postmodern socialism: A reply to Lucie Sauvé. *Canadian Journal of Environmental Education, 4,* 36–45.

Hungerford, H. R., and Volk, T. L. (1990). Changing learner behavior through environmental education. *Journal of Environmental Education, 21*(3), 8–21.

Institute for Learning Innovation (Ed.). (2005, June). *Working group briefs.* Conference proceedings from Free-Choice Learning and the Environment Conference, Shepherdstown, WV.

Interagency Working Group on Ocean Education. (2008). *Toward an ocean literate society: Two year working plan.* Retrieved June 16, 2008 from http://ocean.ceq.gov/about/docs/SIMOR_IWGOE_Implement.pdf.

International Union for Conservation of Nature and Natural Resources. (1971). *IUCN Yearbook: Annual report of the IUCN for the year.* Morges, Switzerland: IUCN.

Isla Earth Radio Series. (2007). *Because earth is an island.* Retrieved September 19, 2007 from www.islaearth.org.

Jacobson, S., McDuff, M., and Monroe, M. (2006). *Conservation education and outreach techniques.* Techniques in Ecology & Conservation Series. New York: Oxford University Press.

Jarvis, P. (1986). *Sociological perspectives on lifelong education and lifelong learning.* Athens: University of Georgia.

Jarvis, P. (1987). Meaningful and meaningless experience: Towards an analysis of learning from life. *Adult Education Quarterly, 37*(3), 164–72.

JASON Project. (2007). *JASON curriculum.* Retrieved September 20, 2007 from www.jason.org/Public/Curriculum/Curriculum.aspx?pos=1.

Jensen, B., and Schnack, K. (1997). The action competence approach in environmental education. *Environmental Research, 3*(2), 163–78.

Joplin, L. (1995). On defining experiential education. In K. Warren, M. Sakofs, and J. S. Hunt, Jr. (Eds.), *The theory of experiential education.* Dubuque, IA: Kendall/ Hunt Publishing Co.

Kahn, P. H., Jr. (1999). *The human relationship to nature: Development and culture.* Cambridge, MA: Massachusetts Institute of Technology Press.

Kals, E., Schumacher, D., and Mondata, L. (1999). Emotional affinity toward nature as a motivational basis to protect nature. *Environment and Behavior, 31*, 178–202.

Kaltenborn, B. P., Bjerke, T., Nyahongo, J. W., and Williams, D. R. (2006). Animal preferences and acceptability of wildlife management actions around Serengeti National Park, Tanzania. *Biodiversity and Conservation, 15*, 4633–49.

Kaplan, M. F. (1991). The joint effects of cognition and affect on social judgment. In J. P. Forgas (Ed.), *Emotion and social judgments* (pp. 73–82). Oxford: Pergamon.

Kaplan, S. (1995). The restorative benefits of nature: Toward an integrative framework. *Journal of Environmental Psychology, 15*, 169–82.

Kaplan, S. (2000). Human nature and environmentally responsible behavior. *Journal of Social Issues, 56*(3), 491–508.

Kaplan, S., and Kaplan, R. (1989). *The experience of nature.* Cambridge, UK: Cambridge University Press.

Kellert, S. R., and Wilson, E. O. (Eds.). (1993). *The biophilia hypothesis.* Washington, DC: Island Press.

Kelly, J. R. (1977). Socialization toward leisure: A developmental approach. *Journal of Leisure Research, 6*, 181–93.

Kelly, J. R. (1983). *Leisure identities and interactions.* London: George Allen and Unwin.

Kerka, S. (1999). *Consumer education for the information age: Practice application brief no. 4.* Columbus, Ohio: ERIC Clearinghouse on Adult, Career, and Vocational Education.

Kimmel, J. R. (1999). Ecotourism as environmental learning. *Journal of Environmental Education, 30*(2), 40–44.

Kirk, E. E. (1999). *Evaluating information found on the internet.* Retrieved June 12, 2007 from http://milton.mse.jhu.edu:8001/research/education/net.html.

Kline, G. F., and Tichenor, P. J. (Eds.). (1972). *Current perspectives in mass communication research.* Beverly Hills: Sage.

Knowles, M. S. (1950). *Informal adult education: A guide for administrators, leaders, and teachers.* New York: Association Press.

Knox, A. (1993). *Strengthening adult and continuing education: A global perspective on synergistic leadership.* San Francisco: Jossey-Bass Publishers.

Knuth, B. A., and Siemer, W. F. (2004). Fostering aquatic stewardship: A key for fisheries sustainability. In E. E. Knudsen, D. D. MacDonald, and Y. K. Muirhead (Eds.), *Sustainable management of North American fisheries* (Symposium 43), (pp. 243–55). Bethesda, MD: American Fisheries Society.

Kola-Olusanya, A. (2005). Free-choice environmental education: Understanding where children learn outside of school. *Environmental Education Research, 11*(3), 297–307.

Kollmuss, A., and Agyeman, J. (2002). Mind the gap: Why do people act environmentally and what are the barriers to pro-environmental behavior? *Environmental Education Research, 8*(3), 239–60.

Koster, E. H., and Schubel, J. R. (2007). Raising the bar at aquariums and science centers. In J. H. Falk, L. D. Dierking, and S. Foutz (Eds.), *In principle, in practice: Museums as learning institutions* (pp.107–20). Lanham, MD: AltaMira Press.

Kotler, P. (2002). *Social marketing: Improving the quality of life.* Thousand Oaks, CA: Sage Publications.

Kramer, L. K. (1994). Cultural elitism vs. cultural diversity in the art museum of the nineties. *Curator, 37*(3), 155–60.

Krosnick, J. A. (2007, May). *Americans' perception of climate change policies.* Paper presented at the Environmental and Energy Study Institute meeting, Washington, DC.

Krosnick, J. A., Lawrence, S., and Giles, C. L. (1999). Searching the web: General and scientific information access. *Communications Magazine, 37*(1), 116–22.

LabVenture! (2005). *Mystery of the fish!* Retrieved March 15, 2008 from http://mystery.gmri.org/about/default.aspx.

LaDoux, J. (1996). *The emotional brain.* New York: Touchstone.

Lave, J. (1988). *Cognition in practice.* Cambridge, UK: Cambridge University Press.

Lave, J., and Wenger, E. (1991). *Situated learning: Legitimate peripheral participation.* Cambridge, UK: Cambridge University Press.

Lazarus, R. S. (1966). *Psychological stress and the coping process.* New York: McGraw-Hill.

Lazarus, R. S. (1991). *Emotion and adaptation.* New York: Oxford University Press.

Lee, J., and Holden, S. (1999). Understanding the determinants of environmentally conscious behavior. *Psychology and Marketing, 16*(5), 373–92.

Lehmann, J. (1999). Befunde empirischer Forschung zu Umweltbildung und *Umweltbewußtsein.* (4). Opladen, Germany: Leske + Budrich.

Leinhardt, G., and Knutson, K. (2004). *Listening in on museum conversations.* Lanham, MD: AltaMira Press.

Leon, W., and Brower, D. (1999). *The consumer's guide to effective environmental choices.* Cambridge, MA: Union of Concerned Scientists.

Leonie, R., Feher E., Dierking, L., and Falk, J. (2003). Toward an agenda for advanced research on science learning in out-of-school settings. *Journal of Research in Science Teaching, 40*(2), 112–20.

Leopold, A. (1949). *A sand county almanac*. New York: Oxford University Press.

Lewis, J. (1985). The birth of EPA. *EPA Journal*, November. Retrieved February 2008 from www.epa.gov/history/topics/epa/15c.htm.

Lieberman, G. A., and Rigby, J. (2005). *Education and the environmental initiative: Model curriculum plan*. Retrieved September 22, 2007 from www.calepa.ca.gov/Education/EEI/documents/ModelPlan.pdf.

Lindsay, J., and Strathman, A. (1997). Predictors of recycling behavior: An application of a modified health belief model. *Journal of Applied Social Psychology, 27*, 1799–1823.

Linville, P. W. (1985). Self-complexity and affective extremity: Don't put all your eggs in one cognitive basket. *Social Cognition, 3*, 94–120.

Locke, E. A., and Latham, G. P. (1994). Goal setting theory. In H. F. O'Neil and M. Drillings (Eds.), *Motivation: Theory and research* (pp. 13–29). Hillsdale, NJ: Lawrence Erlbaum Associates.

Long, H. B., and Zoller-Hodges, D. (1995). Outcomes of elder hostel participation. *Educational Gerontology, 21*(2), 113–27.

Louv, R. (2005). *Last child in the woods: Saving our children from nature-deficit disorder*. Chapel Hill, NC: Algonquin Books.

Louv, R. (2007). Leave no child inside: The growing movement to reconnect children and nature, and to battle "nature deficit disorder." *Orion Magazine*, (March/April).

Lucas, A. M. (1972). *Environment and environmental education: Conceptual issues and curricular implications*. Ph.D. dissertation, The Ohio State University. (UMI No. 73-11531, ED 068 371.)

Lucas, A. M. (1991). "Info-tainment" and informal sources for learning science. *International Journal of Science Education, 5*, 495–504.

Maehr, M. L. (1984). Meaning and motivation: Toward a theory of personal investment. In *Research on motivation in education: Vol. 1. Student motivation*. New York: Academic Press.

Maehr, M. L., and Braskamp, L. A. (1986). *The motivation factor: A theory of personal investment*. Lexington, MA: Lexington Books.

Mainella, F. (2001). Developing a leadership identity: A grounded theory. *National Leadership Journal, 1*(5), 1.

Marsick, V. J., and Neaman, P. G. (1996). Individuals who create organizations that learn. In R. W. Rowden (Ed.), *New directions for adult and continuing education, no. 72. Workplace learning: Debating five critical questions of theory and practice* (pp. 97–104). San Francisco: Jossey-Bass.

Martinsen, C. (2002). *Social marketing: A useful tool or the devil's work*. Unpublished master's thesis. Uppsala University, Stockholm, Sweden.

Maslow, A. (1954). *Motivation and personality*. New York: Harper and Row.

McAdams, D. (1990). *The person: An introduction to personality psychology*. Orlando, FL: Harcourt Brace Jovanovich.

McCombs, B. L. (1991). Motivation and lifelong learning. *Educational Psychologist, 26*(2), 117–27.

McCombs, B. L. (1996). Alternative perspectives for motivation. In L. Baker, P. Afflerback, and D. Reinking (Eds.), *Developing engaged readers in school and home communities* (pp. 67–87). Mahwah, NJ: Erlbaum.

McKenzie, M. (2005). The "post-post period" and environmental education research. *Environmental Education Research, 11*(4), 401–12.

McKenzie-Mohr, D. (2000). Promoting sustainable behavior: An introduction to community-based social marketing. *Journal of Social Issues, 56*(3), 543–54.

McKenzie-Mohr, D., and Smith, W. (1999). *Fostering sustainable behavior: An introduction to community-based social marketing.* Gabriola Island, BC: New Society Publishers.

McTaggert, R. (1991). Principles for participatory action research. *Adult Education Quarterly, 41*(3), 168–87.

Merrian-Webster Online Dictionary. (2008). Retrieved June 22, 2008 from http://merrian-webster.com/dictionary/advocacy.

Meyer, E. M., Bennett, N., Yocco, V., Hause, J., Mony, R. P., and Stuckman, S. (2008, July). *Where am I: Using untours to learn about how under-represented populations experience a visit.* Paper presented at the Visitor Studies Association Annual Conference, Houston, TX.

Meyers, R. B. (2005). A pragmatic epistemology for free-choice learning. *Environmental Education Research, 11*(3), 309–20.

Miles, R. S. (1986). Museum audiences. *International Journal of Museum Management and Curatorship, 5*, 73–80.

Miniwatts Marketing Group. (2007). *Internet world stats.* Retrieved September 22, 2007 from www.internetworldstats.com/stats.htm.

Mocker, D. W., and Spear, G. E. (1982). *Lifelong learning: Formal, nonformal, informal, and self-directed.* Columbus, OH: ERIC Clearinghouse for Adult, Career, and Vocational Education. (ERIC Document Reproduction Service Number ED 220 723.)

Monroe, M. (2003). Two avenues for encouraging conservation behaviors. *Human Ecology Review, 10*(2), 113–25.

Monroe, M., Andrews, E., and Biedenweg, K. (2007). A framework for environmental education strategies. *Applied Environmental Education and Communication, 6*, 205–16.

Mony, R. P. (2007). *An exploratory study of docents as a channel for institutional messages at free-choice conservation education settings.* Ph.D. dissertation, Columbus: The Ohio State University.

Moore, D. E., and Hannon, J. T. (1993). Animal behavior science as a social science: The success of the empathic approach in research on apes. *Anthrozoös, 4*(3), 173–89.

Moore, J. (2005). Barriers and pathways to creating sustainability education programs: Policy, rhetoric and reality. *Environmental Education Research, 11*(5), 537–55.

Mordock, K., and Krasny, M. (2001). Participatory action research: A theoretical and practical framework for EE. *The Journal of Environmental Education, 32*(3), 15–20.

Morrison, J. L., Kim, H. S., and Kydd, C. T. (1998). Student preferences for cyber-search strategies: Impact on critical evaluation of sources. *Journal of Education for Business, 73*(5), 264–68.

Morrow, C., Ross, R. M., et al. (2002). Informal [Earth and space science] education and outreach. In D. Barstow and E. Geary (Eds.), *Blueprint for change: Report from the National Conference on the Revolution in Earth and Space Science Education* (pp. 71–75). Cambridge, MA: TERC.

Myers, O. E., Jr. (2007). *The significance of children and animals: Social development and our connections to other species* (2nd edition). West Lafayette, IN: Purdue University Press. (Original work published 1998)

Myers, O. E., Jr., and Russell, A. (2004). Human identity in relation to wild black bears: A natural-social ecology of subjective creatures. In S. Clayton and S. Opotow (Eds.), *Identity and the natural environment* (pp. 67–90). Cambridge, MA: Massachusetts Institute of Technology Press.

Myers, O. E., Jr., and Saunders, C. D. (2003). Animals as links to developing caring relationships with the natural world. In P. H. Kahn, Jr. and S. R. Kellert (Eds.), *Children and nature: Psychological, sociocultural and evolutionary investigations* (pp. 153–78). Cambridge, MA: Massachusetts Institute of Technology Press.

Myers, O. E., Jr., Saunders, C. D., and Garrett, E. (2003). What do children think animals need? Aesthetic and psycho-social conceptions. *Environmental Education Research, 9*(3), 305–25.

Myers, O. E., Jr., Saunders, C. D., and Birjulin, A. (2004a). Emotional dimensions of watching zoo animals: An experience sampling study building on insights from psychology. *Curator: The Museum Journal 47*(3), 299–321.

Myers, O. E., Jr., Saunders, C. D., and Garrett, E. (2004b). What do children think animals need? Developmental trends. *Environmental Education Research, 10*(4), 545–62.

Naess, A. (1988). Self realization: An ecological approach to being in the world. In J. Seed, J. Macy, P. Fleming, and N. Naess, *Thinking like a mountain* (pp. 19–30). Philadelphia: New Society Publishers. (Originally delivered as the Fourth Keith Roby Memorial Lecture, Murdoch University, Murdoch, Australia, March 12, 1986).

National Audubon Society. (1997). *By-Laws and Constitution of the National Audubon Society, Inc.* Retrieved April 2008 from http://home.att.net/~cgbraggjr/NAS/Bylaws.htm.

National Environmental Education Act P.L 101-619 [S. 3176]; November 16, 1990.

National Environmental Education Advisory Council. (2005). *Setting the standard, measuring results, celebrating successes: A report to Congress on the status of environmental education in the United States*. Washington, DC: U.S. Environmental Protection Agency.

National Environmental Education and Training Foundation/Roper Starch Worldwide. (2001). *The national report card on environmental knowledge, attitudes, and behaviors: The ninth annual survey of adult Americans*. Retrieved September 23, 2007 from www.neetf.org.

National Geographic Society. (2008). *National Geographic Xpeditions: Geography standards in your classroom*. Retrieved March 1, 2008 from www.nationalgeographic.com/xpeditions/standards/index.html.

National Oceanic and Atmospheric Administration Bay Watershed Education and Training Program (NOAA B-WET). (2007). *NOAA bay watershed and training.* Retrieved September 18, 2007 from http://sanctuaries.noaa.gov/news/ bwet/welcome.html.

National Oceanic and Atmospheric Administration (NOAA) Ocean Explorer. (2007). *Learning ocean science through exploration: A curriculum for grades 6–12.* V. Chase (Ed.) Retrieved September 21, 2007 from http://oceanexplorer.noaa .gov/edu/curriculum/welcome.html.

National Oceanic and Atmospheric Administration (NOAA) Ocean Explorer. (2007). *Ocean Explorer: Education.* Retrieved September 21, 2007 from http:// oceanexplorer.noaa.gov/edu/welcome.html.

National Park Service (2007). *Frequently asked questions.* Retrieved September 4, 2007 from www.nps.gov/faqs.htm.

National Research Council. (2002). *New tools for environmental protection: Education, information and voluntary compliance measures.* Washington, DC: National Academy Press.

National Science Board. (2006). Science and technology: Public attitudes and understanding—Information sources, interest, and perceived knowledge. In *Science and Engineering Indicators: 2006* (pp. 1–46). Washington, DC: National Science Foundation.

National Wildlife Federation. (2008). *National Wildlife Federation: History.* Retrieved April 14, 2008, from www.nwf.org/about/history.cfm.

The Nature Conservancy. (2000). The Five-(5) framework for site conservation: A practitioners handbook for site conservation planning and measuring conservation success. Retrieved April 24, 2008 from www.nature.org/summit/files/ five_5_eng.pdf.

The Nature Conservancy. (2008). Retrieved April 25, 2008 from www.nature.org/ wherewework/north americanstates/newyork/misc.

Neisser, U. (1988). Five kinds of self-knowledge. *Philosophical Psychology, 1*, 35–59.

Nickels, A. L. (2008). An exploration of visitors' conservation attitudes, expectations, and motivations at three informal education institutions in Newport, Oregon. Unpublished Master's thesis, Oregon State University, Corvallis.

Nisbet, M. C. (2002). Knowledge, reservations, or promise? A media effects model for public perceptions of science and technology. *Communication Research, 29*(5), 584–608.

North American Association for Environmental Education (NAAEE). (1999). *Excellence in environmental education: Guidelines for learning (K–12).* Washington, DC: North American Association for Environmental Education.

North American Association for Environmental Education (NAAEE). (2004). *Nonformal environmental education programs: Guidelines for excellence.* Washington, DC: North American Association for Environmental Education.

NP Action. (2008). Retrieved May 20, 2008 from www.npaction.org/article/article views/76/1/227.

Ocean Literacy Network. (2005). *Essential principles and fundamental concepts of ocean sciences.* Retrieved September 21, 2007 from www.coexploration.org/ oceanliteracy/documents/OceanLitChart.pdf.

O'Donoghue, R. and Russo, V. (2004). Emerging patterns of abstraction in environmental education: A review of materials, methods and professional development perspectives. *Environmental Education Research, 10*(3), 331–51.

Öhman, A. (1986). Face the beast and fear the face: Animal and social fears as prototypes for evolutionary analyses of emotion. *Psychophysiology, 23*(2), 123–45.

Oskamp, S., Harrington, M. J., Edwards, T. C., Sherwood, D. L., Okuda, S. M., and Swanson, D. C. (1991). Factors influencing household recycling behaviour. *Environment and Behavior, 23*(4), 494–519.

Ostman, R. E., and Parker, J. L. (1986). A public's environmental informational sources and evaluations of mass media. *Journal of Environmental Education, 18*(2), 9–17.

Ostman, R. E., and Parker, J. L. (1987). Impact of education, age, newspapers and television on environmental knowledge, concerns and behaviors. *Journal of Environmental Education, 19*(1), 3–9.

Packer, J., and Ballantyne, R. (2002). Motivational factors and the visitor experience: A comparison of three sites. *Curator, 45*(3), 183–98.

Pantesco, V., Harris, C., and Fraser, J. (2006, June). Sustaining the conservationist: The psychology of working with environmental degradation. Paper presented at the 20th Annual Meeting of the Society for Conservation Biology, San Jose, CA.

Paris, S. G. (1997). Situated motivation and informal learning. *Journal of Museum Education, 22*(2, 3), 22–27.

Paris, S. G., and Cross, D. R. (1983). Ordinary learning: Pragmatic connections among children's beliefs, motives, and actions. In J. Bisanz, G. Bisanz, and R. Kail (Eds.), *Learning in children* (pp. 137–69). New York: Springer-Verlag.

Pekarik, A. J., Doering, Z. D., and Karns, D. (1999). Exploring satisfying experiences in museums. *Curator, 42*, 152–73.

Pew Oceans Commission (2003). *America's living ocean: Charting a course for change. A report to the nation.* Arlington, VA: Pew Oceans Commission.

Pierce, C. J, Steger, M., Steel, B., and Lovrich, N. (1992). *Citizens, political communication, and interest groups.* Westport, CT: Praeger.

Pintrich, P. R., and DeGroot, E. V. (1990). Motivational and self-regulated learning components of classroom academic performance. *Journal of Educational Psychology, 82*, 33–40.

Pintrich, P. R., Marx, R. W., and Boyle, R. A. (1993). Beyond cold conceptual change: The role of motivational beliefs and classroom contextual factors in the process of conceptual change. *Review of Educational Research, 63*(2), 167–99.

Preskill, H., and Torres, R. T. (1999). *Evaluative inquiry for learning in organizations.* Thousand Oaks, CA: Sage Publications, Inc.

Preston, S. D., and de Waal, F. B. M. (2002). Empathy: Its ultimate and proximate bases. *Behavioral and Brain Sciences, 25*, 1–20.

Prochaska, J. O., and DiClemente, C. C. (1986). Toward a comprehensive model of change. In W. R. Miller and N. Heather (Eds.), *Addictive behaviors: Process of change* (pp. 3–27). New York: Plenum Press.

Quadra Planning Consultants, Ltd. and Galiano Institute for Environmental and Social Research. (2004). *Seafood Watch evaluation: Summary report.* Saltspring Island, British Columbia.

Rabb, G., and Saunders, C. (2005). The future of zoos and aquariums: Conservation and caring. *International Zoo Yearbook, 39,* 1–26.

Ramaley, J. (2005). *Integrating research and education: Enriching the undergraduate experience.* Retrieved September 23, 2007 from http://advance.uconn.edu/2005/050124/05012412.htm.

Ramey-Gassert., L., Walberg, H. J., III, and Walberg, H. J. (1994). Reexamining connections: Museums as science learning environments. *Science Education, 78*(4), 345–63.

RARE (2008a). Presentation by RARE staff at Crooked Tree Wildlife Sanctuary. Belize City, Belize: National Audubon Society and Belize Audubon Society.

RARE. (2008b). Retrieved June 21, 2008 from www.rareconservation.org/about/pagephp?subsection=History.

Reid, A., Jensen, B., Nikel, J., and Simovska, V. (Eds.). (2007). *Participation and learning: Perspectives on education and the environment, health and sustainability.* London: Springer.

Reilly, K., and Andrews, E. (Eds.). (2006). *Best Education Practices (BEP) symposium for eater outreach professionals: Defining BEPs, refining new resources and recommending future actions—Report and proceedings.* Madison: University of Wisconsin, Environmental Resources Center.

Rejeski, D., and Salzman, J. (2002). Changes in pollution and the implications for policy. In T. Dietz and P. C. Stern (Eds.), *New tools for environmental protection: Education, information, and voluntary measures* (pp. 17–42). Washington, DC: National Academy Press.

Rennie, J., Feher, E., Dierking, L., and Falk, F. (2003). Toward an agenda for advancing research on science learning in out-of-school settings. *Journal of Research in Science Teaching, 40*(2), 112–20.

Research Resolutions & Consulting. (2007). *Travel activities and motivations survey of U.S. residents: history and heritage tourists.* Victoria, BC: Research Services Tourism British Columbia.

Resnicow, D. (1994). What is Watkins really asking? *Curator, 37*(3), 150–51.

Richardson, L. (2000). Writing: A method of inquiry. In N. K. Denzin and Y. S. Lincoln (Eds.), *Handbook of Qualitative Research, 2nd ed.* (pp. 923–48). Thousand Oaks, CA: Sage Publications.

Rippetoe, P., and Rogers, R. (1987). Effects of components of protection-motivation theory on adaptive and maladaptive coping with a health threat. *Journal of Personality and Social Psychology, 52,* 596–604.

Roberts, L. (2005). Art influencing land preservation: A study of landscape photography. Unpublished master's thesis. Salt Lake City: University of Utah.

Rodriguez, D. A., and Roberts, N. S. (2002). State of the knowledge report: The association of race/ethnicity, gender, and social class in outdoor recreation experiences. *NPS Social Science Program: General Technical Report.* Washington, DC: National Park Service.

Rosenstock, I., Strecher, V., and Becker, M. (1988). Social learning theory and the health belief model. *Health Education Quarterly, 15,* 175–83.

Rounds, J. (2006). Doing identity work in museums. *Curator, 49*(2), 133–50.

Salami, H. (1998, April). Motivation and meaningful science learning in informal settings. Paper presented at the annual meeting of the National Association for Research in Science Teaching, San Diego, CA.

Samdahl, D. M., and Kleiber, D. A. (1989). Self-awareness and leisure experience. *Leisure Sciences, 11,* 1–10.

Sandifer, C. (2003). Technological novelty and open-endedness: Two characteristics of interactive exhibits that contribute to the holding of visitor attention in a science museum. *Journal of Research in Science Teaching, 40*(2), 121–37.

Schauble, L., Leinhardt, G., and Martin, L. (1997). A framework for organizing a cumulative research agenda in informal learning contexts. *Journal of Museum Education, 22*(2, 3), 3–7.

Schiefele, U. (1991). Interest, learning and motivation. *Educational Psychologist, 26*(3, 4), 299–323.

Schoenfeld, A. H. (1999). Looking toward the 21st Century: Challenges of educational theory and practice. *Educational Researcher, 28*(7), 4–14.

Schubel, J. R., Epstein, A. W., Talbot, W., Sloan, P., Duffy, M., Kirby-Hathaway, T., Foster, J. S., McDougall, C., and Muscat, A. (2005, June). *Ocean Literacy.* Paper presented at the Free-Choice Learning and the Environment Conference, Shepherdstown, WV.

Schubel, J. R., Monroe, C., Baker, D. J., et al. (2006, July). *Increasing public ocean awareness and understanding: An aquarium model.* MCRI Aquatic Forum Report Reference Number 2006-5. Long Beach, CA: MCRI.

Schubel, J. R., Monroe, C., and Lau, A. (2005, October). *Public ocean literacy: What residents of Southern California should know.* MCRI Aquatic Forum Report Reference Number 2005-2. Long Beach, CA: MCRI.

Schubel, J. R., Monroe, C., Lau, A., and Cassano, E. (2006, March). *Public ocean literacy: Making ocean science understandable.* MCRI Aquatic Forum Report Reference Number 2006-2. Long Beach, CA: MCRI.

Schulman, M., and Mekler, E. (1985). *Bringing up a moral child.* Reading, MA: Addison-Wesley.

Schultz, P. (2002). Knowledge, information, and household recycling: Examining the knowledge-deficit model of behavior change. In T. Dietz and P. Stern (Eds.), *New tools for environmental protection: Education, information, and voluntary measures* (pp. 67–82). Washington, DC: National Academy Press.

Schultz, W. (2000). Empathizing with nature: The effects of perspective taking on concern for environmental issues. *Journal of Social Issues, 56,* 391–406.

Schutte, N. S., Kenrick, D. T., and Sadalla, E. K. (1985). The search for predictable settings: Situational prototypes, constraint, and behavioral variation. *Journal of Personality and Social Psychology, 51,* 459–62.

Scollon, R. (1998). *Mediated discourse as social interaction: A study of news discourse.* New York: Longman.

Scott, D., and Willits, F. K. (1989). Adolescent and adult leisure patterns: A 37 year follow-up study. *Leisure Sciences, 11*, 323–35.

Scott, W., and Gough, S. (2003). *Sustainable development and learning: Framing the issues*. London: Routledge.

Scott, W., and Gough, S. (2004) *Key issues in sustainable development and learning: A critical review*. London: RoutledgeFalmer.

Seevers, B. S. (1999). *Factors related to teaching style preference of Ohio Cooperative Extension faculty and program staff*. Unpublished doctoral dissertation, Ohio State University, Columbus.

Seng, P. T., and Rushton, S. (Eds.). (2003). *Best practices workbook*. Alexandria, VA: Recreational Fishing and Boating Foundation.

Seydel, J. (2006, October). The role of domestic and wild animals in the ecological identity development of environmental exemplars. Paper presented at the 14th International Conference of the Society for Human Ecology, Bar Harbor, ME.

Sfard, A., and Prusak, A. (2005). Telling identities: In search of an analytic tool for investigating learning as a culturally shaped activity. *Educational Researcher, 34*(4), 14–22.

Shibata, S., and Suzuki, N. (2004). Effects of an indoor plant on creative task performance and mood. *Scandinavian Journal of Psychology, 45*, 373–81.

Sia, A., Hungerford, H., and Tomera, A. (1985). Selected predictors of responsible environmental behavior: An analysis. *Journal of Environmental Education, 17*(2), 31–40.

Sickler, J., Fraser, J., Gruber, S., Boyle, P., Webler, T., and Reiss, D. (2006). *Thinking about dolphin thinking*. WCS Working paper No. 27. New York: Wildlife Conservation Society.

Siemer, W. F., and Knuth, B. A. (2001). Effects of fishing education programs on antecedents of responsible environmental behavior. *Journal of Environmental Education, 32*(4), 23–29.

Simon, B. (1997). Self and group in modern society: Ten theses on the individual self and collective self. In R. Spears, P. J. Oakes, N. Ellemera, and S. A. Haslam (Eds.), *The social psychology of stereotyping and group life* (pp. 318–35). Oxford, UK: Basil Blackwell.

Simon, B. (1998). Individuals, groups, and social change: On the relationship between individual and collective self-interpretations and collective action. In C. Sedikides, J. Schopler, and C. Insko (Eds.), *Intergroup cognition and intergroup behavior* (pp. 257–82). Mahwah, NJ: Lawrence Erlbaum Associates.

Simon, B. (1999). A place in the world: Self and social categorization. In T. R. Tyler, R. M. Kramer, and O. P. John (Eds.), *The psychology of the social self* (pp. 47–49). Mahwah, NJ: Lawrence Erlbaum Associates.

Simon, B. (2004). *Identity in modern society: A social psychological perspective*. Oxford, UK: Blackwell.

Smith, M. K. (1996/2001/2007) Action research. *The Encyclopedia of Informal Education*. Retrieved April 5, 2008 from www.infed.org/research/b-actres.htm.

Smithsonian Institution. (2004). *Results of the 2004 Smithsonian-wide survey of museum visitors*. Washington, DC: Smithsonian Institution Office of Policy and Analysis.

Somekh, B. (1995). The contribution of Action Research to development in social endeavours: A position paper on Action Research methodology. *British Educational Research Journal, 21*(3), 339–55.

Sommer, R. (2003). Trees and human identity. In S. Clayton and S. Opotow (Eds.), *Identity and the natural environment* (pp. 179–204). Cambridge, MA: Massachusetts Institute of Technology Press.

Spitfire Strategies. (2007). Discovering the activation point. Retrieved December 19, 2008 from www.spitfirestrategies.com/tools.

Spitfire Strategies. (2008). Smart Chart 3.0 retrieved June 21, 2008 from www.spit firestrategies.com/tools.

Stapp, W., Wals, A., and Stankorb, S. (1996). *Environmental education for empowerment.* Dubuque, IA: Kendall/Hunt.

Steel, B. (1997). *Public lands management in the west: Citizens, groups, and values.* Westport, CT: Praeger.

Steel, B., Lovrich, N., and Pierce, J. (1992). Trust in natural resource information sources and post-materialist values: A comparative study of U.S. and Canadian citizens in the Great Lakes area. *Journal of Environmental Systems, 22,* 123–36.

Steel, B., Smith, C., Opsommerc, L., Curiela, S., and Warner-Steel, R. (2005). Public ocean literacy in the United States. *Ocean and Coastal Management, 48,* 97–114.

Steele, C. M. (1988). The psychology of self-affirmation: Sustaining the integrity of the self. In L. Berkowitz (Ed.), *Advances in experimental social-psychology: Vol. 21* (pp. 261–302). New York: Academic Press.

Stein, J. (2007, July). *Adapting the visitor identity-related motivations scale for living history sites.* Paper presented at the Annual Meeting of the Visitor's Studies Association, Ottawa, Canada.

Stern, P. C. (2000). Toward a coherent theory of environmentally significant behavior. *Journal of Social Issues, 56*(3), 407–24.

Stevens, M. and Andrews, E. (2006). *Outreach that makes a difference! Target audiences for water education: A research meta-analysis.* Retrieved February 2006 from http://wateroutreach.uwex.edu/beps/MAcoverTOC.cfm.

Stevenson, R. (2007). Schooling and environmental education: Contradictions in purpose and practice. *Environmental Education Research, 13*(2), 139–53.

Stewart, R. (2004). *What every student ought to know about the ocean: A compilation of key concepts.* Retrieved September 23, 2007 from http://ams.confex.com/ams/pdfpapers/85763.pdf.

Storksdieck, M., and Stein, J. (2007, July). *Using the visitor identity-related motivations scale to improve visitor experiences at the U.S. Botanic Garden.* Paper presented at the Annual Meeting of the Visitor's Studies Association, Ottawa, Canada.

Storksdieck, M., Ellenbogen, K., and Heimlich, J. (2005). Changing minds? Reassessing outcomes in free-choice environmental education. *Environmental Education Research, 11*(3), 353–69.

Storksdieck, M., Stylinski, C., Heimlich, J. E., and Bronnenkant, K. (2007, November). Using news media for environmental learning and behavior change. Paper presented at the annual meeting of the North American Association for

Environmental Education, Virginia Beach, VA. Retrieved June 16, 2008 from www.allacademic.com/meta/p188734_index.html.

Strauss, H. (2004). Why your users prefer Disney World to IT. *The Edutech Report, 20*(2). Retrieved May 2008 from www.edutech-int.com/documents/Why%20Your %20Users%20Prefer%20Disney%20World%20to%20IT.htm.

Taylor, N., and Signal, T. D. (2005). Empathy and attitudes to animals. *Anthrozoös, 18*, 18–27.

Tetra Tech. (2003). *Getting in step: A guide to effective outreach in your watershed.* Retrieved October 2005 from www.epa.gov/watertrain/gettinginstep/step1a.html.

Thompson, R. A. (1993). Socioemotional development: Enduring issues and new challenges. *Developmental Review, 13*, 372–402.

Tilbury, D. (1995). Environmental education for sustainability: Defining the new focus of environmental education in the 1990s. *Environmental Education Research, 1*(2), 195–212.

Tolhurst, D. (2007). The influence of learning environments on students' epistemological beliefs and learning outcomes. *Teaching in Higher Education, 12*(2), 219–33.

Tressel, G. (1994). Preface. In V. Crane, *Informal science learning: What the research says about television, science museums, and community-based projects.* Dehham, MA: Research Communications, Ltd.

Turner, J. C. (2001). Using context to enrich and challenge our understanding of motivational theory. In S. Volet and S. Järvelä (Eds.), *Motivation in learning contexts: Theoretical advances and methodological implications* (pp. 85–104). Oxford, UK: Pergamon.

Ulrich, R. S. (1993). Biophilia, biophobia, and natural landscapes. In S. R. Kellert and E. O. Wilson (Eds.), *The biophilia hypothesis* (pp. 73–137). Washington, DC: Island Press.

UNESCO. (1977). Final Report: Intergovernmental conference on environmental education organised by UNESCO in co-operation with UNEP, Tbilisi (USSR), 14–26 October 1977. Retrieved June 12, 2008 from http://unesdoc.unesco.org/ images/0003/000327/032763eo.pdf.

UNESCO-UNEP. (1976). *The Belgrade Charter: A global framework for environmental education.* UNESCO-UNEP Environmental Education Newsletter, 1(1), 1-2.

UNESCO-UNEP. (1978). The Tbilisi Declaration: Final report intergovernmental conference on environmental education. Organized by UNESCO in cooperation with UNEP, Tbilisi, USSR, 14-26 October 1977, Paris, France: UNESCO ED/ MD/49.

University of Wisconsin, Environmental Resources Center. (2004). *National extension water outreach education website.* Retrieved September 2007 from http://wateroutreach.uwex.edu/.

U.S. Commission on Ocean Policy. (2004). *An ocean blueprint for the 21st century: Final report.* Washington, DC: U.S. Commission on Ocean Policy.

U.S. Fish & Wildlife Service. (1999). Get the Lead Out. Brochure retrieved May 2008 from www.fws.gov/contaminants/documents/leadpoisoning2.pdf.

U.S. Fish & Wildlife Service (USFWS) (2007). *2006 National survey of fishing, hunting and wildlife-associated recreation: State report—Preliminary findings.* Washington, DC: USFWS.

U.S. Fish & Wildlife Service. (2008). *Employee pocket guide: FWS fundamentals.* Retrieved April 14, 2008, from www.fws.gov/info/pocketguide/fwsfundamentals.htm.
U.S. Ocean Action Plan. (2004). *The Bush administration's response to the U. S. Commission on Ocean Policy.* Washington, DC: U.S. Ocean Action Plan.
Uzzell, D., and Ballantyne, R. (1998). Heritage that hurts: Interpretation in a postmodern world. In D. Uzzell and R. Ballantyne (Eds.), *Contemporary issues in heritage and environmental interpretation: Problems and prospects* (pp. 152–71). London: The Stationery Office.
Uzzell, D. L., and Rutland, A. (1993). *Inter-generational social influence: Changing environmental competence and performance in children and adults.* Discussion paper for the Second International Workshop on Children as Catalysts of Global Environmental Change, CEFOPE, University of Braga, Portugal.
Van Hemert, M., Wiertsema, W., and van Yperen, M., eds. (1995). *Reviving links: NGO experiences in environmental education and people's participations in environmental policies.* Amsterdam: Both Ends/SME Milieu Adviseurs/IUCN.
Varga, A., Kószó, M. F., Mayer, M., and Sleurs, W. (2007). Developing teacher competences for education for sustainable development through reflection: The environment and school initiatives approach. *Journal of Education for Teaching, 33*(2), 241–56.
Vidart, D. (1978). Environmental education theory and practice. *Prospects: Quarterly Review of Education, 8*(4), 466–79.
Vining, J., and Ebreo, A. (2003). Emerging theoretical and methodological perspectives on conservation behavior. In A. Ts'erts'man (Ed.), *Handbook of environmental psychology* (pp. 541–58). Hoboken, NJ: John Wiley and Sons.
Vittersø, J., Bjerke, T., and Kaltenborn, B. P. (1999). Attitudes toward large carnivores among sheep farmers experiencing different degrees of depredation. *Human Dimensions of Wildlife, 4*(1), 20–35.
Vittersø, J., Kaltenborn, B. P., and Bjerke, T. (1998). Attachment to livestock and attitudes toward large carnivores among sheep farmers in Norway. *Anthrozoös, 11*(4), 210–17.
Wagenet, L., and Pfeffer, M. (2007). Organizing citizen engagement for democratic environmental planning. *Society and Natural Resources, 20*, 801–13.
Wals, A. (1994). *Pollution stinks! Young adolescents' perceptions of nature and environmental issues with implications for environmental education in urban settings.* De Lier, Netherlands: Academic Book Centre.
Watkins, C. A. (1994). Are museums still necessary? *Curator, 37*(1), 25–35.
Weaver, D. B. (2005). Comprehensive and minimalist dimensions of ecotourism. *Annals of Tourism Research, 32*(2), 439–55.
Weintraub, B. A. (1995). Defining a fulfilling and relevant environmental education. *Urban Education, 30*(3), 337–66.
Wertsch, J. (1998). *Mind as action.* New York: Oxford University Press.
Western, D., and Wright, R. (Eds.). (1994). *Natural connections: Perspectives in community-based conservation.* Washington, DC: Island Press.
Westwater, A., and Wolfe, P. (2000). The brain-compatible curriculum. *Educational Leadership: The Science of Learning, 58*(3), 49–52.
Whitehead, A. N. (1929). *The aims of education.* New York: MacMillan.

Whitehead, J., and McNiff, J. (2006). *Action research living theory*. London: Sage Publications, Inc.

Williams, D. R. (2002). Leisure identities, globalization, and the politics of place. *Journal of Leisure Research, 34*(4), 267–78.

Wilson, E. O. (1984). *Biophilia*. Cambridge, MA: Harvard University Press.

Wilson, K. M. (2002). Forecasting the future: How television weathercasters' attitudes and beliefs about climate change affect their cognitive knowledge. *Science Communication, 24*(2), 246–68.

Winther, A., Volk, T., and Hungerford, H. (1994). Issue investigation and citizenship action training: An instructional model for environmental education. In L. Bardwell, M. Monroe, and M. Tudor (Eds.), *Environmental problem solving: Theory, practice, and possibilities in environmental education* (pp. 22–37). Troy, OH: North American Association for Environmental Education.

Wise, G. (1998). Applying U.S. community development process lessons, appendix A. In E. Andrews, *An EPA/USDA partnership to support community-based education: A discussion paper*. EPA 910-R-98-008. Retrieved June 21, 2008 from www .uwex.edu/erc/epacoopextappdx.html.

W. K. Kellogg Foundation. (2004). *Logic model development guide*. Retrieved May 2008 from www.wkkf.org/Pubs/Tools/Evaluation/Pub3669.pdf.

Wolcott, H. (1991). Propriospect and the acquisition of culture. *Anthropology and Education Quarterly, 221*(3), 251–73.

Wood, D. (1990). *How to plan a conservation education program*. Washington DC: U.S. Peace Corps Information and Exchange Program.

Woodcock, D. M. (1982). *A functionalist approach to environmental preference*. Unpublished doctoral dissertation, University of Michigan, Ann Arbor.

Woodward, K. (2002). *Understanding Identity*. London: Arnold.

World Wildlife Fund (2008) *A guide to socioeconomic assessments for ecoregion conservation*. Washington, DC: World Wildlife Fund.

Yob, I. M. (1997). The cognitive emotions and emotional cognitions. In H. Siegel (Ed.), *Reason and education: Essays in honor of Israel Scheffler* (pp. 43–57). Dordrecht: Kluwer Academic Publishers.

Zint, M., Kraemer, A., Northway, H., and Lim, M. (2002). Evaluation of the Chesapeake Bay Foundation's conservation education programs. *Conservation Biology, 16*(3), 641–49.

Index

action research, defined, 107
affect, 35, 40, 42, 159–60, 165–66. *See also* emotion
American Association for the Advancement of Sciences, 124
American Fisheries Society, 145
Anniston Museum of Natural History, 28
Aquarium of the Pacific, 127, 128, 134
Association of Science-Technology Centers, 130
Association of Zoos and Aquariums, 18, 89, 100, 130
attitudes, 35; toward conservation, 53
AZA, *See* Association of Zoos and Aquariums

behavior: change, 28, 62–63, 65–68, 145–46, 159–60; conservation, 49–50, 57; empathy and, 48–49; environmental behavior, 59, 64; knowledge and, 64; measuring behavioral impacts, 162; self-efficacy and, 61–62, 65. *See also* planned behavior, theory of
Belgrade Charter, 6
Biltmore Estate, 28
biophilia, 41–43. *See also* emotion

California Science Center, 28
citizen science, 93
Colonial Williamsburg, 28
community-based environmental education (CBEE) model, 148–51
conservation: action, 16, 57–59, 87–89; action paralysis and, 168; action resources and, 169–70; empathy and, 49, 53–54; goals, 98–99; qualities of stewardship programs, 145; social strategies for, 91–96
Conservation International, 89
contextual model of learning , 31, 60, 105–6, 108, 110–11, 143, 157
Cooperative State Research, Education and Extension Service (CSREES), 174

Department of Interior, 173, 174
Disney's Animal Kingdom Theme Park, 2, 89, 100
Disney World, 78

EarthWatch Institute, 129
education, defined, 96
education for sustainable development (ESD), 114–15

emotion, 39–41, 47, 64, 160; role in
    free-choice learning, 39, 41; theory
    of, 40. *See also* biophilia
empathy, 39–55; biological basis for,
    45; conservation and, 49, 53–54;
    defined, 44–45; for animals, 49,
    50–53; variables effecting, 46–48
environment: defined, 6; learning about,
    14; restorative properties, 42, 43
environmental education, 37,
    58, 71, 97, 141–42, 175; best
    practices in, 143, 144, 152–55,
    166–67; community and, 147–51;
    constraints, 19–21; defined, 6, 94;
    empathy and, 44, 53–55; factors
    in researching, 106; participatory
    action research and, 110–11,
    116–18; ocean literacy and, 132–33;
    organizational mission and, 78;
    sources of, 16, 18–19; value of, 12;
    youth programs, 133–34
environmental learning, aspects of,
    159–60
environmental policy, 172–73, 175–76,
    179
EPA, *See* U.S. Environmental Protection
    Agency

formal education, 11, 89
free-choice learning, 15, 21; behavior
    change and, 69–70; contextual model
    of learning and, 143, 157; definition,
    5–6; elements of, 15, 60, 63; identity
    and, 34; generally and specifically
    environmental, 158; methodological
    issues in researching, 162–64, 165
Free-Choice Learning and the
    Environment Conference, vii, 1–2,
    146–48, 192

goals, organizational, 79

health belief model, 66–67
Henry Ford Museum and Greenfield
    Village, 28

identity, 31–33, 43; free-choice learning
    and, 34
informal education, 5, 14
Interagency Working Group on Ocean
    Education (IWGOE), 132
Institute for Learning Innovation, ii, 2,
    146
interpretive planning, 80–81

Kellogg Foundation, 80

learner: motivations, 30–31. *See also*
    visitors
learning, 13; definition, 6, 11; emotion
    and, 41, 47; family, 31; free-choice
    (*see* free-choice learning); learning-
    exchange theory, 12; lifelong, 11,
    15; socially mediated, 12, 13, 16, 20;
    situated, 13
leisure activities, 26–27, 32
literacy, 11; environmental, 57, 123,
    175, 177, 179–80; ocean literacy
    defined, 124–25; U.S. National
    Conference on Ocean Literacy, 131

media: literacy and, 134-36; role of, 18,
    129, 134; social, 135–37
message, organizational, 12–13 15–16,
    19
mission, organizational, 19–21, 57–58,
    60, 71, 77, 102–4; drift, 83–85;
    performance and, 78–81. *See also*
    goals, organization; message,
    organizational; vision statements
Monterey Bay Aquarium, 73, 77, 79–80
motivation, 31, 34–35; emotion and, 44,
    47–48; theories of, 161–62

National Aquarium in Baltimore, 169
National Association for Interpretation,
    79
National Association of Research in
    Science Teaching (NARST), 111
National Audubon Society, 89, 90, 92,
    93

National Environmental Education Act, 175–76
National Environmental Education Training Foundation, 2
National Environmental Policy Act, 172
National Marine Educators Association (NMEA), 130
National Museum of Natural History (NMNH), 25
National Park Foundation, 2
National Park Service, 18, 174
National Oceanic and Atmospheric Administration (NOAA), 2, 179
National Science Foundation, 133, 174–75
National Wildlife Federation, 89
The Nature Conservancy, 89, 99
New York Aquarium, 133
NOAA, *See* National Oceanic and Atmospheric Administration
nonformal education, 14; definition, 5
normative beliefs, 65, 160
North American Association for Environmental Education (NAAEE), 2, 141–43

objectives, organizational, 80
Ocean Project, 130
Ohio State University, 2, 100

participatory action research, (PAR): defined, 107; key characteristics of, 109, 116–17; learning outcomes and, 106; problems of PAR in environmental education, 120
perceived value, 29–30
perception-action model (PAM), 45
personal meaning-mapping (PMM), 163
planned behavior, theory of, 160–61

RARE, 95, 99
reasoned action, theory of, 66
Recreational Boating and Fishing Foundation (RBFF), 143

responsible environmental behavior, model of, 67–68

Serengeti National Park, 52
Sierra Club, 89
Silent Spring, 172
Smithsonian Institution, 24, 25, 131
social cognitive theory, 66
socialization, 12, 42, 54
social marketing, 68–69, 93-94, 97, 100–1, 166
social media. *See* media
South African Development Community Regional Environmental Education Programme (SADC REEP), 111–12
Students and Teachers Restoring a Watershed (STRAW), 98

Tbilisi Declaration, 6, 97, 159
transtheoretical model of behavior change, 67

U.S. Commission on Ocean Policy, 132
U.S. Department of Agriculture, 145, 174
U.S. Environmental Protection Agency, 2, 7, 89, 145–46, 172, 174, 179
U.S. Fish & Wildlife Service, 1, 2, 89, 92, 100, 104, 143–44, 176, 178
U.S. Ocean Action Plan, 132

Virginia Museum of Fine Arts, 28
vision statements, 79
visitors: demographics of, 24–26; emotions, 49–50; motivations for visiting, 23, 28–30, 34–35; purpose of visit, 17, 31; socioeconomic status, 24; values of, 16–17

Wilderness Society, 89
wildlife: direct encounters with, 51; mediated, 52
World Wildlife Fund, 92, 95, 99

About the Contributors

Janet Ady is chief of the Division of Education Outreach for the U.S. Fish & Wildlife Service at the National Conservation Training Center in Shepherdstown, West Virginia. She worked as the regional environmental education specialist in Alaska and at the San Francisco Bay National Wildlife Refuge at the environmental education center in California. She holds degrees in natural resources and environmental education from Humboldt State University and from San Jose State University.

Nicole Ardoin is assistant professor of environmental education at Stanford University, where she holds a joint appointment with the School of Education and the Woods Institute for the Environment. Her research focuses on motivations for environmental behavior, with a recent emphasis on the links among sense of place, geographic scale, and behavior. Nicole serves on the board of directors of the North American Association for Environmental Education and the EPA's National Environmental Education Advisory Council.

Elaine Andrews (M.S., M.A.T.) is director of the Environmental Resources Center in the College of Agricultural and Life Sciences at the University of Wisconsin where she is a specialist in environmental education, focusing on community and the environment. She is the former executive director of the North American Association for Environmental Education, a principal investigator for over twenty national or multistate projects, and the author of numerous publications.

Roy Ballantyne is head of the School of Tourism at the University of Queensland in Brisbane, Australia. He has over thirty years of experience

in teaching and researching in tertiary institutions; has a well-established international reputation for his work in environmental/heritage interpretation, environmental education, and visitor research; and is presently seeking to extend interpretation and visitor research within the tourism area. He is a coeditor of the *Australian Journal of Environmental Education*.

Sarah M. Bexell is director of Conservation Education and Communications at the Chengdu Research Base of Giant Panda Breeding, China. She has a B.A. in biology/environmental studies, M.A. in physical anthropology, M.Ed. in science education, and Ph.D. in early childhood education and conservation sciences. Her career has focused on effective education about endangered species and ecosystems for their conservation. She combines her background in both animal behavior and education to facilitate the human–animal bond in hopes of inspiring wildlife and environmental stewardship.

Judy Braus has been actively involved in national and international environmental education efforts for more than twenty-five years. She is currently vice president of education and centers for the National Audubon Center and project manager for TogetherGreen, a project focused on building leadership and engaging diverse communities in conservation. Before coming to Audubon, she was director of education for the World Wildlife Fund-US (WWF), where she managed a variety of education initiatives, including "Windows on the Wild," the Russell Train Education for Nature Program, and WWF's Community Outreach Program.

Lisa Brochu is associate director of the National Association for Interpretation (NAI). Her thirty-year career includes a successful consultant practice in interpretive planning, writing, and training before starting employment with NAI in 2002. She is the author of *Interpretive Planning: The 5-M Model for Successful Planning Projects* (2003) and the coauthor of *Interpretation by Design* (2008).

Michael Brody teaches courses in environment, science education, and educational research at Montana State University. He is a research associate of the Museum of the Rockies in Bozeman, Montana and a member of the North American Association for Environmental Education (NAAEE) Research Commission. He received the NAAEE Outstanding Contributions to Research Award in 2006. He is the executive editor of *Arexpeditions*, an on-line action research journal for professional educators.

Kerry Bronnenkant received a B.S. degree in marine biology from Roger Williams College and her M.E. in museum education and evaluation from

Lesley College. She spent seven years working at the New England Aquarium in Boston before joining the Institute for Learning Innovation in 2003. Her research and evaluation interests lie in the environmental science field and in working with behavioral change research.

John H. Falk, Sea Grant Professor of Free-Choice Learning at Oregon State University, is known internationally for his expertise on free-choice learning—the learning that occurs in settings like parks, museums, and the Internet. He has authored over one hundred scholarly articles and chapters in the areas of learning, ecology, and education and more than a dozen books. He helped to create several nationally important environmental out-of-school educational curricula.

Susan Foutz is research associate at the Institute for Learning Innovation. Since joining the Institute in 2003, she has coordinated *In Principle, In Practice* and *Free-Choice Learning and the Environment*, two Learning Innovation Initiatives. Her research interests include positive youth development, family learning in museum exhibitions and programs, and the use of technology and media in the pursuit of free-choice learning. She received an M.A. in museum studies from the University of Nebraska.

Joe E. Heimlich is a specialist with OSUExtension@COSI and a professor in the School of Environment and Natural Resources and Environmental Studies Graduate Program at the Ohio State University. He also is senior research associate with the Institute for Learning Innovation in Edgewater, Maryland. His research focus is visitor outcomes in free-choice environmental settings specializing in adult learning of cognition and affect.

Tim Merriman has been executive director of the National Association for Interpretation (NAI) in the United States since 1995. NAI has 5,200 members in 30 nations. He earned a Ph.D. in communications along with zoology, botany, and education degrees. He is coauthor with Lisa Brochu of *Personal Interpretation* (2002), *Management of Interpretive Sites* (2005), and *History of Heritage Interpretation in the United States* (2006).

Corinne Monroe's love of nature's watery world started in her childhood where she experienced the wonders of the Great Lakes and Michigan rivers and streams. Then a professional career in laboratory medicine in which an important part of her responsibilities was teaching the sciences of medical technology. An active advocate for protection of the ocean and its resources, she now assists the president of the Aquarium of the Pacific in identifying programs that will foster stewardship of the ocean through ocean awareness and literacy.

Olin E. Myers Jr. is associate professor at Huxley College of the Environment at Western Washington University, where he offers courses in conservation psychology, human ecology, and environmental ethics, and is extensively involved in undergraduate and graduate programs in environmental education. He applies his training in psychology and human development to probe the roles of nonhuman animals across the lifespan and how interest in them may link to conservation action.

Jan Packer is a senior research fellow in the School of Tourism at the University of Queensland. She has a strong background in education research and has published broadly in the area of educational psychology over many years. The current major focus of her research is in applying the principles of educational, environmental, and positive psychology to understand and facilitate visitor experiences in tourism and leisure settings. She is currently the editor of *Visitor Studies*.

Ginger Potter is the senior education specialist for the U.S. Environmental Protection Agency (EPA), responsible for research, evaluation, and program assessment as well as strategic planning in the Office of Environmental Education. She also serves as the designated federal officer for the National Environmental Education Advisory Council. Before coming to the EPA, she was a research chemist for the U.S. Geological Survey.

She is also the founder of an organization development consulting firm specializing in strategic planning and project development, change management, team building, leadership development, personal coaching, and international relations. She has degrees in chemistry, business administration, and organization development.

Carol D. Saunders is a core faculty member in the Department of Environmental Studies at Antioch University New England. Previously she directed the Communications Research Department at the Chicago Zoological Society. She received a Ph.D. in behavioral biology from Cornell University and a master's degree in psychology from the University of Virginia. With interests in animal behavior, human–nature relationships, and biodiversity conservation, she has helped lead efforts to advance the new field of conservation psychology.

Jerry R. Schubel, Ph.D, has been president of the Aquarium of the Pacific in Long Beach, California, since 2002. He is president emeritus of the New

England Aquarium, and from 1974 to 1994 was dean of Stony Brook University's Marine Sciences Research Center. He has written extensively for scientific journals and for general audiences; the emphasis has been on exploring alternatives for solving major environmental problems of the coastal ocean, and more recently on ocean and environmental literacy.

Kathryn A. Schubel, Ph.D., has a long history in higher education. She has taught students a variety of geoscience, environmental science, and oceanography courses, both in person and online. For the past two years she has been project manager and curator of content for exhibits at the Aquarium of the Pacific, Long Beach, California. She is committed to inspiring people to understand Earth processes with the sincere hope that they translate that knowledge into action.